METAMORPHISM

Ákos Moravánszky

META MORPH ISM

Material Change in Architecture

Birkhäuser
Basel

CONTENTS

FOREWORD:
ANOTHER BRICK
IN THE WALL

I want to speak about bodies changed into new forms.
You, gods, since you are the ones who alter these,
and all other things, inspire my attempt,
and spin out a continuous thread of words,
from the world's first origins to my own time.
Ovid, Metamorphoses[1]

My membership of the *Tégla-brigád* (Brick Brigade) was one of the most formative experiences of my earlier life as a young architect in Budapest. Back then, the cityscape was much more strongly shaped by brick façades than it is today. Above all, the many empty plots that had been left behind by the Second World War exhibited fire walls of an expressively raw materiality. [Fig. 0.1] In the large state-owned architectural office in Budapest which specialized in the design of public buildings and where I was employed after receiving my diploma the ateliers of the leading architects were referred to as socialist brigades. Although most brigades in the office bore the names of celebrated architects (amongst others there was a Vitruvius Brigade), the head of our atelier, who was well known in Hungary as an architect as well as being the editor-in-chief of the country's most important architecture magazine, found great pleasure in choosing the unheroic sounding name of a humble building material. He was a connoisseur of English and Scandinavian brick architecture and did everything he could to use this material in his projects, although it was unpopular and, indeed, often rejected due to the large amount of work involved in its use and the low wage norms for bricklaying work in the state building industry. At the time I was involved in the development of a prefabricated brick-clad panel system that was intended for use in the construction of an institute building at Budapest University of Technology. The fact that employees of the construction company were allowed to travel to Denmark in order to study relevant models certainly wasn't detrimental to the acceptance of the new technology.

There was yet another reason for this choice of name which can only be explained by reference to late socialism's tendency towards irony. The heroic ring of "Brick Brigade" appeared to fit well with Lenin's definition of the role of the union as the drive belt in the production plant with which the party could spur the "working intelligentsia" to work even harder. The laying of bricks, a subject in treatises and illustrations since the very birth of printing became, in the early 20th century, an area of experimentation designed to investigate methods of working more efficiently. [Fig. 0.2] Around 1900 the American pioneer of *time and motion studies*, Frank Bunker Gilbreth filmed the work of a bricklayer and then analyzed his movements before making suggestions for how to make them more efficient.[2] In the Soviet Union the Stakhanov Movement, which was

0.1 Fire wall in Budapest, Dessewffy utca.

named after Alexey G. Stakhanov, planned to motivate bricklayers to work at record levels by improving standards. However, one could also understand the term brick as a reference to the conspiratorial history of the workers' movement out of which the brigades had emerged. This movement had labeled the informant "embedded" amongst the enemy as a brick: someone who only appears to identify with an organization. In the context of state socialism, however, this expression naturally had yet another meaning and this was exactly our boss' intention, although not noticing this was also part of the rules of the game.

Such ambiguity was one of the tools of political art and architecture in Eastern and Central Europe in the 1970s. A favorite tactic of the so-called dissidents of the time was to provoke the bureaucratic state machinery by confronting it with the rhetoric of its own revolutionary beginnings. In our case we achieved this objective using the ambivalence of the brick. And yet, this oscillation between integration and individuality and then on to opposition and even subversion also says a lot about the complexity of the meanings which, while associated with brick as a building material, were also an integral part of the daily life of the intelligentsia under socialism.

The label "brick" has a metaphorical meaning in many languages. "She was a perfect brick" is a way of saying that the strengths of the person referred to include reliability and warmth and that they slip willingly into a family or group. However, the obedience of the *perfect brick* is not required if one is no more than *another brick in the wall* (Pink Floyd). Found in many languages, the expression "adding one's own brick to the collective structure" means making one's own contribution towards the achievement of a shared objective.

Such expressions refer to the bonding process that gives masonry and, hence, the brick, its meaning. Without this, the geometrically cut lump of clay would hardly be capable of evoking so many complex associations. Or maybe it would: Unlike a block of masonry, a brick is associated with human qualities "in itself". In contrast with such, one could say, superhuman characteristics as the hardness of granite and the eternal nature of marble, the hand-made and hand-laid brick awakens feelings of warmth. Yet, at the same time, the brick is

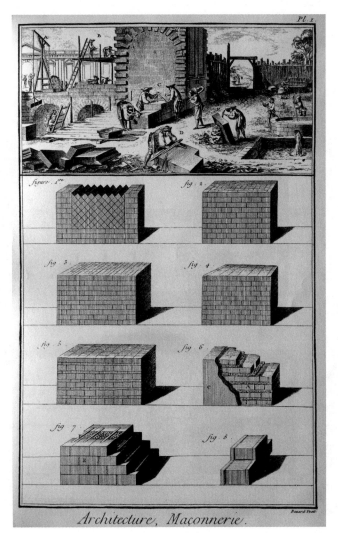

0.2 Illustration to the article on masonry (Maçonnerie) in the *Encyclopédie. Recueil de planches, sur les sciences, les arts libéraux, et les arts méchaniques, avec leur explication*, Paris, 1769.

an industrial product: Its dimensions are standardized, it is made from mineral raw materials (just like its cultural antithesis concrete, which is often described as "inhuman" and used as a scapegoat for the destruction of nature) and both its manufacture and laying are industrial processes. Alvar Aalto used this as a starting point for a summary of his understanding of architecture: 'I was once in Milwaukee with my old friend Frank Lloyd Wright who gave a lecture which he opened as follows: 'Ladies and gentlemen, do you know what a brick is? It is a small, worthless, ordinary thing which costs 11 cents but has a peculiar quality. Give me this brick and it immediately becomes worth its weight in gold.' It was the first time that I had heard an audience told so bluntly and expressively what architecture is. Architecture is the turning of a worthless stone into a nugget of gold."[3] Adolf Loos was equally convinced of the relative value of materials to the artist: "Which is worth more, a kilo of stone or a kilo of gold? [...] The artist will answer: For me, all materials are equally valuable. [...] The artist [...] has just one ambition: To master the material in such a way that his work

9

0.3 The façade of Gantenbein
Winery in Fläsch in-filled with
brick elements laid by a robot.
Architecture: Bearth & Deplazes,
façade: Gramazio & Kohler, 2006.

becomes independent of the value of the raw material."[4] Ludwig Mies van der
Rohe formulated his interpretation of the value of architecture in another way,
but the proposition sounds similar: "Whether we build vertically or horizontally, with steel and glass, says nothing about the value of this building. [...] But
it is precisely this question of value that is decisive."[5]

The transformation of a worthless stone into a golden one, architecture as
alchemy: That would be a potential interpretation of Gottfried Semper's theory
of *Stoffwechsel* (material transformation), which explains the ability of materials to undergo change by considering the products of human *téchne*.[6] Today,
this process of transformation is accelerating as a result of the new opportunities offered by the research carried out by the building materials industry. An

0.4 Robot assembling a façade element.

ancient craft rooted in the piling up or joining together of blocks of stone and logs has become a precision technology which, however, continues to invoke the mythical origins of building.

The ambiguity of brick illustrated by the example of the Brick Brigade is more than merely linguistic. It has to do with the ambivalence of this material itself. Where does the brick belong: to the craft tradition or to industry? Is it the abstract, three-dimensional modular network that becomes architecture in the well-known axonometric drawings of the houses of Mies van der Rohe? Is it the presence of fired clay as in the façade of Aalto's dormitory at MIT? Or does the careful work of the bricklayer predominate? Which aspect is the architect thinking about as he sits at the screen copying stretcher and header courses into a brick pattern with a couple of clicks of the mouse? Is brick still a "signifier" or is it exclusively dependent upon the visually conveyed but thoroughly haptic appeal of the surface, as suggested recently by a number of architects?

The widespread image of the solid brick is being confronted with the reality of its dematerialization or liquefaction. Brickyards can transform clay into bricks of wildly differing forms and formats, which robots or computer-controlled drones then assemble and fix with synthetic adhesives. The office of Fabio Gramazio and Matthias Kohler was aided by robots as it developed prefabricated masonry elements which were then inserted into concrete frames at the Gantenbein Winery in Fläsch by Bearth & Deplazes Architekten. [Figs. 0.3, 0.4] The bricklaying robot was programmed in such a way that it rotated the bricks according to a pattern, creating a textile-like sculptural surface. As the bricks were fixed together by synthetic two-component glue applied by the robot there are no horizontal joints. The vertical joints are, conversely, open, which lends the wall an air of lightness.[7] The resilience of the brick which, earlier, was understood as a moral quality lives on here on a meta-level, even though the invisible layer of glue is stronger than ceramic stone. Although the format that was adapted to the bricklayer's craft is no longer an issue for the bricklaying robot or, indeed, for the bricklaying drone which has also been developed by Gramazio and Kohler, the "traditional" brick remains indispensable because the architects continue to need the craft-related meanings associated with the brick in order, at the very least, to establish a tension between its original solid and new sculptural identities. As we have seen, this identity has little to do with modern production methods. It is a product of history, is reproduced in the media and is used by the brick industry for marketing purposes.

Now that we have become aware of the negative impact that picture book postmodernism has had on our cities, the pendulum is swinging in the opposite direction in that we are making a fetish of materials or spectacularizing them by emphasizing their ability to convey atmosphere. Regardless of whether we reduce material to a media construct or to processes of production, both approaches are similarly fundamentalist. They ignore those intermediate areas in which concept and material are engaged in a constant process of transformation in which material, craftsman, worker, technician, machine, image and meaning determine and influence each other. Even the motion of the bricklayer as he takes a brick, turns it into position, applies mortar and adds the brick to a rising wall in keeping with the rules of a particular bond is much more than a mere manual gesture and, rather, a movement which is also standardized in terms of both mechanical and industrial methods. On the "traditional" building site this motion only made sense when it was carried out in time with the rhythms and chronology of the building process; a process which the individual steps of the bricklayer's work both managed and deferred to. For us, the brick continues to embody these movements and gestures, even if these "traditional" building sites have largely been taken over by machines and software.

Today, many see the qualities of the idealized craftsman, as he was described by Richard Sennett with a certain amount of misty-eyed romanticism. However, Sennett's complaint that computerization is transforming the human being into a passive spectator and consumer and that this separation between hand and head is destroying the crafts is unfounded. As demonstrated by the example of the bricklaying robot, the development of such a program also demands craftsmanship.[8] The fact that the figure of the "honest brick" is constantly being used in Sennett's book when discussion turns to the moral foundations of the profession only shows how little we know about the interrelationships of contemporary architectural production.

Ovid's *Metamorphoses* were the first attempt to put into verse the ancient myths about transformation which have echoed through the arts for centuries. In first-century Rome the poet experienced a period of political revolution that confirmed to him that, although everything flows and every form is subject to constant change, such transformations are not random because they obey consistent rules that govern the acts of emergence and development. For Ovid, who initially dedicated his poems to love and the art of love, desire and passion were the triggers for transformations which fate then steered into happy or unhappy trajectories.

This book is about metamorphoses, about the alchemical transformation of materials in architecture. The brick-clad panel system all those years ago in Budapest and the digital materiality of today's wall elements by Gramazio and Kohler are two stages in this process – but it is a process which is far from linear. It is much more about the oscillation of matter between nature and technology, fetish and foe, science and sensuality. This contribution to architectural theory is *another brick in the wall,* albeit one which should explain how the material brick is, itself, a "construct". In this context, "construction" refers not to the technological manufacturing process but, rather, to the manner in which a building material becomes a cultural object and to the theoretical discussion that justifies and regulates its use. In short, this book is about the construction of the meaning of building materials and, hence, about a historical process. Even this discussion is a microcosm, in which all important areas of architectural theory – tradition, temporality and site-specificity, for example – are represented.

The work on this book was a long and continuously interrupted process. I started to collect the material during my stay at the Zentralinstitut für Kunstgeschichte in Munich between 1986 and 1988 and continued this work at the Getty Center for the History of Art and the Humanities in Santa Monica, California. Over the course of the more than 20 years during which the manuscript emerged I was supported by many colleagues at these research institutes and then at the Eidgenössische Technische Hochschule (Federal Institute of Technology) in Zurich.

My conversations with architects and engineers were immensely valuable to me. I would particularly like to thank Marianne Burkhalter, Adam Caruso, Andrea Deplazes, Tom Emerson, Annette Gigon, Fabio Gramazio, Mike Guyer, Adolf Krischanitz, Peter Märkli, Boris Podrecca, Joseph Schwartz, Jonathan Sergison, Christian Sumi, and Jo Tailleu. In addition to this I am extremely grateful to all those individuals and institutions that have made documents and images available to me. In addition to the architectural offices which are listed in the picture credits I would also like to offer a particular mention to Markus Joachim, Head of the Building Library of the ETH, Daniel Weiss of the gta Archiv, Shigeru Ban, Leon Faust, Ricardo Joss, Karl R. Kegler, Bertalan Moravánszky, Katalin Moravánszky-Gyöngy, Damjan Prelovšek, Johannes Schmitthenner, Adam Shaw and Jonas Wirth. My special thanks are also due to Judith Hopfengärtner, my team colleague at the Chair for the Theory of Architecture. This publication would not have been possible without the help of the Architecture Department and the Institute for the History and Theory of Architecture (gta) of the ETH Zürich. The support of Birkhäuser Verlag and its staff in Basel and Vienna, in particular David Marold and Angelika Heller, was equally important.

The book is dedicated to the memory of Elemér Nagy (1928–1985), the architect, critic, magazine editor, printer of books, maker of kites and musical instruments, and inventor and leader of the Brick Brigade.

Notes

1   Publius Ovidius Naso, *Metamorphoses,* Translated by A. S. Kline Copyright 2000 All Rights Reserved.

2   Frank B. Gilbreth, *Motion Study. A Method for Increasing the Efficiency of the Workman,* New York: D. Van Nostrand Company, 1911.

3   Alvar Aalto, "Between Humanism and Materialism" (1955), in: Aalto *Synopsis. Painting Architecture Sculpture.* Basel, Boston, Stuttgart: Birkhäuser Verlag, 1980, pp. 36–38, here p. 38.

4   Adolf Loos, "Die Baumaterialien" (1898), in: Loos. *Ins Leere gesprochen 1897–1900*. Paris, Zurich: Éditions Georges Crès, 1921. Reprinted, Vienna: Georg Prachner Verlag, 1981, pp. 133–138, here p. 133. Translation by R. H.

5   Ludwig Mies van der Rohe, "Die neue Zeit", Closing words of a speech delivered to the Vienna meeting of the Deutscher Werkbund, 22nd to 26th June 1930, in: Fritz Neumeyer, *Mies van der Rohe. Das kunstlose Wort. Gedanken zur Baukunst.* Berlin: Siedler Verlag, 1986, pp. 372–373, here p. 372. Translation by R. H.

6   Regarding the translation of the term *Stoffwechsel*: see p. 26, note 1.

7   Fabio Gramazio, Matthias Kohler, *The Robotic Touch. How Robots Change Architecture.* Zurich: Park Books, 2014.

8   Richard Sennett, *The Craftsman.* New Haven: Yale University Press, 2008

1.
INTRODUCTION: KNITTING-ON

In the 19th century, the term "metabolism" moved beyond its scientific origins and reverberated widely across the areas of economics, technology, art, and architecture. These waves are still (or, perhaps, are once again) in motion. The German architect Gottfried Semper (1803–1879) elevated the theory of *Stoffwechsel* (metabolism, material transformation) to the central element of his "practical aesthetic".[1] In doing so he was labeling a phenomenon which is familiar in the history of architecture and design: the transfer of forms that were originally connected with the way in which one material was processed to other materials.

Semper backed up his theory with numerous examples. Although all forms and motifs can be traced back to certain primary techniques and materials related to their origins, they become estranged from these origins as soon as they come into contact with new materials and technologies in a new environment. As an example he mentions "timber style" as a formal language which corresponds with the characteristics of wood but which, after several metamorphoses, can develop into "stone style".[2] The wall of a building woven from textile fibers or branches is echoed in a brick pattern or a painted imitation of fabric. The forms of a wooden roof structure can be transferred to iron. Thus, the memory of the original texture remains inscribed into the form or the skin of the object, the direct determinacy by a material and manufacturing process is supplanted by a symbol.

Propositions related to the theory of *Stoffwechsel* such as the textile origins of the wall and the principle of dressing accompanied the development of architecture throughout the 20th century. Semper's writings and, in particular, his main work, *Style in the Technical and Tectonic Arts; or, Practical Aesthetics*, are much more than mere historical documents pertaining to 19th-century architectural history.[3] They offer new impulses to the philosophy of technology, the theory of digital manufacturing, and, above all, the teaching of construction. Semper proposed an inspiring alternative to technical treatises on questions of aesthetics and design. He considered objects from various periods and places, described how they were made and used, and established often playful associations and connections between them as he drew far-reaching conclusions for the act of design. It is thus little wonder that the strands that Semper identified as he developed "technical and tectonic arts" and described in his theory of *Stoffwechsel* have been taken up and used by many architects. The fact that new buildings with façades of woven copper sheet and wooden slates can be described in today's architecture magazines as "monumental wickerwork" demonstrates the long-term effect of Semper's technical aesthetics.

The relationship between form and material that is addressed by Semper and his theory of *Stoffwechsel* on the basis of his observations of buildings, constructional details, and everyday objects throughout the history of architecture has always been a central theme of architectural theory. The subject was dealt with in construction handbooks which, starting from the notion of the "truth to materials", codified knowledge about material, construction and form.[4] Widely regarded in schools and architectural offices as basic know-how, these books left little room for doubt or interpretation. They mostly focus on the joint as a key to understanding the principle of the entire construction. For Semper (as, later, for Konrad Wachsmann, see pp. 222–223), the joint as "knot" plays a primary role in the thought process, albeit a role that he understands as being less about disclosure than about disguise. In his suggestive drawings of the labyrinthine form of knots, Semper offers us a hint of their symbolic power. And yet modern teaching manuals seek to codify and solidify knowledge about building construction. It is only in recent years that building handbooks have appeared which, freeing themselves from the dogma of being true to materials, have ventured into open, not completely secured territory and, in doing so, readdressed the theory of *Stoffwechsel*.[5] The architect is a "'professional dilettante', a kind of alchemist, who tries to generate a complex whole, a synthesis from most diverse conditions and requirements of dissimilar priority [...]," writes Andrea Deplazes in his handbook *Constructing architecture* – a statement which would have been unimaginable earlier in similar publications.[6]

Today it is no longer possible to talk about materials in architecture in an exclusively technical and economic sense without addressing the question of their meaning and sensuality. Our collective memory is full of images of the sensory qualities of materials. Stone walls, clay pots, steel blades, woolen cloth, and golden jewelry are, however, more than mere mental pictures. They emanate warmth and cold, power and intimacy – meanings that stretch far beyond not only the physical characteristics but also the purely visual appearance of the materials. The philosopher Theodor W. Adorno writes that materials are much more than simple natural phenomena "as an unreflective artist might easily presume. History has accumulated in them, and spirit permeates them."[7] It is as if it is precisely this unwillingness of matter to dissolve into a stream of images that nourishes its ability to store memories. One must add, however, that we are not primarily referring here to raw materials such as stone, wool or metal but, rather, to products which reveal the sensory qualities of materials as a result of such human work as weaving, layering or forging. The fact that such products as masonry or fabric bear the visual traces of this work goes without saying. Today, most raw materials are processed by machines in a way that leaves neither a seam nor any other trace and yet such seams and joints are often simulated in order to trigger visual memories of a manual production method, even in objects that have been manufactured in one piece.

The Swiss architect Peter Zumthor describes carefulness, ability and the respectful joining together of constructional elements as "work within things": "I believe that the real core of all architectural work lies in the act of construction. At the point in time when concrete materials are assembled and erected, the architecture we have been looking for becomes part of the real world."[8] At the other end of the spectrum of ways of dealing with materials we find the desublimation that is pursued by, for example, the Spanish artist Lara Almarcegui. Her works are poured rather than assembled: hundreds of cubic meters of excavated material, clods of earth and rubble which she seeks to show (not represent) as the real material of the real world, fully devoid of idealization.[9] Both of these gestures share an almost nostalgic desire to slice a path to individual experience through the forest of our homogenized media culture; the raw material, as something which cannot be broken up by communication networks, becomes a talisman of resistance. And this sense of insurgency has far-reaching consequences for the methods with which artistic and architectural theory approach their subject.

The fields of artistic study that address the role of the material as a bearer of meaning in art and architecture are the iconography and iconology of materials. These investigate the various ways in which materials are used in an aesthetic context and belong to the broader art historical methods of iconography and iconology that seek to reconstruct the former meaning of a work of art with the help of pictorial and written sources. Iconography (*eikon* = image, *graphein* = to write) seeks concrete evidence and deciphers symbols and allegories whereas iconology (*logos* = meaning) interprets the deeper associations of a work of art by addressing a cultural background of which even the artist himself was possibly not even aware. The German art historian Günter Bandmann was the first to also use the methods of iconography and iconology to investigate the material out of which works of art are created. In this regard, his studies of the shift in the way in which materials are evaluated in art are seminal. In his text "Bemerkungen zu einer Ikonologie des Materials" ("Notes on an iconology of materials") he criticizes the widespread attitude of art appreciation that "treats the material as an unimportant quantity," because it simply sees this material as the medium which "is required by an idea which has an urgent need to be made tangible."[10] According to Bandmann it was the appreciation "of the pure, unclad material in its natural state as a means of expression and the understanding of the material as a contributory factor in the emergence of style" during the 19th century that consummated the turn from idealism to materialism.[11] For artistic and architectural practice this meant a shift from the "sublimation" of the material to the maxim of the appropriate use of materials in design. For architecture, however, Bandmann's categories are misleading. The powerful material effects exemplified by Henry Hobson Richardson's use of roughly hewn stone masonry has nothing to do with materialism, and much more to do with American transcendentalism, a form of romantic natural religion centered around the figure of Ralph Waldo Emerson (see Chapter 5). It would be wrong to attempt to contrast Richardson's Ames Gate Lodge in North Easton, Massachusetts (1880/81) with Auguste and Gustave Perret's Notre-Dame du Raincy (1922/23), the church known as "Sainte-Chapelle of reinforced concrete", as examples of materialism and idealism, respectively. Both Richardson and the Perret brothers deploy materials with precision and extreme technical skill but neither example can be associated with materialist philosophy. [Figs. 1.1, 1.2, 1.3]

The iconology of materials has established itself as a field of artistic study since the 1960s. In his book *Die Sprache der Materialien* (*The Language of*

Materials), Thomas Raff attempts to offer an "introduction to an iconology of materials."[12] The bulk of his work deals with the expressive potential of materials which, in connection with their physical, medicinal-magical, and symbolic characteristics determine, amongst other things, their appreciation and artistic use. Such research has meanwhile reached the field of architectural history. In his book *Beton Klinker Granit – Material Macht Politik: Eine Materialikonographie* (*Concrete Brick Granite – Material Power Politics: An Iconography of Materials*) Christian Fuhrmeister undertakes a detailed analysis of the political symbolism of these materials in the period between 1918 and 1945, drawing attention to the ideological baggage carried by the term *Werkstoff* (literally "work-matter", a German synonym for *Material*) as a result of its use under National Socialism.[13] The investigations started by Bandmann are continued in new publications which provide important approaches and methods for considering materiality in architecture.[14] However, the iconographic-iconological method alone cannot do justice to the material-based processes of architectural production. The very term "iconology" is, indeed, an indication of the fact that we are dealing here with the analysis of images – representations – of materials, despite the fact that the presence of a material cannot be reduced to its visual manifestation.

In the 1960s iconology was joined by semiotics, a method for analyzing the cultural phenomenon as a system of signs which had its roots in linguistics. The very title of Raff's book *The Language of Materials,* suggests that one can understand the meaning of materials in the same way that one understands the words and sentences of a language. Semiotics was used by postmodernism as a means of criticizing the linguistic deficits of modernism: its inability to communicate meanings that can be decoded and understood. It is about reading signs: literary texts, advertising, body language, medical symptoms and, not least, architecture. These signs were the territory of semiotics in the 1970s. Within a short period this became a methodology which enabled one to interpret a vast range of phenomena from everyday culture to urban planning. Regardless of whether one was dealing with a column, a portal, a residential building or an entire urban district, semiotics employed methods and ideas which had their origins in Ferdinand de Saussure's *Cours de linguistique général* (1906–1911) and had been subsequently developed further by theorists such as Umberto Eco.[15] In the 1990s this doctrine worked like a well-oiled machine which could be called upon at any time to deliver interpretations, but the impulse to reconstruct the underlying "meaning" increasingly supplanted the act of seeing. This methodology of interpretation had a direct influence on artistic and architectural practice. The postmodernism of Michael Graves or Charles Moore, with its use of historical "quotations", demonstrated with particular clarity the consequences of translating the methodology of art history and literary theory into architecture, as demonstrated by Charles Jencks in his book *The Language of Post-Modern Architecture.*[16]

The consideration of architecture as language reduces its impact on the communicative act. The shortcomings of applied semiotics as a theory of sign-based communication became increasingly clear during the final years of the 20th century. In the special issue of the Berlin architecture magazine *Daidalos* entitled "Magic of Materials" Caroline Bos writes: "Perhaps ours is the first generation for whom material and meaning are completely and ef-

1.1 Nave of the Parish Church of Notre-Dame du Raincy near Paris, the "Sainte-Chapelle of reinforced concrete." Auguste and Gustave Perret, 1922/23.
1.2 Ames Gate Lodge on the country estate of the Ames family in North Easton, Massachusetts. Henry Hobson Richardson, 1880/81.
1.3 Arched gateway of Ames Gate Lodge.

fortlessly disconnected."[17] UNStudio, the Dutch architectural office of Caroline Bos and Ben van Berkel, designed the Mercedes Benz Museum in Stuttgart (2001–2006) with a façade assembled from materials, primarily aluminum and glass, which are used in the production of car bodies. Here, meaning and material are not separated in any way because they simply cannot be. [Fig. 1.4] Instead of the impossible task of contrasting the direct, immediate presence of

the material with the search for meaning, ways should be found of overcoming this dichotomy.

The question of the separability of material and meaning was also posed by Swiss architecture at the end of the last millennium. "Beyond the symbols" ("Jenseits der Zeichen", literally "Beyond the signs") was the title of a sub-chapter in Zumthor's collection of texts *Thinking Architecture* which was first published in 1998.[18] The Swiss architect and architectural historian Bruno Reichlin published an essay with the same title in 2001 in which he reports on the "growing aversion" of the younger generation of architects "to any theoretical construct, conclusion or explanation which attempts to record in any sort of rational discourse either the creative interpretation of the design phase or the critical reception of the work …"[19]

Reichlin seeks to use semiotics as an explanatory model in order to give a voice to dissatisfied younger generations. In the essay quoted above he contrasts the rationality of the method with the directness and warmth that they are seeking. He shows much empathy in presenting the reasons for their dissatisfaction but is also critical, suspecting that their pithy words about a new aesthetic of immediacy and presence are driven by anti-intellectualism. He remarks, for example, that the "speculation" about synesthesia, which should smooth the path of subjectivist approaches in aesthetics, has a thoroughly ideological character: "[…] certain artists," he writes, "are awarded the almost shamanic role of creating such objects using their intuition rather than the knowledge of a technician and scientist."[20] In his contribution, Reichlin refers to recent developments in Swiss architecture such as buildings by Zumthor. One is tempted, he writes, to consider the impression left by the "physical/material characteristics of the object" as a "purely sensory impression, which is experienced beyond any cultural and cognitive influence."[21]

The virtual impossibility of separating the search for an architecture which is "beyond signs" and its opposite, the "cascade effect of references," is demonstrated by Zumthor's architecture. Referring to the conversion of the Gugalun House, a 17th-century farmhouse in the mountains of the Grisons (1990–1994), Zumthor coins the term "knitting-on" (in German: *Weiterstricken*). [Figs. 1.5, 1.6] He retained the part of the old building containing the main rooms which overlooked the valley, removed later cladding and added a new kitchen part and a transverse corridor with a staircase in keeping with the traditional sequence of three sections in the farmhouses of the mountain villages of the region. The horizontal planks on the façade of the new part of the building appear like the supporting threads of a piece of fabric. Rather than clearly separating old and new as prescribed by the then dominant conservationist paradigm, the textile-based analogy of knitting-on allows them to be formally connected. The term also refers to a building technique that is widely found in the Grisons. The houses built of solid, interlocking logs are known as "knitted buildings" ("Strickbauten"). The notched interconnection of the logs creates a solid, single-layered structure which requires no further bracing or cladding.

1.4 The curved steel and glass façade of the Mercedes-Benz Museum in Stuttgart. UNStudio, 2001–2006.

These layers overlap each other alternately at the corners of the building from which they protrude.

Zumthor's essay "The hard core of beauty" was written while he was working on the Gugalun House.[22] The metaphors that he uses in the text come from the world of alchemy and literature. The subject is the *materia prima*, the underlying substrate that, as in the beautiful text "De materia" by the Mallorcan mystic Ramón Llull (or Raimundus Lullus, 1232–1316), begins to speak and explain its own essence.[23] "The hard core of beauty: concentrated substance," writes Zumthor, and the visitor to the house believes that he understands what he means: the consistent elimination of figurative details, a radical reduction.[24] As a result of this, the traditional interpretative mechanisms of the critic, obsessed as they are with images, are no longer effective. "It is the reality of building materials, stone, cloth, steel, leather …, and the reality of the structures I use to construct the building whose properties I wish to penetrate with my imagination, bringing meaning and sensuousness to bear […]."[25] But as visitors to Gugalun do we truly find ourselves "Beyond the symbols"? A brief *excursus* will seek to answer this question.

Semper describes log construction as an archaic technique in comparison with half-timbered construction. It is an "invention of inhabitants of mountainous areas rich in the conifers they used as motives in house building, that is, as reminiscences of older social conditions already established before they immigrated."[26] Semper gathered much of his information about log and "knitted" building techniques from the research of his Zurich colleague Ernst Gladbach (1812–1896). Gladbach was professor of building construction at the Zurich Polytechnic School (today Eidgenössische Technische Hochschule) and published his painstakingly drawn pictures of buildings under the title *Der Schweizer Holzstyl* (*The Swiss Timber Style*) in two volumes (1868 and 1883). He also identified a certain similarity with the anonymous architecture of the Mediterranean: The roofs of the solid timber buildings had a shallow "gradient which corresponded with those of the far south in order to be able to support the shingle roof with its load of heavy stones."[27] [Fig. 1.7]

The gabled façade of the old part of the building overlooking the valley, graying and patched in places, seems, for all its humble "materiality," to evoke in us the idea of a classical culture of the Mediterranean "far south". In Gugalun, these references to Mediterranean stone building are intentional – starting with the inscription "Et in Gugalun ego" which, engraved into a flat block of stone as a threshold to the site, seeks to awaken memories of the mythic Arcadia. More than anything else, however, it is the interplay between similarity and difference, old and new, stone and wood, and north and south, that addresses the notion of "knitting-on". In contrast with the historical "quotations" of postmodern architecture Zumthor creates historical continuity through the technical metaphor of "knitting-on" and through an immediately perceptible materiality in the façades and internal spaces which, while highlighting differences, is connecting the old and new parts of the building. The seam as a place of connection, as the joint between old and new, thus becomes a key to the understanding of the continuous whole. At Zumthor's Kolumba Diocesan Museum in Cologne which, like Gugalun, also integrates existing building elements, this seam is similarly articulated in the symbolic form of textile "knitting-on". [Figs. 1.8, 1.9]

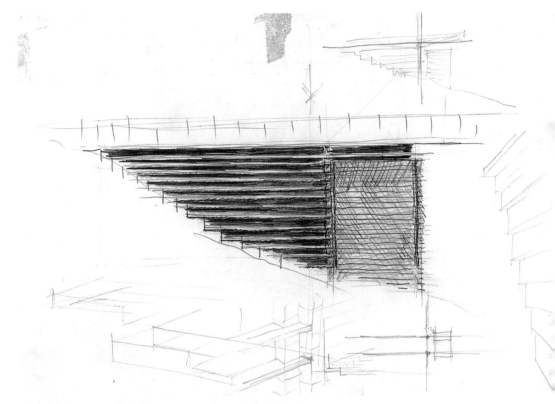

1.5 Peter Zumthor's sketch of the façade of the Gugalun House near Versam in the Grisons, 1990–1994. **1.6** East façade of the Gugalun House.

However much the architect attempts to steer clear of the "artificial world of symbols," the observer will associate forms with his own social and cultural experience.[28] It is precisely this rootedness in the wealth of meanings of the real world that gives architecture its social relevance – quite apart from the world of signs and symbols. The sensory world cannot be completely understood in terms of concepts because there are aspects of perception that are beyond the scope of reflection. This is perhaps what Zumthor means by the "Hard core of beauty." As a program, knitting-on doesn't just mean connecting old and new

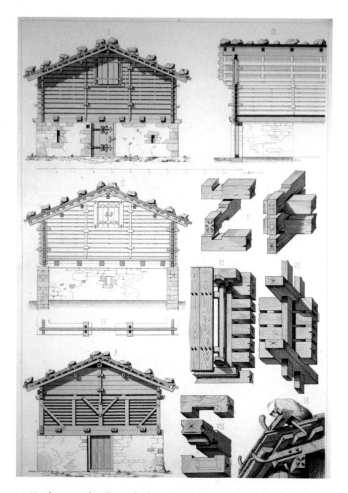

1.7 Hay barns and stalls in Flüelen, from Ernst Gladbach, *Der Schweizer Holzstyl in seinen cantonalen und constructiven Verschiedenheiten vergleichend dargestellt mit Holzbauten Deutschlands*, 1st Series, Zurich, 1882.

but, in particular, focusing on the very question of production and perception. On the basis of these examples we could claim that image and meaning, favorite themes of postmodernism, may play just a secondary role here, but the technique of "knitting-on" is symbolically present in the image of the seam.

The interpretation of material outlined in this introduction progresses from constructional principles via cultural meaning to sensory experience. Accordingly, the technical literature is progressively complemented by texts which use the power of material as an argument for a post-human materialism and as a tool for the ecologization of culture. This book is neither a construction handbook nor a work of architectural history, neither a treatise on the iconology of materials nor a plea for a new materialism. By focusing our attention on ideas that have arisen in close connection with the practice of design it seeks to significantly advance the discourse about material. The examination of Semper's

1.8, 1.9 Joint between old and new: Gugalun House, 1990–1994, and Kolumba Museum in Cologne, 1997–2007, by Peter Zumthor.

theory and the presentation of theoretical discussions about materiality cannot be separated from the investigation of architectural examples. The recognition of materiality can counter the dematerialization as a phenomenon of globalization.

These tasks are reflected in the structure of the book. After an opening chapter covering material concepts in philosophy and their influence on architecture the book turns to the scale of geology. Natural materials are transformed into the built environment; into gardens, cities, buildings, and objects. The observation and the theoretical and aesthetic interpretation of this transformation, this "development of the earth" (Rudolf Schwarz), is the subject of the second chapter. The system for the classification of materials drawn up by the early scientists was based on the theory of the four elements and this also formed the basis for Semper's proposition of the four elements of architecture. The search for an aesthetic which corresponded with the essence of materials led to the establishment of the "law" of truth to materials that then provided the context for Semper's theory. However, the theory of *Stoffwechsel* is based on an approach which starts with the ability of a form to slip from one material to another. The theory of mimesis which was formulated by the Greeks as a basic gesture of all art appears to contradict the law of being true to materials. The notion of evolution, the idea of progress and development, also includes mimesis, transfer, and transformation. The discussion of these subjects forms the starting point for the description of the theory of *Stoffwechsel* and the principle of dressing which represent the main theses of Semper's theory. An entire chapter is devoted to the "apes of materials": arbitrarily shapeable plastic materials such as rubber or concrete which, due to their lack of a clear identity, could not be associated with any specific formal language. Finally, two closely related subjects will be discussed. Dematerialization began with the use of iron as a material and is continuing today due to newly developed "ultra-materials". Its doppelganger, formlessness, was first expressed as a program in surrealist art. In architecture, the sense of the disappearance of materials is also leading to a counter movement: the aesthetic upgrading of formless masses of matter and the notion of material "ecstasies" as a source of atmosphere. This thematic structure results in a non-chronological treatment of the subject which, rather than merely permitting, even demands the inclusion of examples from the 20th and 21st centuries.

With his theory of *Stoffwechsel* Semper laid tracks along which, as the Austrian architectural critic Friedrich Achleitner writes, trains continue to travel.[29] Today, more than 150 years after the appearance of Semper's *Style*, it is clear that these tracks have grown into a widely branched and intertwined network. The role of this book is to map this network and open up new lines of understanding.

Notes

1   The German term *Stoffwechsel*, which literally means "change of matter", was introduced in 19th-century biology to describe the circulation of materials in nature, a process known as metabolism. In architectural history, however, the term Metabolism signifies a movement in post-war Japanese art and architecture whose representatives, who included Kenzo Tange, Kiyonori Kikutake, Kisho Kurokawa and Fumihiko Maki, considered the lifecycle of natural organisms as a model for an architecture that is open for change. To avoid confusion, Semper's theory of *Stoffwechsel* is generally translated in scholarly literature into English as "material metamorphosis", "material change" or "material transformation". For the sake of clarity, we have decided in this book to use the German term *Stoffwechsel* in untranslated form. Á. M.

2   Gottfried Semper, *Style in the Technical and Tectonic Arts; or, Practical Aesthetics*, transl. by Harry Francis Mallgrave and Michael Robinson. Los Angeles: Getty Research Institute, 2004, p. 371.

3   Ibid.

4   One historic and one currently used building handbook are offered here as representative examples: G[ustav] A[dolf] Breymann, *Allgemeine Baukonstruktionslehre mit besonderer Beziehung auf das Hochbauwesen*. 3 volumes. Leipzig: J. M. Gebhardt's Verlag, 1896–1902; Nabil Al Fouad (ed.), *Lehrbuch der Hochbaukonstruktionen*. 4th edition. Wiesbaden: Springer Vieweg, 2013.

5   Comp. Andrea Deplazes (ed.), *Constructing Architecture. Materials Processes Structures. A Handbook*. Basel, Boston, Berlin: Birkhäuser, 2008.

6   Ibid., p. 19.

7   Theodor W. Adorno, "Functionalism Today," transl. by Jane Newman and John Smith in: Peter Eisenman et al (eds.) *Oppositions 17*. Cambridge, Mass.: Institute for Architecture and Urban Studies and MIT Press, (Summer 1979), pp. 31–44.

8   Peter Zumthor, "A Way of Looking at Things" (1988), in: Zumthor, *Thinking Architecture*, transl. by Maureen Oberli-Turner. Basel, Boston, Berlin: Birkhäuser, 2010, pp. 7–27, here p. 11.

9   Ines Goldbach (ed.), *Lara Almarcegui*. Exhibition Catalog. Kunsthaus Baselland. Basel: Christoph Merian Verlag, 2015.

10 Günter Bandmann, "Bemerkungen zu einer Ikonologie des Materials", in: *Städel-Jahrbuch, Neue Folge*. Volume 2. Munich: Prestel Verlag, 1969, pp. 75–100, here p. 75. Translation by R. H.

11   Ibid., p. 76. Translation by R. H.

12   Thomas Raff, *Die Sprache der Materialien. Anleitung zu einer Ikonologie der Werkstoffe.* Munich: Deutscher Kunstverlag, 1994.

13   Christian Fuhrmeister, *Beton Klinker Granit – Material Macht Politik. Eine Materialikonographie.* Berlin: Verlag Bauwesen, 2001, p. 12.

14   Monika Wagner, *Das Material der Kunst. Eine andere Geschichte der Moderne.* Munich: C. H. Beck, 2001; Dietmar Rübel, *Plastizität. Eine Kunstgeschichte des Veränderlichen.* Munich: Verlag Silke Schreiber, 2012; Dietmar Rübel, Monika Wagner, Vera Wolff (eds.), *Materialästhetik: Quellentexte zu Kunst, Design und Architektur.* Berlin: Dietrich Reimer Verlag, 2005.

15   Umberto Eco, *A Theory of Semiotics.* Bloomington: Indiana University Press, 1978.

16   Charles Jencks, *The Language of Post-Modern Architecture.* London: Academy Editions, 1977.

17   Caroline Bos, "Painful Materialism", in: *Daidalos,* Special Edition "Magic of Materials II", August 1995, pp. 20–25, here p. 22.

18   Zumthor, "A way of looking at things", (see note 8), pp. 16–17.

19   Bruno Reichlin, "Jenseits der Zeichen", in: *Der Architekt,* March 2001, pp. 61–69, here p. 62. Translation by R. H.

20   Ibid., p. 63. Translation by R. H.

21   Ibid. Translation by R. H.

22   Peter Zumthor, "The hard core of beauty", in: Zumthor, *Thinking Architecture* (see note 8), pp. 27–34.

23   Raimundus Lullus, "Über die Materie", in: Sigrid G. Köhler, Hania Siebenpfeiffer, Martina Wagner-Egelhaaf (eds.), *Materie. Grundlagentexte zur Theoriegeschichte.* Frankfurt am Main: Suhrkamp Verlag, 2013, pp. 25–28.

24   Zumthor, "The hard core of beauty", (see note 8), p. 28.

25   Ibid., p. 34.

26   Semper, *Style,* (see note 2), p. 689.

27   Ernst Gladbach, *Der Schweizer Holzstyl in seinen cantonalen und constructiven Verschiedenheiten vergleichend dargestellt mit Holzbauten Deutschlands.* 2 Volumes. Hannover: Curt R. Vincentz, 1868, 1883. Reprint Hannover: Verlag Th. Schäfer, 1984, Introduction without page numbers. Translation by R. H.

28   Zumthor, "A way of looking at things", (see note 8), p. 16f.

29   Friedrich Achleitner, "Franks Weiterwirken in der neueren Wiener Architektur", in: *UM BAU 10,* August 1986, p. 125.

2.
PATHS TO MATTER

The victory of speed over the heaviness and inertia of the past was celebrated by modernism as a victory over matter. And yet, following this triumphal moment of acceleration, the supposedly vanquished matter doggedly returned and it was precisely this heaviness that seemed to confirm its authenticity and integrity, its timeless presence. Louis I. Kahn was able to successfully combine his interest in the monolithic and compact forms of antiquity with the program for a new monumentality that he published in 1944.[1] Manifestations of heaviness have accompanied modernism's enthusiasm for lightness like a shadow. In an age of globalization Jean-Luc Nancy is seeking a "transcendental aesthetic of heaviness," something that does not dissipate in images and communication: "The existence of the slightest pebble already overflows. However light it may be it already weighs this excessive weight."[2]

The megaliths of Stonehenge, the menhirs on the Breton coast or the tombs of Mycenae appear to later observers to be an architecture borne directly of matter, as the primary way of creating space from and with material. Erecting a huge stone is not only a gesture designed to mark a physical center but also back-breaking work which is carried out to the limit of transportability of the extremely heavy material. This is how indestructible buildings came about, those buildings which have outlived mankind to date and will probably do so definitively. [Fig. 2.1] This is precisely why such buildings never stop stirring the imagination. The Dutch Benedictine monk and architect Dom Hans van der Laan addressed the relationship between "solid and void" in his book about built space and in his architecture; Stonehenge was one of his models.[3] In the Benedictine abbey near Vaals (1956–1968) he combined the form of a brick with the form of the building by speaking about the dialectic between the limited material and the unlimited solid.[4] [Fig. 2.2] With the help of the architect Fritz Gerhard Mayr, the Austrian sculptor Fritz Wotruba built the Church of the

2.1 The megaliths of Stonehenge, 2,500–2,000 B.C.

2.2 Church nave of St. Benedictusberg Abbey near Vaals. Dom Hans van
der Laan, 1956–1968.

Most Holy Trinity (1965–1976) out of huge concrete blocks on a raised plateau
in Vienna. The powerful building, that also brings Stonehenge to mind, is a
conscious antithesis to the aesthetic of cladding and opulence of the Viennese
architectural tradition. [Fig. 2.3]

Flowing matter

The megaliths, built forms from an age without history, resemble matter frozen
in time. And yet material has also been associated with dynamic and movement since antiquity. In the didactic poem *De rerum natura* (*On the nature of
things*), which he wrote in the first century B.C., the Roman poet-philosopher
Lucretius created a cosmology which, alongside a description of the material
universe, also portrayed not only the position of mankind in the spatial world
but also the development of human culture, all in dactylic hexameter. He assumes that no single particle of original matter in the universe is fixed: "space

2.3 The Church of the Most Holy Trinity, Vienna. Fritz Wotruba with Fritz Gerhard Mayr, 1965–1976.

spreads out without bound or limit / immeasurable toward every quarter everywhere" while "unceasing, diverse motion" drives the bodies.[5] Lucretius' work was widely reprinted and read in later centuries, in particular the 17th century, even though the atomic theory of Epicurus upon which Lucretius had based his lines were already considered outdated when he wrote them. The poem's popularity was arguably a result of the vivid language which must have come across as highly suggestive in contrast with Aristotle's much more complex and abstract argumentation. The vision of a world filled with constantly moving matter conveyed by the poem inspired the imaginations of artists from Leonardo da Vinci to Robert Smithson and has now become an emblem for an ecological worldview.[6] New books about materiality such as Jane Bennett's *Vibrant Matter* embody a post-humanist philosophy which places the vitality of material at the heart of "political ecology".[7] In contrast, a history of the representation of inert matter as an embodiment of real, heavy, physical objects that cast shadows has yet to be written.

Materia

The word "matter", materia, is derived from the root mater which, in Latin, means not only "mother" but also the wood that, freed of bark and branches, is processed in sawmills. On this basis, the term *materia* describes all matter that is used in the manufacture of objects. In Vedic Sanskrit the word *mātrā* (material) is derived from the root *mā-* which linguists connect with two meanings. The first has to do with "making", "manufacturing", and "creating" as in, for example, the word *māna* (to build, altar). The word *mātr* (mother) is related to this meaning. We find the same root in the name of the ancient goddess Demeter, a sister of Poseidon and Zeus, who makes the earth fertile and covers it with the beauty of nature. The other area of meaning has to do with measurement: *mātrā* also means "dimension", and this is also the origin of the ancient Greek term *metis* – "acumen", "practical knowledge", "craftsmanship". It is no coincidence that this reference to measurability, a characteristic that requires material stability, finds itself close to "manufacture" and "materiality". In one of his introductory lectures to psychoanalysis Sigmund Freud uses this etymological argument to interpret matter in general as the generative principle of tangible reality, writing that: "The material out of which something is made, is at the same time its mother-part. In the symbolic use of wood for woman, mother, this ancient conception still lives."[8] There is a further connection between the womb and the ship (*naval, nave, Nabel*, the German word for the umbilicus). As a result of the beauty of their form ships are regarded as feminine and the corporeality of the timber structures of *architectura navalis,* naval architecture, is quite obvious. [Fig. 2.4]

The often unclear terminological differentiation between "matter" and "material" is largely a consequence of the relationship between their subsequent treatments. This difference has little to do with technical processing but is epistemological and related to the conceptualizing of the world. "Material" is always the material of something that is intended for processing whereas processing is something that also occurs at the discursive level as a result of naming, systematizing and evaluating. Material is thus not only an object of technology but also of culture, which is why one also speaks of "thematic" or "psychological" material. "Matter", on the other hand, is a correlative term for form. Matter becomes material. The process of transformation takes place not only on the physical level exemplified by, for example, the sawing up of a tree trunk. It begins much earlier with the intention to build and the gathering of the knowledge required in order to be able to do so. The extent to which this knowledge can be complex, precise, and ritualized down to the tiniest detail is described by the Hungarian writer László Krasznahorkai in his literary report on the periodic rebuilding of the Ise Shrine in Japan.[9] The finely woven nature of the structure of this knowledge is reflected in the ingenious timber joints and the hundreds of special woodworking tools, the saws, planes, carving tools, and chisels, that are used in the process.

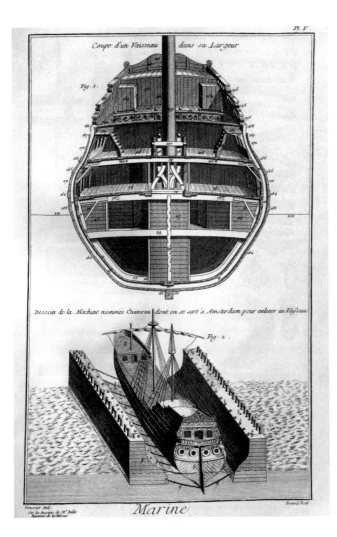

Form and matter

Inspired by the ideology of Plato which he fought against in other contexts, Aristotle's philosophy employed the now widely used concept of the duality of "form" (*eidos* or *morphé*) and "matter" (*hylé*), a term which he coined himself. As the antonym of "form", "matter" is shapeless, unformed substance, the "substratum" (*hypokeimenon),* the origin of all visible things. For Aristotle, "matter" represents potential, the unlimited options for movement, appearance, and disappearance inherent to the process of formation and degeneration of structured states. Without the continuum of indefinite possibility structure is unthinkable: *Physis*, as the origin of movement, cannot exist as a medium without matter. As potential, matter is a symbol of divine creation which, at the same time, cannot be considered separately from the soul. In the system of Aristotelian metaphysics a chain leads from the lowest step of pure, inert matter via inorganic things, plants, animals and people to God as the principle of all movement.

For Aristotle, matter never has the concrete shape exemplified by wood or stone in which the continuum of matter has already adopted a structure. This demonstrates an important difference between the term "matter" as used by Aristotle and as found in the earlier materialism of Democritus and Epicurus and amongst the later materialists, who equated matter with the real. For Aristotle, shape is already incorporated into matter – but as the basic structure of its capacity for movement rather than as a specific form; even a material such as iron alters its characteristics, color and consistency as soon as it is heated. With this notion, Aristotle established a school of thought regarding the observation of materials which is still prevalent amongst the media artists of today and which focusses on the object as transformed material and on the idea that determines this process of transformation. Ovid put these ideas in a nutshell in his *Metamorphoses* when he described the representation of a castle on an ivory, gold, and silver relief and eulogized it with the oft-quoted words: "Materiam superabat opus" (the workmanship surpassed the material) – words which, according to Bandmann, are the quintessence of the idealistic material aesthetic.[10]

As a substratum matter is, thus, a category of thinking. But it is also an object of engineering science which is investigated by instruments and worked on by tools. The building site as a place of transformation is, at the same time, a place in which theory can emerge – *theoria* as contemplative observation of the world.[11] In his book *Anaximander and the Architects* Robert Hahn convincingly demonstrates that the connection between philosophical speculation and constructional practice is not a one-way street.[12] For the early pre-Socratic philosophers the site of the temple was a place that delivered hypotheses and concepts for their interpretations of the cosmos. Anaximander of Miletus observed material and its processing, geometry, mathematics, building technology, and ritual as parts of a complex but rational interrelated whole. The conclusions drawn from the building process could be transferred to the explanation of the world. Hahn even claims that the rationality, organization, and cooperation that were necessary for the construction of the temple eventually destroyed the power of those aristocratic patrons whose interests should originally have been served by the huge temple complexes.[13] Seen from this point of view there was hardly a more appropriate place for understanding the relationships between nature, matter, and weight on the one side and visual perception, eurhythmics, dimensions, and proportions on the other as the building site where huge blocks of stone were shifted, shaped, and precisely connected to create stable and durable structures. Our philosophical terms "world", "space", and "matter" were molded on the building sites of antiquity, where theory – in the form of contemplative observation – and experiment were inseparably interconnected.

Fabrica and *ratiocinatio*

The pre-Socratic notion of matter was revived in Rome. In the preface to the ninth of his *Ten Books on Architecture* (*De architectura*) Vitruvius emphasized the significance of Lucretius; the story of the origins of architecture is inspired by the fifth book of *De rerum natura*. Vitruvius' distinction between the two forms of architectural knowledge which he described as *fabrica* and *ratiocinatio* was decisive for later discussion, particularly in the Renaissance. Like the Greek *téchne*, the former addressed the manual-material aspects of design while the latter focused on linguistic-immaterial aspects. Vitruvius called *fabrica* "the continuous and regular exercise of employment where manual work is done with any material according to the design of a drawing."[14] *Ratiocinatio* is, on the other hand, "the ability to demonstrate and explain the productions of dexterity on the principles of proportion," or, so to say, conception and deliberation.[15] For this reason it is important that the architect is also experienced in using his hands because "those who relied only upon theories and scholarship were obviously hunting the shadow, not the substance."[16] From the starting point of this diagnosis Vitruvius then deduced that it was necessary for the architect to master a wide range of disciplines. This differentiation between *fabrica* and *ratiocinatio* corresponds with the division of knowledge into the technical-constructional and the theoretical disciplines. Design is the mediator between these two areas, establishes a relationship between matter and form, and develops a notion on the basis of the wealth of ideas in the space of material reality. Matter and form enjoy a dialectical relationship, matter is unimaginable without form and vice versa. This gave Vitruvius enough to present a detailed, scientifically-grounded introduction to building materials in *De architectura* which was based on the theories of such pre-Socratic thinkers as Thales of Miletus, Heraclitus, Epicurus, and Democritus.

Neo-Platonism and the cult of light

The emergence of Christian thought led to the increasing questioning and even combatting of the rationalism of antiquity. However, the Neo-Platonism of Plotinus enabled the philosophy of antiquity to live on in a form that met the contemporary need for reflection on the transcendence of the divine. Following in the footsteps of Aristotle, Plotinus assumes that matter is shapeless, pure potential about which one can only formulate negative statements in the sense that one can only say what it is not. Arguably influenced by Christian theology Plotinus interpreted matter as something evil and ugly that can only be redeemed by the spiritual energy stored within it. It is the role of art to enable the reflection of the divine to shine through this material shroud.[17] *Aisthesis* enables this beauty to be experienced in the suddenness of sensory perception. In the writings known as *The Enneads* Plotinus uses figurative language to describe his vision: He asks how the material corresponds with the immaterial and answers that, disregarding the stones, the house corresponds with the idea. It may be structured in its materiality but the inherent, undivided idea still appears, despite this plurality.

Plotinus' theory is important if one is seeking to understand Byzantine aesthetics. His pupils developed the system further and *Corpus Areopagiticum*, a collection of texts whose name is derived from that of its author Dionysios Areopagita, appeared in the 6th century. The central theological question in the work is the relationship between light (*phos*) and matter (*hylé*). The *Corpus* is a semantically precise system of terms which communicates the vision of a sensorially perceptible but rationally intangible world perfused with divine light. In this vision the ray of primordial light is initially reflected in the finest substratum of the "first matter"; in the heavy, dark matter this ray of light can only be perceived very weakly. In Areopagite aesthetics *Marmarygé* is the name given to the shimmer of marble and also the glow "left behind on the 'first matter' by the primordial light through all the phases of being."[18] The marble cladding in the interior of the Basilica San Vitale in Ravenna (535–547) suggestively communicates the metaphysics of light of the Areopagites. [Fig. 2.5]

The relationship between matter and form became a contentious issue during the Middle Ages. Some philosophers assumed that matter was defined by form and others that form developed from matter. The *artifex*, the creator of art, permits the observer to directly perceive the characteristics of the material as defined by God. The common basis is the theory of viewability which is a characteristic of the material object. Thomas Aquinas is the most important representative of a scholastic theory supported by the teaching of Aristotle which considers *perfectio* (the integrity of form), *proportio* (or *consonantia),* and *claritas* as the most important aspects of beauty. The highest principle of physical-material beauty is light, *claritas,* in the physical sense, which reminds us of the neo-Platonic aesthetic. This cult of light in the Middle Ages reached its highpoint in the spiritualization and dematerialization of the Sainte-Chapelle in Paris, a highpoint which was also approached or even reached much later by modernist architects with the use of new structural possibilities (steel, reinforced concrete) (see pp. 18–19). Abbot Suger's reports of the rebuilding of the Cathedral of Saint-Denis emphasize that the beauty of the building is a result of the visibility of the *physis* of the matter that is based in the perfection of divine creation: "The weak spirit becomes a true one through material things /and with the light it lifts itself longingly from its submersion."[19] Here, the beauty of the material largely depends upon clarity, color, and the incidence of light or, so to say, visually perceptible qualities. The Catalan architect Antoni Gaudí refers to Thomas Aquinas in writing that: "Beauty is the splendor of truth. Everyone is drawn to splendor—this is why art is universal. Science and reason are, on the other hand, only accessible to a certain mind."[20] When Ludwig Mies van der Rohe repeated this quotation – *pulchritudo est splendor veritatis* (beauty is the splendor of truth) – he was, consciously or otherwise, building a bridge from scholastic aesthetics to Plotinus and the neo-Platonists.[21] Accordingly, the opulent marble panels in the rooms of the Villa Tugendhat or the German Pavilion at the Universal Exposition in Barcelona glow with the *marmarygé* of the Byzantine basilicas. Beauty is described here not in terms of *venustas,* the word used by Vitruvius that reached back to antiquity and the Roman goddess Venus, but the scholastic term *pulchritudo* which is connected with the recognition of God. [Figs. 2.6, 2.7] The demand for *decorum* (appropriateness) has also belonged to the criteria of good architecture since Sebastiano Serlio. The combination of reduced forms with noble cladding materials in the building of new town halls across Scandinavia was justified by the dignity of public administration. Arne Jacobsen, for instance, clad the façades of the town halls of the municipalities of

2.5 Marmarygé: shimmering marble walls in the Basilica San Vitale in Ravenna, 537–547.

2.6 Alpine green marble and travertine surfaces in the Barcelona Pavilion. Ludwig Mies van der Rohe, 1929, rebuilt 1983–1986.
2.7 Wall panel of onyx doré in the Barcelona Pavilion.

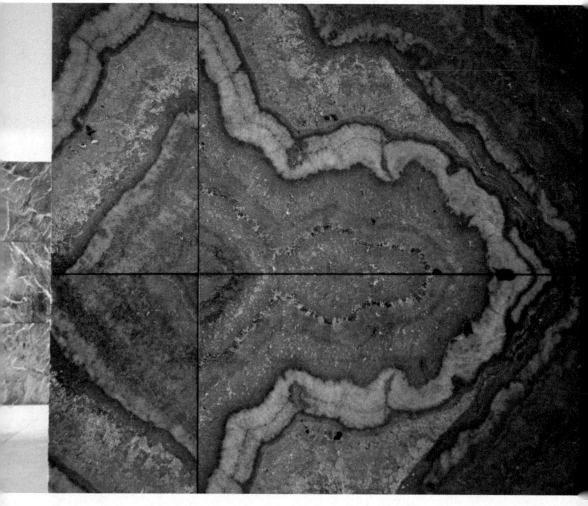

Søllerød (1939–1942, with Flemming Lassen) and Aarhus (1937–1942, with Erik Møller) with pink Porsgrunn marble panels from Norway. [Fig. 2.8]

Dark matter

Unlike the scholastics, religious rigorists such as St. Donatus of Besançon fought against the cult of light and claimed the dominance of the color black.[22] The aesthetic ideal of using the appropriate *téchne* as a means of expressing the *physis* of matter – a connection that had more-or-less disappeared by the time of Hellenistic, neo-Platonic aesthetics – defined the religious buildings of the Cistercians. Here, the relationship between light and stone was completely different to that of the interior of the Basilica of Ravenna. Fontenay, Alcobaça and other Cistercian abbeys inspired modern architects. [Fig. 2.9] The French architect Fernand Pouillon was in prison when he wrote his novel *The Stones of the Abbey* about the building of the Cistercian Le Thoronet Abbey

2.8 Façade of the assembly room of the town hall of Søllerød (now Rudersdal) near Copenhagen. Arne Jacobsen and Flemming Lassen, 1939–1942.

2.9 Church nave of the Cistercian abbey at Alcobaça in Portugal, 1178–1252.

in the form of the journal of the abbey's master mason.[23] Between 1950 and 1953 Pouillon built residential buildings and offices in the old port of Marseille using huge stone blocks with precise joints but grainy surfaces, as described in the words that he ascribed to his alter ego, Guillaume Balz, the builder of Le Thoronet. In the Résidence Victor Hugo, a large housing complex in Pantin outside Paris (1955–1957) Pouillon inserted panels of red marble between the pilasters. [Fig. 2.10] The contrast between the huge, heavy blocks and the finely balanced surfaces and colors differentiates his work from that of Le Corbusier. The influence of Cistercian architecture on the work of the latter is best embodied in the notion of communal living and the rhythm of light and shadow as strikingly photographed by Lucien Hervé.[24]

An even more powerful antithesis to the transcendence of Mies van der Rohe is the "as found" material aesthetic of the British Brutalists for whom it was important to show that a material belonged to the real world and appeared to be neither opulent nor a product of sophisticated craftsmanship. Alison and Peter Smithson reconsidered the materiality of simple anonymous buildings "not in the craft sense but in intellectual appraisal [...] a poetry without rhetoric."[25] The magical radiance of the ordinary is the result of an appreciation of the materials of the built world.[26]

2.10 Marble and limestone façade in the main courtyard of the Résidence Victor Hugo in Pantin near Paris. Fernand Pouillon, 1955–1957.

The renaissance of antiquity

In the 15th century, interest in the Classical principally involved the direct use of ancient sources, unmediated by the authors of Neo-Platonism. Accordingly, the attention of the humanists was no longer focused on the notion of God but on nature. Religion plays no role in Leon Battista Alberti's *Treatise on Architecture*. In contrast with Vitruvius and his *De architectura*, Alberti titled his work *De re aedificatoria*[27] because, as Françoise Choay shows, the figure of the *aedificator* presents him with a concept on the basis of which he can postulate an analogy between the Creation and the human act of building.[28] Alberti found his confirmation that the art of antiquity could be not only matched but even outclassed in such ingenious and audacious masterworks of Renaissance Florence as Filippo Brunelleschi's cathedral dome. His own built work and, in particular, the Tempio Malatestiano in Rimini, the conversion of a Gothic church into a reliquary for the Malatesta family, demonstrates his attempts to combine ancient-pagan and Christian elements (façade 1453–1460). [Fig. 2.11]

In *De re aedificatoria* Alberti differentiates between the work of the designer and the craftsman, between intellect and hand: "The intellect is responsible for choice, distribution, arrangement, and so on, which give the work dignity; the

2.11 Façade of the Tempio
Malatestiano in Rimini. Leon
Battista Alberti, 1453–1460.

hand is responsible for laying, joining, cutting, trimming, polishing, and such
like, which give the work grace [...]."[29] In accordance with his attitude to the
division of labor between the architect and craftsman he entrusted the execution of his buildings in Rimini and Mantua to local builders. Every type of construction consists of "the ordered and skilful composition of various materials"
such as stone or timber into an "integral and unified structure."[30] It is the architect and not the craftsman who lends the material a form that corresponds with
his design in the manner of the demiurge, the creator god in Plato's dialogue
Timaeus. This ordering, theory-based activity also differentiates the architect
from other artists, from painters and sculptors.

Alberti emphasizes "that the building is a form of body, which like any other
consists of lineaments and matter, the one the product of thought, the other of
Nature [...]."[31] Placing one stone upon the next is not enough. The composing
and ordering activity of the spirit is required in order to ensure that a building
is defined by *coerenza* and *necessità,* the characteristics of correct construction.
Hence, the building must be shaped like an organism and have a relationship

2.12 Marble incrustation on the façade of the church of Santa Maria Novella in Florence. Leon Battista Alberti, 1456–1470.
2.13 The Chapel of the Holy Sepulchre of the Rucellai Family in the former church of San Pancrazio in Florence. Leon Battista Alberti, 1457–1467.

2.14 Competition project for the remodeling of the Zedlitzhalle in Vienna, façade. Josef Frank, 1907.

with the city. According to Alberti's theory, beauty and *concinnitas* – the structural congruity that Cicero deemed to be a law of nature – are the outcome of a mental process. Starting at the geometrical level, the resulting harmonic effect is transferred to all parts of the building at the material level. The strict separation between the *lineamenti,* the geometrical organization of the lines in the architect's mind (the subject of the first book of his treatise on architecture), and the materiality of the external reality (the subject of the second book) corresponds with the perspective model that also brings together the mental and material worlds with the help of projection lines. "It is quite possible to project whole forms in the mind without any recourse to the material [...]", writes Alberti in the chapter about the lineaments.[32] It is in this spirit that he covers the surface of Santa Maria Novella (1456–1470) and the Chapel of the Holy Sepulchre (1457–1467) in Florence with "speaking" ornamentation made from white Carrara marble and green Serpentine from Prato, which demonstrates his knowledge of both antiquity and Christian symbolism. [Figs. 2.12, 2.13]

Alberti's differentiation between the naked work of the craftsman and the dressing which was designed by the architect according to strict rules lays a path which leads via the imagery of the body in Classicism to Gottfried Semper and, further, to Otto Wagner, Wagner's followers, and Adolf Loos. To this extent it is not surprising that the Vienna architect Josef Frank wrote his dissertation on the subject of Alberti.[33] Both this decision and the dissertation itself

2.15 Detail from the interior of the Church of Santa Maria dei Miracoli, Venice, around 1481–1489.

were influenced by Frank's professor at the College of Technology Carl König and König's assistant Max Fabiani, a colleague of Wagner. Frank's precisely colored ink drawings of the façades with rich incrustations are perhaps the most important part of the dissertation. They show how certain basic aspects of the architectural space – its typology, geometry, and rhythm – can also be recog-

2.16 Façade of the Villa Thiene in Quinto Vicentino by Andrea Palladio, around 1545.

nized in the scale of the ornamental treatment of the surface of the façade. This question of the relationship between space and surface which he investigated in his dissertation with graphic means rather than language was subsequently pursued by Frank in his work as an architect and designer of furniture and textiles. While it is still rich in Art Nouveau detail, his early competition entry for the remodeling of the Zedlitzhalle in Vienna (1907) already demonstrates his interest in composition. [Fig. 2.14] The interior space of Haus Beer in Vienna (1929/30) appears like a cross-section, a technical framework, which only becomes living space upon the addition of furniture and fabrics.

Alberti's separation of the mental and material processes of building was taken further by Andrea Palladio who noticed that buildings tended to be more valued for their forms than for their materials (*Le fabriche si stimano più per la forma che per la materia*).[34] Naturally, this does not mean that manual aspects do not have to be addressed with care and precision. Palladio, however, did not share Alberti's interest in opulent, polychromatic dressing. His buildings are mostly built of brick; their façades and columns covered in marble plaster (*marmorino*) in order to create the effect of a stone surface. Palladio's appreciation of the *non-finito* effect of unplastered, raw façades as exemplified by the Villa Thiene in Quinto Vicentino (1st phase around 1545) can perhaps be traced back to the power of the ruins of ancient walls. [Fig. 2.16] His capitals are often

VIII

PALATIN

2.17 Axonometric projection of a vault on the Palatine, Rome, from Auguste Choisy, *L'art de bâtir chez les Romains*, Paris, 1873.

assembled from terracotta elements and then whitewashed – as at the Il Redentore church in Venice (1577–1592).

Cartesian and baroque perspectives

The notion of matter as something completely independent of – or even opposite to – spirit is a guiding principle of modern thinking and was first systematically posited by René Descartes (1596–1650). The French philosopher, who is held responsible for the dissolution of the Aristotelian-scholastic world view, regarded mind and matter, *res cogitans* and *res extensa,* as two separate parts of reality which only come together in the human consciousness. *Res extensa* describes the measurable material world which spreads infinitely and homogenously like a geometrical field. *Res cogitans* is that thinking substance which reflects this world and, as a result, becomes a reflection of this material reality; our senses can use this *res extensa,* of which our bodies are also part, as a means of communicating impressions but not explanations. This concentrates matter into a measurable object which – unlike *res cogitans* – can lay claim to expansion, but not to movement.[35] Modernist thinking has extended this spirit-matter dichotomy even further. It attributes life, movement, quality, and subjectivity to the one pole of spirit and inertness, resilience, quantity, and objectivity to the other pole of matter.

The invention of central perspective in the 16th century predated Descartes as a consequence of the rationalization of seeing. The notion of the outside world as a spatial extension is made accessible by the new norm of *costruzione legitima* and communicated by the observing eye of thinking substance. The surface of projection, on which the rays of light coming from the outside world portray an image of reality, separates the image space from the object space – thus paving the way for the Cartesian postulate. This was subsequently further consolidated by the French mathematician Gaspard Monge, who presented descriptive geometry as an alternative "objective" method of projection, which was not tied to the spatial position of the observer. Axonometric projections display the composition rather than the sensory quality of the technical object. The axonometric representations of Roman and Byzantine constructions produced by Auguste Choisy float in geometrical space like graphic models of perfectly built vaults, visions of the tangible material world of *res extensa.*[36] [Fig. 2.17]

Although Descartes' postulate is regarded as the paradigm of modern scientific thinking, his concept of material was far from uncontroversial. Gottfried Wilhelm Leibniz soon rejected Descartes' equalization of matter and expansion and replaced Cartesian expansion with the notion of the filling of space in a way that is only imaginable due to the effect of some force; one such force being, in his view, the human imagination. In this way Leibniz, for whom the link between mind and matter is a question of both consciousness and memory and, hence, bound up with the dimension of time, severed Descartes' connection between matter and spatial-mechanical reality. In his analysis of Leibniz's ideas the French philosopher Gilles Deleuze discovered an attempt to reconstruct classical, pre-Cartesian rationality with a wealth of inflections and dissonances – a baroque drapery, in the folds of which one obtains a glimpse of the diversity of the world. According to Deleuze the Baroque interpreted the idea of the "fold" in two ways: "as if infinity were composed of two stages or floors: the pleats of matter and the folds in the soul."[37] Echoing Plato's allegory of the cave he presents us with two levels of reality. In baroque architecture we find both a delight in the joining together or contrasting of different materials and surfaces – as exemplified by the work of Gianlorenzo Bernini and the brothers Cosmas Damian and Egid Quirin Asam – and a tendency towards homogenization and the suppression of the differences, even between "real" and "represented" materiality. [Fig. 2.18]

According to Hans Sedlmayr "the material in which Borromini's structures are imagined" is "not an actual, specific material."[38] In his *Opus Architectonicum* Borromini does indeed report that he had seen an ancient tower with walls of flat, finely-cut bricks next to the Porta del Popolo in Rome. On the

2.18 Interior of the Church of St. Johann Nepomuk in Munich. Cosmas Damian Asam and Egid Quirin Asam, 1733–1746.

basis of this he decided to design the façade of the oratory of San Filippo Neri (1620–1637) in such a way that the observer can hardly differentiate between brick and joint. He writes "that it would be wonderful if one could build a tower out of fired materials that consisted of one single piece, without any joints."[39] However, given that this is not possible, "one can at least make the joints much less visible by using small bricks; and thus I first had the flat bricks […] cut into a rectangular form and then used these to build the entire façade."[40] In this way, the brick is transcended and the individuality of the individual block suppressed in favor of the folds and curves of the façade. [Fig. 2.19]

The relationship between matter and form, continuum and structure postulated by Aristotle was reexamined in the philosophy of Immanuel Kant. Kant speaks of matter in two senses: on the one hand as substance, something that persists and, on the other hand, as appearance, something that, in contrast with substance, moves and changes. The fact that matter fills a space has nothing to do with its mere existence but, rather, with its "expansive force." The effect of this force-based and movement-based definition of matter can be found today in the rejection of the Cartesian concept of material which accompanies Bruno Latour's idea of lines of force as an alternative to the notion of material. Such non-Cartesian or even decidedly anti-Cartesian material concepts have been with us continuously since Aristotle.

Materialism versus idealism

It is often asserted that the "idealistic" first half of the 19th century was followed by the "materialistic" second half. At any rate, the period after 1850 was characterized by a realism that rejected the exuberance of the romanticists. A second enlightenment now celebrated its victory in the name of science and reality, a victory that reached a broad swathe of the population in the form of popular scientific literature. At the time, materialism was understood as an attempt "to comprehend the world as a whole and to rise above shared sensory illusion."[41] Key contributions to the so-called materialism controversy, which included Carl Vogt's *Physiologische Briefe* (*Letters on Physiology*, 1845) and his pamphlet *Köhlerglaube und Wissenschaft* (*Blind Faith and Science*, 1854), Jakob Moleschott's *Der Kreislauf des Lebens* (*The Circuit of Life*, 1852), Ludwig Büchner's *Kraft und Stoff* (*Force and Matter*, 1855), and Heinrich Czolbe's *Neue Darstellung des Sensualismus* (*New Account of Sensualism*, 1855), appeared around 1850.[42] Written in the self-confident tone of the Enlightenment, most of these works positioned themselves as recipes for salvation which sought to replace the old myths with a new scientific worldview. However, one still cannot speak of a general shift towards materialism; theories described as "magical idealism" also appear in the second half of the 19th century as offshoots of the romantic philosophy of identity. By selecting the notion of *Stoffwechsel* (as metabolism) as the most important element of his style theory Semper positioned himself very clearly vis-à-vis the idealists and materialists, apparently on the side of the latter – but only apparently. His main work *Style in the Technical and Tectonic Arts* emerged during the materialism controversy. The introductory prolegomena to the first volume in 1860 may reveal Semper's intention of overcoming the speculative romantic aesthetic of Schelling and moving towards an empirical artistic theory but his rejection of the teachings of the radical materialists was equally decisive.

Gottfried Semper's concept of material

Material – whether in the more general sense of theme, subject, object or in the form of an actual, physical material – is, for Semper, just one of the "outward influences acting upon the performance of a work of art" which, thus,

2.19 Detail of the façade of the Oratory of S. Filippo Neri, Rome. Francesco Borromini, 1620–1637.

contribute to determining its style.[43] In this way he distances himself from the then widely held definition that had been formulated by the German art historian Carl Friedrich von Rumohr in his book *Italienische Forschungen* (*Italian Investigations*). Rumohr invokes the origins of the word "style" in the Greek *stylos,* stylus, a tool with which a writer also engraved his own personal writing style in the wax tablet, as a means of rejecting interpretations that understand style as a formal consistency in the work of a master or a school that can be identified with the benefit of hindsight. He declares style to be "*a deference to the internal demands of the material which has become habitual* [...] *according to which the creator truly shapes his forms, the painter makes them appear.*"[44] Style emerges "solely from the correct, but necessarily humble and sober sense of the external limitation on art placed by the rough and, in relationship to the artist, *formless* material."[45] Like Georg Wilhelm Friedrich Hegel in his *Aesthetic*[46] – Semper quotes Rumohr's definition but then immediately distances himself from it, despite paying extensive tribute to the historian elsewhere in his writings.[47]

In the slender volume *The Four Elements of Architecture,* which appeared in 1851, Semper had already taken a clear stance against the view that saw the forms of architecture "as mainly conditioned by and arising from the material" and architecture as thus being defined – indeed, as being "placed in fetters" – as construction. "Architecture, like its great teacher, nature, should choose and apply its material according to the laws conditioned by nature, yet should it not also make the form and character of its creations dependent on the ideas embodied in them, and not on the material?" he asks.[48] With reference to numerous authors who, since Vitruvius, have sought to expound the timber origins of the construction of the Greek temple, he criticizes the "materialistic way of thinking" which has led to "strange and fruitless speculations".[49] In his work *Style* he sharply attacks the "coarsely materialistic" position "that holds architecture's essence to be nothing but improved construction – illustrated and illuminated statics and mechanics, as it were – or mere materiality"[50] that he associates with the Neo-Gothic and that he wants to clearly dissociate from his own "constructional-technical" notion of the origin of the basic forms of architecture.

In the prolegomena to *Style* Semper criticizes the damaging effect on art of the capitalist economy. Products "scarcely introduced" age quickly, before they can be technically or artistically exploited: "Something new, not necessarily better, always takes their place."[51] He opposes three architectural schools of thought: the "materialists", the "historians" and the "schematists". The ideas of the "materialist" school, which is influenced by natural sciences and mathematics can be criticized, according to Semper, "for fettering the idea to the material too much by accepting the false premise that the world of architectural forms arises solely from structural and material conditions and that these alone supply the means for further development."[52] According to Semper the material school also included those architects, who "favor the so-called naturalistic style of ornament" rather than observe the "basic stylistic and structural principles of adornment."[53] Here, he was probably referring to buildings to which ornament was freely applied and which appeared to have no relationship with the influences which should determine the form. "Every work of art is a *result,* or [...] it is a *Function* of an indefinite number of quantities or powers, which are the variable coefficients of the embodiment of it," he writes, summarizing this with a formula: U = C x, y, z, t, v, w. U represents the overall result, the form or the style, and x, y, z, t, v, w. represent the "different kinds of influences which act upon the embodiment of an artistic work."[54]

Semper differentiates between two classes of influence: those that "are based upon certain laws of nature and necessity, which are the same at all times and under every circumstance"[55] and those that define the work of art from outside. He divides the latter into three groups: firstly, materials and forms of execution, "the things, and the early forms in which these fundamental ideas have been clothed," secondly, the local and ethnological influences and "Influences, such as the climate and physical constitution of a country, the political and religious institutions" and, thirdly, "individual personality," which can refer to the artists or the practical producers of the work.[56]

Material as resistance

Semper's thoughts on the role of material were fundamentally misunderstood by subsequent generations and rejected as materialism. The Viennese art historian Alois Riegl was certainly careful to direct his criticism not against Semper but against the Semperians (and probably, most of all, against Otto Wagner): "Whereas Semper did suggest that material and technique play a role in the genesis of art forms, the Semperians jumped to the conclusion that all art forms were always the direct product of materials and techniques."[57] Despite this however, Riegl held Semper and his followers responsible for the dangerous cultural tendency of overvaluing technology: "'Technique' quickly emerged as a popular buzzword; in common usage, it soon became interchangeable with 'art' itself and eventually began to replace it. Only the naive talked about 'art'; experts spoke in terms of 'technique'."[58] Riegl accused the Semperians of having replaced the "free and creative artistic impulse" with an "essentially mechanical and materialist drive to imitate."[59]

In his work *Late Roman Art Industry*, which has an important place in the annals of art history, Riegl also found it necessary to attack the "older view": this is the theory "that is used in connection with the name of Gottfried *Semper* and according to which the work of art should be no more than a mechanical product consisting of a practical purpose, raw materials and technique."[60] This "dogma of materialistic metaphysics" deserves "to be finally discarded to history."[61] Riegl himself sees the work of art as "the result of a specific, purposeful artistic volition" (*Kunstwollen*) which "is victorious in the battle with practical purpose, raw materials and technique. Thus, the positive-creative role that so-called *Semperian* theory gave to these latter three factors is replaced by a much more limiting and negative one: as if they represent the coefficient of friction within the overall product."[62] For Riegl, however, this artistic volition was not something that could be derived. Hence, only metaphysical speculations could offer any insight into the emergence of this aesthetic urge.[63] One can only surmise as to why this depiction of Semper's position was so patently false. As we have seen, material and technique featured, for Semper, amongst those external factors that an artist must take into account, but any talk of a "mechanical product" is completely out of place. It is possible that Riegl wanted to emphasize the originality of his own idea of *Kunstwollen* as a driver of stylistic development; perhaps he regarded *Artis sola domina necessitas* (the only master of art is necessity), the slogan that Otto Wagner had borrowed from Semper, as a threat to the artistic imagination. In any case he rejected every material-technical explanation of ornamental forms. In his book *Problems of Style* he presents the "very delicate and intricate spiraling forms" of the facial tattoos of the Maoris as proof: "What this example does point out is [...] that, quite to the contrary, technical processes did not have to play a major role in the formation of these motifs at all."[64] Here he develops his own position by offering a cartoon-like simplification of the theory that he is criticizing.

The art historiography of the National Socialists rejected Semper's theory using arguments that were similar to those of Riegl but which were clearly based on even less understanding of his writings. "The train of thought of Semper's statements were so materialistic that no real historian who believes in human beings and great figures as the only true driving forces behind historical lives and events would want to work with them," wrote Albert Stange in 1940 in his study *The Significance of Materials for German Art (Die Bedeutung des Werkstoffes in der deutschen Kunst).*[65] He quotes the art historian Wilhelm Waetzoldt: "The creative drive of the artist also asserts itself against material, tool and purpose."[66] In the eyes of this ideology, materialism was the enemy. One of the relevant handbooks stated that "the more materialism took hold, the more it fed the growth in cultural deterioration which, in turn, seemed set to lead to national and ethnic dissolution."[67] Stange's use of the German term "Werkstoff" was no coincidence, because the alternative "Material" had to be avoided due to its proximity to the "communist" notion of materialism.[68]

Spirit and matter

In his philosophy Martin Heidegger rejected the dualistic idea of spirit and matter. He sought to overcome the traditional aesthetics which made the experience of the observer the focus of theoretical reflection. He criticized the dichotomy of form and material as a crude reduction of reality: The labeling of form as rational and matter as "ir-rational" and the linking of the dual notion of form-matter with the subject-object relationship, created a division that left us with a universally applicable mechanism for interpretation, a highly simplified "conceptual machinery".[69] The truth of a Greek temple is rooted not in the aesthetic experience of the observer but in the way in which the work was produced. Rather than becoming purely "subservient" or being consumed during the manufacturing process, a material uses that process as an opportunity to develop and to reveal its true being: " [...] the rock comes to bear and rest and so first becomes rock; metals come to glitter and shimmer, colors to glow, tones to sing, the word to speak. All this comes forth as the work sets itself back into the massiveness and heaviness of stone, into the firmness and pliancy of wood, into the hardness and luster of metal, into the lighting and darkening of color, into the clang of tone and into the naming power of the word."[70]

Peter Zumthor refers to Heidegger when he claims that a good answer to the question of "what the use of a particular material could mean in a specific architectural context" could be to "throw new light on both the way in which the material is generally used and its own inherent sensuous qualities."[71] "If we succeed in this" he writes, "materials in architecture can be made to shine and vibrate."[72] With the power of his imagination he wants to dig deep into the characteristics, into the "reality of building materials" and the "reality of the structures [...] bringing meaning and sensuousness to bear so that the spark of a successful building may be kindled."[73] His conclusion that "there are no ideas except in things"[74] is related to his differentiation between the thing and the material: "I believe that they [the materials, Á.M.] can assume a poetic quality in the context of an architectural object, although only if the architect is able to generate a meaningful situation for them, since materials in themselves are not poetic."[75]

Almost 100 years earlier Henry van de Velde had made a comparable remark upon finding that the inspiring power that makes a material beautiful was first released by human craftmanship: "No material is beautiful in itself [...]. Wood, metal, stone, and precious stones owe their unique beauty to the life that is bestowed upon them by processing, by the traces of tools and by the various ways in which those who work upon them express their inspired passion and sensitivity. There is no limit to the scale of this breathing of life into material and the result can trigger emotions ranging from the subtlest charm to complete inebriation."[76] For Van de Velde this "breathing of life into the material" signifies a sensitive empathizing with the characteristics of the material: "You should subordinate forms and structures to the essential use of the materials that you employ,"[77] he writes in his credo. He states that "the most significant, most indispensable condition for the beauty of a work of art consists of the life that is manifest in the material out of which it is made."[78] The process of working on the material represents the imbuing of the material with the subjective attributes of the genius: "In the hands of a simple worker or of any person without genius, wood, stone, clay, metal, glass and piping embody no more than their practical value. [...]."[79] For him, the challenge is to realize potential, to breathe life into a material and this requires a feeling of empathy with the material's very essence. There is no doubt that Zumthor is also convinced of the transformative power of careful work which can lend poetic expressive power to a material "in the context of an architectural object."[80] But for Van der Velde, images of streaming matter were, at the same time, the creative gesture of the empathetic artist that Loos had already criticized as the superfluous addition of the decorator. Rather than such decorative extras, Zumthor is interested in a reduction of formal resources as a way of presenting the material in a state of limbo between a faceless raw material and a cultural object. Weight and surface finish, but also associations with warmth, energy or symbolic economy connect the factual with the mythical as demonstrated by the use of felt or honey in the work of the German artist Joseph Beuys.

In the 1960s minimalist artists as Donald Judd and Robert Morris attempted to eradicate any immaterial ideas which were hidden within a material. "When I sliced into the plywood with my Skilsaw, I could hear, beneath the ear-damaging whine, a stark and refreshing 'no' reverberate off the four walls: no to transcendence and spiritual values, heroic scale, anguished decisions, historicizing narrative, valuable artifact, intelligent structure, interesting visual experience," wrote Morris retrospectively.[81] According to the minimalists the work should not be protected and controlled by the methods of memory (preservation, museum) but anonymous and at the mercy of its surroundings. The illusion of a life supported by the psychological theories of empathy should also be abandoned. This is why these artists preferred such industrial surfaces as plywood or concrete rather than materials such as grained wood or veined stone which display growth, deposits, and organic processes. The "specific object" (Judd) produced against this background should have a presence which is completely free of references except to itself. Mistrust of artistic subjectivity, enthusiasm for phenomenology – one would think that the contrast with enactment, the art of staging could not be greater. But even minimalism cannot survive without enactment. At the end of the day anonymity and serial production also have to be recognized as qualities of this art.

New Materialism

The vitalistic concept of material is gaining a new significance today in a time of disappearing resources. In the light of the feared ecological catastrophe, which is described by authors such as Bruno Latour as the ultimate criticism of modernism, categories such as matter or nature are being fundamentally reconceived (although the actual 'novelty' of these ideas has already been questioned in connection with Kant's concept of material). Feminist artistic theory (*gender studies*) interprets the form-matter duality postulated by Plato and Aristotle in a gender-specific way that is already explicitly present in those ancient theories. Aristotle writes that material requires a form like "a woman longing for a man, or what is ugly longing for what is beautiful."[82] Judith Butler suggests that design should be understood as materialization rather than as construction.[83] From her point of view, materialization is a discursive process that is related to performative acts. This is the perspective from which Donna Haraway investigated the world of material objects in the search for an alternative to vitalistic and mechanistic explanations and conceded that these objects had the capacity to act.[84] Such studies divert attention onto the cultural productivity and meaning of material objects. Authors of more recent studies of materiality often understand the so-called *material imagination* as the origin of the form: "Certainly, already in the corbelling of Neolithic dolmens, one finds evidence for an imagination that permits architects to *dream with matter,* not as a surrogate to form but as the *sine qua non* for its being," writes Matthew Mindrup.[85] He suggests that architects, through their approach to materials, had insight into the hidden productive characteristics of matter. Jane Bennett follows the same line even more rigorously in claiming that "so-called inanimate things have a life, that deep within is an inexplicable vitality or energy" and identifies that these material things have a "thing-power".[86]

Which brings us full circle. Bennett refers to Lucretius and his poem *De rerum natura*, with which we opened this chapter. Influenced by Latour's concept of the Parliament of Things Bennett emphasizes the opportunities that are opened up to us by Lucretius' realism: The opportunity, for example, to divert our view, which up until now has been blocked by concepts of subjectivity or of the image, towards the vitality of the material.[87] She describes vitality as the ability of things – products, materials, foodstuffs etc. – to act as agents, which have their own tendencies or energy. At this point many questions arise regarding this vitality: Is it a characteristic of the material or a result of a process of anthropomorphization? Bennett links the vitality of material with the historic interpretations of nature found in such works as Antonio Vivaldi's *Four Seasons*.[88] It is difficult to connect such speculations with new insights from science or system theory. There is hardly any representative of New Materialism who appears ready to do so for fear of slipping into the esoteric. On the one hand, the new interest in gnostic, animistic, and vitalistic theories demonstrates growing fear and unease in the face of dwindling ecological resources. On the other hand, however, the mystification of material fails to offer any instrument with which these dangers can be countered with solutions. If it is true that – as Latour claims – we never were modern,[89] then it is high time to become modern and to bridge the gap between material research, with its philosophically unconsidered yet concrete technological results, and a theoretical debate for which these results are generally something to be ignored.

Notes

1   Louis I. Kahn, "Monumentality", in: Paul Zucker (ed.), *New Architecture and City Planning. A Symposium*. New York: Philosophical Library, 1944, pp. 77–88.

2   Jean-Luc Nancy, *The Gravity of Thought*, transl. by François Raffoul and Gregory Recco. New Jersey: Humanities Press, 1997, p. 78.

3   Hilde de Haan, Ids Haagsma, *Gebouwen van het Plastische Getal. Een lexicon van de "Bossche School"*. Haarlem: Architext, 2010, pp. 97–100.

4   Dom H[ans] van der Laan, *Architectonic Space. Fifteen Lessons on the Disposition of the Human Habitat*. Leiden, New York, Cologne: E. J. Brill, 1983, p. 39.

5   T. Lucretus Carus, *On the Nature of Things*, transl. by Cyril Bailey. Oxford: Clarendon Press, 1910, p. 68.

6   Ruggero Pierantoni, *Vortici, atomi e sirene. Immagini e forme del pensiero esatto*. Milan: Mondadori Electa, 2003.

7   Jane Bennett, *Vibrant Matter. A Political Ecology of Things*. Durham, London: Duke University Press, 2010.

8   Sigmund Freud, *A General Introduction to Psychoanalysis* (1917), transl. by G. Stanley Hall. New York, Boni and Liverlight, 1920, 10. "Symbolism in the Dream", p. 132.

9   László Krasznahorkai, "The Rebuilding of the Ise Shrine", in: Krasznahorkai, *Seiobo There Below*, transl. by Ottilie Mulzet, New York: New Directions Books, 2013, pp. 373–422.

10   Publius Ovidius Naso, *Metamorphoses II, 5*, transl. by Stanley Lombardo. Indianapolis: Hackett Publishing Company, p. 33.

11   Comp. Ákos Moravánszky, "Architectural Theory. A Construction Site", in: Moravánszky, *Lehrgerüste. Theorie und Stofflichkeit der Architektur*. Zurich: gta Verlag, 2015, pp. 14–27.

12   Robert Hahn, *Anaximander and the Architects. The Contributions of Egyptian and Greek Architectural Technologies to the Origins of Greek Philosophy*. Albany: State University of New York Press, 2001.

13   Ibid.

14   Vitruvius, *Ten Books on Architecture*, transl. by Morris Hicky Morgan. Cambridge: *Harvard University Press*, 1914, p. 5.

15   Ibid.

16   Ibid.

17   Wolfgang Röd, *Der Weg der Philosophie von den Anfängen bis ins 20. Jahrhundert*. Volume 1: *Altertum, Mittelalter, Renaissance*. Munich: C. H. Beck 1994, p. 248.

18   Konrad Onasch, *Lichthöhle und Sternenhaus. Licht und Materie im spätantik-christlichen und frühbyzantinischen Sakralbau.* Dresden, Basel: Verlag der Kunst, 1993, p. 87. Translation by R. H.

19   Abbot Suger von Saint-Denis, "Verse für das Portal der Kathedrale von Saint-Denis", in: Rosario Assunto, *Die Theorie des Schönen im Mittelalter.* Cologne: Verlag M. DuMont Schauberg, 1963, p. 150. Translation by R. H.

20   Antoni Gaudí, "Auswahl aus den Handschriften", in: Maria Antonietta Crippa (ed.), *Gaudí. Interieurs, Möbel, Gartenkunst.* Ostfildern-Ruit: Hatje Cantz Verlag, 2001, pp. 101–107, here p. 104. Translation by R. H.

21   However, in his inaugural address as Director of the Architecture Department of the Armour Institute of Technology in Chicago on 20th November 1938, Mies van der Rohe referred not to Thomas Aquinas but to St. Augustine, who regarded beauty as "The splendor of order" *(pulchritudo splendor ordinis).* Comp. Fritz Neumeyer, *Mies van der Rohe. Das kunstlose Wort. Gedanken zur Baukunst.* Berlin: Siedler Verlag, 1986, pp. 380–381, here p. 381. (English edition: Neumeyer, *The Artless Word: Mies van der Rohe on the Building Art,* transl. by Mark Jarzombek. Cambridge, Mass.: The MIT Press, 1991.)

22   Comp. Rosario Assunto, *Die Theorie des Schönen im Mittelalter.* Cologne: Verlag Du Mont Schauberg, 1963, p. 74.

23   Fernand Pouillon, *Les pierres sauvages.* Paris: Seuil, 1964. English Edition: Pouillon, *The Stones of the Abbey,* transl. by Edward Gillott. New York: Harcourt, Brace & World, 1970.

24   Lucien Hervé, *Architecture du vérité.* London: Phaidon, 2001.

25   Alison and Peter Smithson, *Without Rhetoric. An Architectural Aesthetic 1955–1972.* Cambridge, Mass.: The MIT Press, 1973, p. 6.

26   Ibid.

27   Leon Battista Alberti, *De re aedificatoria* (Florence 1486), *On the Art of Building in Ten Books,* transl. by Joseph Rykwert, Neil Leach, Robert Tavernor. Cambridge, Mass.: The MIT Press, 1988.

28   Françoise Choay, "De re aedificatoria als Metapher einer Disziplin", in: Kurt W. Forster, Hubert Locher (ed.), *Theorie der Praxis. Leon Battista Alberti als Humanist und Theoretiker der bildenden Künste.* Berlin: Akademie Verlag, 1999, pp. 216–231.

29   Leon Battista Alberti, *On the Art of Building* (see note 27), p. 159.

30   Ibid., p. 61.

31   Ibid., p. 5.

32   Ibid., p. 7.

33   Josef Frank, "Über die ursprüngliche Gestalt der kirchlichen Bauten des Leone Battista Alberti. Dissertation zur Erlangung des Doktorgrades der technischen Wissenschaften, vorgelegt bei Professor Carl König, Technische Hochschule Wien 1910", in: Frank, *Schriften in zwei Bänden,* ed. Tano Bojankin, Christopher Long, Iris Meder. Volume 1: *Veröffentlichte Schriften 1910–1930.* Vienna: Metroverlag, 2012, pp. 47–119.

34   Andrea Palladio, *Scritti sull' architettura (1554–1579),* ed Lionello Puppi. Vicenza: N. Pozza, 1988, p. 124.

35   René Descartes, "2. Meditation", in: Descartes, *Meditationen über die Grundlagen der Philosophie,* ed. Artur Buchenau. Hamburg: Felix Meiner, 1958, pp. 22–24.

36   Auguste Choisy, *L'art de bâtir chez les Romains.* Paris: Ducher et Cie, 1873.

37   Gilles Deleuze, *The Fold. Leibniz and the Baroque.* transl. by Tom Conley. London, New York: Continuum, 1993, p. 3.

38   Hans Sedlmayr, *Francesco Borromini.* 2nd Edition, Munich: Piper, 1939, p. 93f. Translation by R. H.

39   Francesco Borromini, *Opus Architectonicum. Erzählte und dargestellte Architektur. Die Casa die Filippini in Rom im Stichwerk von Sebastiano Giannini (1725) mit dem Text von Virgilio Spada (1647),* ed. Monika Küble, Felix Thürlemann. Sulgen, Zurich: Niggli, 1999, p. 94f. Translation by R. H.

40   Ibid. Translation by R. H.

41   Friedrich Albert Lange, *Geschichte des Materialismus und Kritik seiner Bedeutung in der Gegenwart.* 2nd Edition, Iserlohn: Verlag von J. Baedeker, 1873, p. 3. Translation by R. H.

42   Carl Vogt, *Physiologische Briefe für Gebildete aller Stände.* Gießen: J. Ricker'sche Buchhandlung, 1854. Vogt, *Köhlerglaube und Wissenschaft. Eine Streitschrift gegen Hofrath Rudolph Wagner in Göttingen.* Gießen: J. Ricker'sche Buchandlung, 1954. Jac[ob] Moleschott, *Der Kreislauf des Lebens. Physiologische Antworten auf Liebig's Chemische Briefe.* Mainz: Verlag von Victor v. Zabern, 1852. Louis [Ludwig] Büchner, *Kraft und Stoff. Empirisch-naturphilosophische Studien. In allgemein-verständlicher Darstellung.* Frankfurt a. M.: Meidinger Sohn,

1855. Heinrich Czolbe, *Neue Darstellung des Sensualismus. Ein Entwurf.* Leipzig: Hermann Costenoble, 1855.

43   Gottfried Semper, "London Lecture of November 11, 1853", ed. with a commentary by Harry Francis Mallgrave, foreword by Joseph Rykwert, in *Res 6* (Autumn, 1983) pp. 5-22, here p. 11. Semper's text was subsequently translated into German by his son Hans and published in Semper, *Kleine Schriften,* ed. Hans and Manfred Semper. Berlin, Stuttgart: Verlag W. Spemann, 1884.

44   C[arl] Fr[iedrich] von Rumohr, *Italienische Forschungen,* ed. Julius Schlosser, Frankfurt am Main: Frankfurter Verlags-Anstalt A.-G., 1920, p. 59f. Translation by R. H.

45   Ibid. Translation by R. H.

46   Georg Wilhelm Friedrich Hegel, *Introductory Lectures on Aesthetics,* ed. Michael Inwood, transl. by Bernard Bosanquet. London: Penguin Classics, 1994.

47   Semper, "London Lecture of November 11, 1853" (see note 43), p. 15.

48   Gottfried Semper, "The Four Elements of Architecture", in: Semper, *The Four Elements of Architecture and Other Writings,* transl. by Harry Francis Mallgrave and Wolfgang Herrmann, Cambridge: Cambridge University Press, 1989, p. 102.

49   Ibid.

50   Gottfried Semper, *Style in the Technical and Tectonic Arts; or, Practical Aesthetics,* transl. by Harry Francis Mallgrave and Michael Robinson. Los Angeles: Getty Research Institute, 2004, p. 106.

51   Ibid., p. 75.

52   Ibid., p. 77.

53   Ibid., p. 78.

54   Semper, "London Lecture of November 11, 1853" (see note 43), p. 11.

55   Ibid.

56   Ibid., p. 11f.

57   Alois Riegl, *Problems of Style. Foundations for a History of Ornament.* transl. by Evelyn Kain. Princeton, New Jersey: Princeton University Press, 1992, p. 4.

58   Ibid.

59   Ibid.

60   Alois Riegl, *Spätrömische Kunstindustrie.* Vienna: Druck und Verlag der österreichischen Staatsdruckerei, 1927, p. 8. Translation by R. H.

61   Ibid.

62   Ibid., p. 9.

63   Hans Sedlmayr, "Einleitung", in: Alois Riegl, *Gesammelte Aufsätze.* Augsburg, Vienna: Dr. Benno Filser Verlag, 1928, pp. XI–XXXIV.

64   Alois Riegl, *Problems of Style* (see note 57), p. 77f.

65   Albert Stange, *Die Bedeutung des Werkstoffes in der deutschen Kunst.* Bielefeld, Leipzig: Velhagen und Klasing, 1940, p. 7.

66   Wilhelm Waetzoldt, *Deutsche Kunsthistoriker.* 2nd Volume, 1924, p. 132, quoted in: Stange (see note 65), p. 8.

67   Reichsjugendführung der NSDAP, *Werkhefte für den Heimbau der Hitler-Jugend.* 2nd Volume: *Die Gestaltung des Innenraumes.* Leipzig: Verlag von Erwin Skacel, 1938, p. 282.

68   Comp. Christian Fuhrmeister, *Beton Klinker Granit, Material Macht Politik. Eine Materialikonographie.* Berlin: Verlag Bauwesen, 2001, pp. 10–12.

69   Martin Heidegger, "The Origin of the Work of Art", in: Heidegger, *Basic Writings from Being and Time (1927) to The Task of Thinking (1964),* ed. David Farrell Krell. San Francisco: Harper & Row, 1977, pp. 143–187, here p. 158.

70   Ibid., p. 171.

71   Peter Zumthor, "A way of looking at things" (1988), in: Zumthor, *Thinking Architecture.* Basel, Boston, Berlin: Birkhäuser, 1999, p. 11.

72   Ibid.

73   Peter Zumthor, "The hard core of beauty" (1991), in: Zumthor, *Thinking Architecture* (see note 71), p. 34.

74   Ibid.

75   Zumthor, "A way of looking at things", (see note 71), p. 11.

76   Henry van de Velde, "Die Belebung des Stoffes als Prinzip der Schönheit" (1910), in: van de Velde, *Essays.* Leipzig: Insel-Verlag 1910, pp. 5–38, here p. 13. Translation by R. H.

77   Henry van de Velde, "Das Streben nach einem Stil, dessen Grundlagen auf vernünftiger, logischer Konzeption beruhen", in: van de Velde, *Zum neuen Stil,* Munich: Piper, 1955, pp. 148–155, here p. 150. Translation by R. H.

78   Van de Velde, "Die Belebung des Stoffes" (see note 76), p. 28. Translation by R. H.

79   Ibid. p. 12f.

80   Zumthor, "A way of looking at things", (see note 71), p. 11.

81   Robert Morris, "Three Folds in the Fabric and Four Autobiographical Asides as Allegories (or Interruptions)", in: Morris, *Continuous Project Altered Daily. The Writings of Robert Morris.* Cambridge, Mass.: The MIT Press, 1993, pp. 259–285, here pp. 263–265.

82   Aristotle, *Physics*, ed. David Bostock, transl. by Robin Waterfield. Oxford: Oxford World's Classics, 2008, p. 31.

83   Judith Butler, *Bodies that matter: On the Discursive Limits of "Sex".* Hove: Psychology Press, 1993.

84   Donna Jeanne Haraway, *Crystals, Fabrics, and Fields. Metaphors That Shape Embryos.* Berkeley: North Atlantic Books, 1976.

85   Matthew Mindrup, "Editor's Note. Interrogating the Gap Between the Material and Formal Imagination: An Introduction", in: Mindrup (ed.), *The Material Imagination. Reveries on Architecture and Matter.* Farnham: Ashgate, 2015, pp. 1–9, here p. 3.

86   Jane Bennett, *Vibrant Matter* (see note 7), p. 18.

87   Ibid., p. 19.

88   Ibid., p. 117.

89   Bruno Latour, *We Have Never Been Modern.* Cambridge, Mass.: Harvard University Press, 1993.

3.
THE MATTER OF NATURE

The concept of metamorphosis in architecture, which also underlies Gottfried Semper's theory of *Stoffwechsel*, is based on the observation of nature. Marc-Antoine Laugier's renowned description of the so-called primitive hut, which was published in 1753, refers explicitly to the simplicity of this model as a natural principle: "Such is the course of simple nature; by imitating the natural process, art was born."[1] [Fig. 3.1] Imitation refers here not to the external appearance but to nature's way of working. According to Laugier it is important

3.1 Charles Eisen, allegory of the return of architecture to its natural model. Frontispiece to M.-A. Laugier, *An Essay on Architecture*, 2nd Edition, Paris, 1755.

3.2 Vault of the St. Nicholas Church in Leipzig. Johann Carl Friedrich Dauthe, 1784–1797.

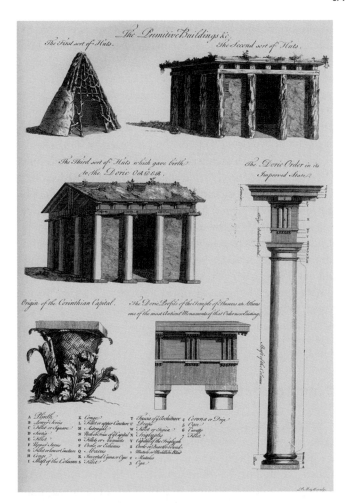

3.3 William Chambers, plate from
*A Treatise on the Decorative Part of
Civil Architecture*, London, 1759.
3.4 The royal saltworks at Chaux in
Arc-et-Senans by Claude-Nicolas
Ledoux, 1775–1778.

to ask fundamental questions about things rather than just questions about the classical orders which, until then, had been the main subject of architectural treatises. His demand had a huge impact across Europe in the second half of the 18th century and even the engraving by Charles Eisen that Laugier used as a frontispiece influenced the architecture of the time: Leipzig's city architect Johann Carl Friedrich Dauthe used fluted columns with capitals of palm fronds when remodeling the interior of the St. Nicholas Church (1784–1797). [Fig. 3.2] However, the young Johann Wolfgang von Goethe (in his essay "On German Architecture", 1773) and the English architect William Chambers (in his book *A Treatise on the Decorative Part of Civil Architecture,* 1st edition 1759) decidedly rejected Laugier's "Manifesto of Classicism". Nature is imperfect and cannot be a model for architecture, or, even better: It is precisely in its whims and diversity that the magic of nature is to be found, writes Chambers as he illustrates his book with not just one but three primitive huts.[2] [Fig. 3.3] Chambers, like Goethe, was an admirer of the Gothic, whose qualities of lightness and structural audacity could never have been achieved by the architecture of antiquity.[3] Even Giovanni Battista Piranesi in his essay in the form of a dialogue, "Parere sull'architettura" (1765), poured scorn on the search for the one true principle in view of the fantastic abundance of architectural forms.[4]

Creating and created nature

The term "nature" has a dual meaning in Western thought that can be traced back to Aristotle and his medieval interpreters. *Natura naturans* means: creating nature, nature as a creative principle and can be traced back to the Latin root of the word *nasci,* "to be born". *Natura naturata* is the result, the born, created nature. In antiquity this was already associated with the image of the grotto: the uterus of the earth, the entrance to the underworld which was venerated by the Greeks as the place of the oracle. It is thus no surprise that buildings related to work imitate such forms.

The salt town of Chaux in Arc-et-Senans, which was designed by the architect Claude-Nicolas Ledoux and completed in 1778, is an ensemble which includes not only the saltworks but also the workers' accommodation. [Fig. 3.4] The reduction of brine was a dangerous process that claimed many victims due to the fact that the workers had to walk on planks which were laid above the evaporating basins. The – largely symbolic – visual control of the working process by the supervisors determined the layout of the complex. Ledoux presented the result as *architecture parlante:* a rigorous classicism, in which tectonic refinement is replaced by crystalline sharpness, combined with narrative details that naturalize the industrial process of crystallization. The use of Doric columns without bases in Chaux was to be understood as a form of industrial classical order. In his essay "L'architecture considérée sous le rapport de l'art, des moeurs et de la legislation" (Architecture considered in relation to art, morals, and legislation, 1804) Ledoux describes nature as a nourishing, creative force which brings benefits to mankind that can unfold in the form of a harmonic collaboration with industry: "[…] even the earth fructifies industry."[5] The façades of the buildings in Chaux feature a petrified salt solution

3.5, 3.6 The royal saltworks at Chaux.

gushing from circular openings and one enters the ideal city through a grotto below a Propylaean gateway with tightly packed columns which also invokes the underground crystalline world of nature. [Fig. 3.5] The hard labor in the fumes of the factory sheds was thus glorified as the human contribution to the fructification of the earth in a similar way to the pollination of flowers by bees. Supervision and discipline had to appear just as natural in Ledoux's ideal city as the classical orders, which were presented in an inorganically-petrified state, stripped of their humanistic refinement. [Fig. 3.6]

occasionner ni ruptures ni déformations, ni même une pose difficile ou des retouches au burin sur le tas.

13

Il est évident que dans une construction de ce genre, tout doit être

3.7, 3.8 Drawing of a cast-iron joint and a design for a hall. Illustrations from Viollet-le-Duc, *Entretiens sur l'architecture*, Paris, 1863–1872.

It is the gatehouse, the point of entry to the world of industry, where *Natura naturans* is interpreted as a rugged, rocky grotto. The American architect Henry Hobson Richardson chose this pictorial eruption of raw blocks of stone as the theme for the façade of Ames Gate Lodge in the industrial town of North Easton near Boston (1880/81). The building forms the entrance to the grounds of the country home of Frederick Lothrop Ames, son of the "railway baron" Oliver Ames, and contains apartments for the gardener and for guests (see Figs. 1.2, 1.3). The interpretation of the gateway as geological architecture can be understood here as some sort of symbolic compensation for the large-scale destruction of nature that began with the construction of the railways. The building acts like an as-found formation of rocks, a natural bridge that, with minimal intervention, was transformed into architecture. Richardson's pyramidal monument to Oakes and Oliver Ames was created in the same way: The natural formation known as Reed's Rock was sawn up and the result-

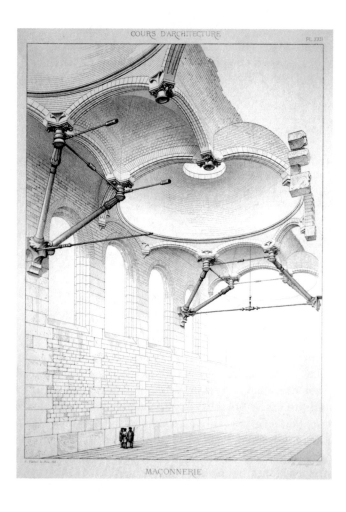

3.9 Masonry with cast-iron supports. Plate from the atlas of the *Entretiens sur l'architecture* by E. E. Viollet-le-Duc, Paris, 1864.
3.10 Façade of the Sacré-Coeur School, Paris. Hector Guimard, 1895.

ing granite blocks, with their untreated surfaces and weight of several tons, were transported by ox cart to the monument's location in Sherman. Richardson was delighted by the fact that passengers on passing trains assumed that the monument was a natural object and he believed that the frequent heavy storms in the State of Wyoming could only be good for his work.[6]

While Richardson used the forms of *Natura naturata* (see p. 64) as a model, the French architect and restorer Eugène Emmanuel Viollet-le-Duc (1814–1879) worked on the theory of an architecture which, rather than imitating nature, appropriated the formal principles of creating nature. In comparison with Semper, who had sought to achieve this objective through a practical aesthetic organized in material categories, Viollet-le-Duc set out his theory in the ten-volume *Dictionnaire raisonné de l'architecture française du XIe au XVIe siècle* (1854–1868), an encyclopedia of medieval architecture which regarded the rationality of the Gothic as analogous with the more elevated rationality of the laws of nature and, hence, proposed this as the proper basis for the architecture of the modern age.[7] Despite their different stylistic ideals, Viollet-le-Duc and Semper were both influenced by the comparative anatomy of the French natural scientist Georges Cuvier and endeavored to make use of the comparative methods of the zoologist in their investigations into architectural forms (see p. 164). Cuvier's starting point was the observation of the correlation of the organs in an organism, the question of how they join together as a whole, in terms of both form and function. [Fig. 3.7] Viollet-le-Duc identified a similar chain of causalities in the structure of a gothic cathedral. For him, style was the unity of structure and form, in both nature and architecture. "If the mode of construction changes, the form necessarily differs but there is not a Greek unity, a Roman unity, nor a unity of the Middle Ages. An oak does not resemble the stem of a fern, nor a horse a hare; yet plants and animals obey the organic unity that governs all organized individuals."[8] This form of anatomical obser-

3.11 Hanging model for the church of the Colònia Güell by Antoni Gaudí, reconstruction 1982.

vation dictated Viollet-le-Duc's thinking as a restorer of medieval buildings for which he used the same deductive methods as those used by Cuvier when reconstructing the physical build of extinct animals from their fossilized remains. He describes the cathedral as an organism at a certain point of its evolutionary history and thus not at its end. Most chapters of the *Dictionnaire* address "the logical process of thought and the unity of principle as applied by the masters of the Middle Ages."[9]

Viollet-le-Duc was convinced that the Gothic which he admired was not the ultimate peak of architectural excellence. Quite the contrary, the latest breakthroughs in engineering science and the use of iron meant that gothic rationality could be developed further. In his series of essays *Entretiens sur l'architecture* (Lectures on Architecture), a summary of his teachings on design published between 1858 and 1870, Viollet-le-Duc explains his idea of a modern iron architecture which is suitable for the building of large spaces.[10] The ornamental joints of the iron framework are shaped in line with the model of the joints of the human skeleton. For some strange reason, however, Viollet-le-Duc's concept of unity appeared to attach no importance to that correlation between the

3.12 View of the vault of the Basilica of the Sagrada Familia by Antoni Gaudí in Barcelona during construction. The execution commenced in 1882.
3.13 Façade of the crypt of the unfinished church of the Colònia Güell in Santa Coloma de Cervelló by Antoni Gaudí, 1908–1914.

3.14 Façade of the Casa Batlló,
Barcelona, as remodeled by Antoni
Gaudí between 1904 and 1906.

parts that, according to Cuvier, results from the living conditions of an organism. In Viollet-le-Duc's bold and often bizarre designs for new structures it is precisely this unity, the most important objective of a style, which is missing.[11] [Fig. 3.8] One of his structural ideas, the use of diagonal steel supports, was taken up by Hector Guimard in the façade of his Sacré-Cœur School in Paris (1893–1895) as a means of opening up the ground floor as much as possible. [Figs. 3.9, 3.10] Semper had read Viollet-le-Duc's *Dictionnaire* and commented critically upon the work.[12] The issue about which the two most influential 19th-century theoreticians differ greatly is the evaluation of gothic architecture. For Viollet-le-Duc, Gothic was the embodiment of constructional rationalism – and for Semper it was, for precisely this reason, a tyrannical principle that clapped the freedom of the "divinatory purpose of the artist" in irons. For Viollet-le-Duc the crystal was the object that embodied the logical principle of

3.15 Fallingwater (Kaufmann Residence), Bear Run, Pennsylvania. Frank Lloyd Wright, 1935–1939.
3.16 The fireplace in Fallingwater.

abb. 17 metallstruktur. elektrolyteisen durchgebrochen   foto: kramer

(2¹/₄mal vergrößert)

abb. 18 struktur. salzlagerstätte. spanien   foto: kaiser-wilhelm-institut (metallografie)

36

nature and architecture in a primary form. Semper, on the other hand, saw the knot, the basic motif of the weaving of fabric, as "the oldest technical symbol" (see Chapter 8).[13] The stringent form of the crystal, dictated by natural laws, is confronted by the diversity of decorative textile patterns which emerges from the rules of weaving and the fantasy of the artist. The Gothic is dominated by the framework, while the walls – regarded by Semper as the primary elements of architecture – dissolve in the form of stained glass windows. It is for this reason that Semper regarded the purely decorative use of tracery in the late Gothic as some sort of ironic self-criticism of the style: "The principle itself, interpreted with the utmost sophistry, encouraged the greatest arbitrariness; in its dotage the system became comical and played humorous games with its own nature!"[14] This criticism has a certain currency today in the light of the gymnastic feats of engineering that are rendered possible by the computer.

Viollet-le-Duc's work convinced the Catalan architect Antoni Gaudí to search for the roots of a national architecture in the local landscape, in its flora and fauna and the intrinsic manual skills of its people. Gaudí studied the forms of growth of plants and the rock formations of Catalonia and used the results in his designs for buildings such as the Sagrada Familia in Barcelona (start of construction 1882). [Fig. 3.11] In his notes about nature, Gaudí described both *Natura naturans* and *Natura naturata* as principles and models.[15] Viollet-le-Duc's *Entretiens sur l'architecture* strongly influenced the Catalan architect although, at the same time, he doubted whether everything in architecture really was dictated by rational laws and necessity.[16] Thus, the study of nature in his

abb. **23** textur
ein 130 jähriger amerikaner von
minnesota

im grunde ist diese fotografie eine zeitraffer-
aufnahme der epidermiswandlung: eine flug-
zeugaufnahme der zeit.

abb. **24** textur
ein fauler, mit pilzen besetzter
apfel

foto: weltspiegel

foto: haus und garten

6 moholy-nagy

41

foto: pestry tyden

foto: koralle

abb. **26** faktur
ulmenrinde, durchbohrt von dem sco-
litus multistriatus

abb. **27** faktur
von dem „buchdrucker" zerfressene
fichte

die „künstliche einwirkung" ist hier die zerstörungsarbeit der käfer: auch faktur.

6*

43

3.17 a, b, c *Struktur, Textur*
and *Faktur*. Pages from László
Moholy-Nagy, *Von material zu
architektur*, Munich, 1929.

work led to formal results which, unlike the designs of the French architect, had an organic air.

Gaudí's experiments with what he described as "stereostatic" hanging models are often cited as examples of material self-production.[17] Although the load-bearing capacity of structures had already been investigated as part of building practice long before Gaudí – we have already referred to the relevance of the building site of antiquity in terms of the development of theory – this is the first occasion in the history of building in which experiment becomes a form-generating factor. Gaudí built models in which the loadbearing structural members of a church, the columns and ribs, for example, correspond with the strings that were hung from the ceiling of his workshop. He weighed down the knots in the string polygon with small bags of lead shot which approximately modeled the expected loads. The spatial form that was assumed by the string structure under the weight of the bags was regarded by Gaudí as the naturally determined form of the loadbearing structure, which then had to be covered with a skin-like façade. He compared this process with the act of creation in which flesh and skin are applied to a skeleton.[18] [Fig. 3.12] Most of his buildings are "overgrown" by organic, skin-like surfaces while climbing plants complete his work. [Fig. 3.13] The Casa Batlló in Barcelona is the remodeling of an existing residential building (façade 1904–1906) for the surfaces of which Gaudí developed a broad spectrum of geological-organic forms. The façade is covered with a plastered skin in which glazed ceramic shards are embedded and out of which painted circular ceramic discs project. In front of this pointillist, colorfully glowing façade, which recalls the shimmering surfaces of the plant-covered ponds of the paintings of Claude Monet, the stone structure of the lower-level balconies stands like a series of enormous bones. This moving façade composition is crowned with a roof that is covered with glazed ceramics which resemble the scales of a reptile. [Fig. 3.14]

While Viollet-le-Duc was convinced that rationality was the common principle shared by the Gothic on the one hand and by a modern architecture which worked with industrial materials on the other, Gaudí's experimental methods were designed to permit the direct use of natural laws to determine forms, without the subjective creative input of the architect. He spoke of an "intel·ligència angelica", of the wisdom of the angel, referring to the angelic ability to directly address the notion of space without the need for intermediation in the form of two-dimensional drawings.[19] In Gaudí's view it is nature itself, this inscrutable force that can never be reduced to mere formulas, that determines the optimal form of the loadbearing structure in his model-based experiments. In reality, both the design of the experiment itself (such as the choice of the points from which the rope is hanged) and the interpretation of the results leave enough room for architectural subjectivity. It is thus no surprise that these buildings tend to be seen as the eccentric creations of a lonely genius rather than the results of scientific experimentation. "The principle itself, interpreted with the utmost sophistry, encouraged the greatest arbitrariness; in its dotage the system became comical and played humorous games with its own nature!" Can Semper's ironic criticism of Viollet-le-Duc also be applied to Gaudí's stereostatics?[20]

Gaudí's experiments with models were taken up by such post-war architects and engineers as Frei Otto, Sergio Musmeci and Heinz Isler. For Otto, however, it was clear that even if a model-based experiment resulted in a form, this

3.18 Detail of the courtyard of Alvar Aalto's summer house in Muuratsalo on Lake Päijänne, 1952/53.

form was still a long way from being an architectural project. For him, the experiment was thus more a trigger for a thought process than a solution to the design problem.[21]

Avant-garde materials

The vitality of nature can be seen in modern dress in Frank Lloyd Wright's Fallingwater. The weekend house in the Allegheny Mountains to the south of Pittsburgh was built for the department store mogul Edgar J. Kaufmann (1935–1939). Rather than meaning something like 'the house on the waterfall' the name "Fallingwater" is derived from the plunging, dynamic element of water. Earlier, Ledoux had designed a waterfall house for the surveyors of the River Loue near his salt town which, demonstratively technical, was to have had the air of a classicist machine. Fallingwater is a picturesque antithesis to the industrial city of Pittsburgh. This notion has been familiar since the Baroque but Wright developed the thematic possibilities with grandiose modern orchestration, a form of spatial ornamentation which is fractal right down to the last detail and interlaced with natural *objets trouvés*. The floor of the living level is paved with *flagstones* which are polished with wax in such a way that they glisten as if bathed in a thin film of water. Boulders upon which the family used to sit and picnic before the house was built emerge from the floor alongside the fireplace. The dialectical counterpart to the fireplace is a glass *hatch* with a door and sliding lid from which an open stair leads down to the stream. When this *hatch* is open the living space should be filled with the "music of the water". [Figs. 3.15, 3.16]

As the dynamization of a natural element and a visual embodiment of time flowing inexorably by, Wright's Fallingwater combines the cult of sources of Art Nouveau (the areas of concrete on the terrace which are now rendered in a peach color were originally to have been covered in gold leaf!) with an avant-gardist activation of the material.[22]

3.19 Rock salt from Wieliczka, Galicia. Photograph from Alfred Ehrhardt, *Kristalle*, Hamburg, 1939.

In his Bauhaus book *Von material zu architektur* (1929, first American edition: *The new vision: from material to architecture,* 1930) László Moholy-Nagy emphasizes that intensive engagement with the material would "increase one's assurance in measuring sensations."[23] The title of the book is important: According to Moholy-Nagy it is not knowledge about history, style or detailed forms but the (in no way merely scientific-technical) study of material that leads to contemporary architecture. The optically and haptically discernible traces of workmanship, the so-called *Faktur* (translated in the American edition as "surface aspect"), overlapped with the *Textur* (texture), the structure of the final surface, determine our relationship with the material. The internal *Struktur* (structure) of a piece of wood is visible in cross-section; a piece of bark has a natural *Textur,* and if it has been perforated by woodworm one can speak of *Faktur*. Moholy-Nagy combines examples such as the cell structures of paper wasps, the fur of a cat or the haptic quality of a field of rye after harvest with images from the "technical world" in which machines and tools, steel frames, and concrete structures are selected to communicate the aesthetic of modernism. [Figs. 3.17 a, b, c]

For Moholy-Nagy the biological was the regulator *par excellence*: The apogee of spatial creation is "its significance from the biological standpoint."[24]

Moholy-Nagy's and Alvar Aalto's studies of material (the latter were influenced by the book by Moholy-Nagy cited above) are comparable with experiments in the VKhUTEMAS workshops in Moscow, not least as a result of their shared interest in the psychological effect of processed materials – as exemplified by curved pieces of laminated wood. Aalto was convinced that the solution to a design problem was a process. He intended "to underline variation and growth – similar to that of natural organic life – as the most profound characteristic of architecture."[25] His Finnish Pavilion at the World Fair in New York in 1939 was pure interior architecture in a box-like space that was created at the same time as his Villa Mairea in Noormarkku. The narrative aspect was important in both projects. In New York, the basic spatial idea consisted of a clearing in a Finnish forest – as mythical nature and, at the same time, the raw material of the timber industry – together with the atmospheric *mis-en-scène* of the Aurora Borealis.

The reconciliation between the endless wealth of formal variants of a type in nature and the inflexibility of the technical prototype was one of Aalto's major rhetorical achievements. While he was still advocating standardization in architecture in his speech of 1938 his address to the Nordic Building Conference in Oslo just three years later criticized the sort of standardization that "creates uniformity and formalism."[26] In 1941 Aalto delivered a lecture in several Swiss cities about post-war European reconstruction. He emphasized that standardization in architecture had to occur in line with biological models rather than the principles of the automobile industry: "Nature is the most remarkable standardization institute of all. [...] Every blossom is made up of innumerable apparently uniform proto-cells, but these cells have a quality that permits the most extraordinary variety in the linkage of cells."[27] True standardization must

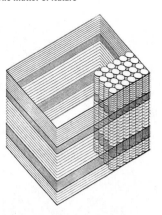

3.20 Illustration from the book *Von der Bebauung der Erde* by Rudolf Schwarz, Heidelberg, 1949.
3.21 Façade of the church of S. Giovanni Fuorcivitas in Pistoia, with bands of white marble and green serpentine from Prato. 1119, expanded until 1344.

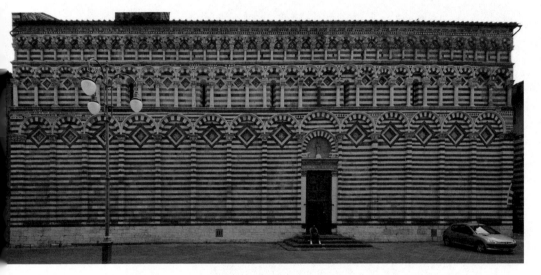

be conceived in such a way that the standardized elements permit the greatest possible number of combinations. The model for this is nature, in which "standardization" only occurs in the smallest entity, the cell. The result of this is that identical cells "with the capacity to form an astounding variety of combinations can thus produce a tremendous wealth of forms in the final product; yet these forms are all based on a specific system."[28] The brick was given the role of being a cell. The curved form of Aalto's Baker House, the student residence of Massachusetts Institute of Technology in Cambridge (1946–1949), and the deformed and partly kiln-damaged bricks which were used in its construction, sought to illustrate this idea: Thus, a metaphor was materialized.[29] Aalto used his summer house in Muuratsalo on Lake Päijänne (1952/53) as a laboratory, an experiment with various building materials which "were tested from both the aesthetic and the practical points of view."[30] He clad the courtyard façades of his house with several types of brick and ceramic tiles in order to communicate the joy of juxtaposing their varying haptic and optical qualities. Here, the experiment should not be understood in the scientific sense: It cannot fail because it promises experience rather than results and this is a promise which is certain to be kept.[31] On the other hand: the example demonstrates how we can broaden

3.22 Façade of St. Anna's Church in Düren, Rudolf Schwarz, 1951–1956.
3.23 Interior of St. Anna's Church in Düren.

the notion of the "modern experiment" in order to enable the processes of reality to become part of the structure of the experiment – to "contaminate" it with earth and moss. [Fig. 3.18]

3.24 Parish Church of St. Florian in Vienna, Rudolf Schwarz, 1957–1963.
3.25 Interior of the Parish Church of St. Florian.

Visions of the earth

In his later years Viollet-le-Duc dedicated himself to a truly gigantic project: the theoretical and graphic restoration of the Alps. Numerous mountain hikes around Mont Blanc – one of which ended when he fell into a crevice – and his

Cuvier-inspired anatomical viewpoint enabled him to see the organic whole behind every fragment. Viollet-le-Duc's *Le massif du Mont Blanc. Étude sur sa constitution géodésique et géologique sur les transformations et sur l'état ancien et moderne de ses glaciers* appeared in 1876.[32] Mountaineers and geologists had already drawn attention to the erosion of the mountains. Now, the architect took the task of restoring the architecture of the mountains seriously and prepared a series of detailed drawings in order to determine the crystalline logic of the morphology which could serve as the basis for the recreation of the original situation. As soon as the scientific eye of the architect has recognized the large-scale geometric order of nature he can reverse the destruction of the erosion in order to return the Alps to their original condition – at least in the form of drawings and watercolors. This equating of nature with rationality, with clear rules which are merely waiting to be discovered, was an Enlightenment idea that Viollet-le-Duc applied rigorously. But this connection between the history of the earth and the history of architecture does not start with Viollet-le-Duc's study. The Renaissance fascination with veins in rocks which show cities or landscapes and which are then introduced into architecture already suggests potential reciprocities between geology and architecture. "Objective" scientific photography, sharp close-ups of plants and crystals and photographs of microorganisms and landscapes were truly magical images – and important sources of inspiration - for architects in the 1920s and 1930s. This way of looking at natural forms that was associated with New Objectivity began with the work of Karl Blossfeldt who enjoyed global success with his photographs of seemingly ornamental plant forms (*Urformen der Kunst*, 1928).[33] The former Bauhaus student Alfred Ehrhardt was one of the most important representatives of the new "objective" photography of nature. [Fig. 3.19] Albert Renger-Patzsch significantly expanded this new pictorial world in that he also captured technical objects and industrial buildings. In 1928, the architect Rudolf Schwarz (1897–1961) published a book, the first – and final – volume in the series *Aachener Werkbücher* (Aachen Workbooks), with the ambiguous title *Wegweisung der Technik* (*Guidance for Technology* as well as *Guidance by Technology*) that he illustrated with 74 full-page photographs by Renger-Patzsch.[34] The fact that technology and nature do not come across in the book as incompatible opposites is not only down to Schwarz's text which, from its very first lines, evokes the might and magnitude of the energy in both worlds. It is also confirmed by the eye of the photographer: The crown of a Brazilian papaya tree and the gothic pillars of St Mary's Church in Zwickau exhibit a similarly steely monumentality.

A truly global vision of the material and formal continuity of the natural and urban worlds was then presented by Schwarz in the book *Von der Bebauung der Erde* (*Of the Development of the Earth*, 1949) that he had written during the war years. The architect argues that mankind builds "in order to find a home in the uninhabitability of space," through a process of "building layers" analogous to the geological layering of the earth.[35] As a result of movements, this layered earth stretches in two directions: "[...] the vertical path, which the earth climbs in order to counter gravity, and the horizontal expansion," which Schwarz also describes as "cleavage and graining."[36] The geological tectonics of the "material of the world" has its parallels in architectonics: The higher the building, the denser the lower layers and the more delicate the upper ones. "The building

3.26 Arantzazu pilgrimage church near Oñati. Francisco Sáenz de Oiza with Luis Laorga, 1950–1954.
3.27 Interior of the Arantzazu pilgrimage church, altar wall by Lucio Muñoz, 1962.

3.28 Erdman Hall at Bryn Mawr
College, Bryn Mawr, Pennsylvania.
Louis I. Kahn, 1960–1965.

is also more elegant as one rises within it, heavy strands and columns seem to taper towards the top, swelling surreptitiously like Doric columns."[37]

Schwarz illustrated his text with simple axonometrics and sections. Some, which illustrate the process of layering, trigger associations with the striated marble façades of Italian medieval churches whose combination of white Carrara marble and gray Pietra Serena suggestively visualizes the rhythm of layered masonry. [Figs. 3.20, 3.21] Another of Schwarz's drawings shows a section through a rocky conglomerate that he associates in the text with both fabric and concrete: "The depth of the earth is torn open and water gushes from the edges of the wound. The glowing rock rises from even deeper cracks and causes the landscape to shudder. In those places where [...] fragments of rock, sand and pebbles collect together to form piles of debris one finds disparate, colorfully mixed remains lying side-by-side like new concrete. A bewildering, multicolored carpet which is woven together from conflicting elements in the landscape yet still achieves coherency."[38]

3.29 Light-gray profiles from Woodbury granite framing white, translucent panels of Vermont marble on the façade of the Beinecke Rare Book Library, Yale University, New Haven. Gordon Bunshaft, Skidmore, Owings & Merrill, 1959–1963.
3.30 Interior of the Beinecke Rare Book Library.

The church buildings which Schwarz constructed after the Second World War reveal how this understanding of nature and materials also influenced his architecture. St. Anna's Church in Düren was built between 1951 and 1956 on the site of a gothic church that had been completely destroyed during the war. When Schwarz visited the ruins he found the "piles of ancient stones"

3.31 Interior of St. Pius' Church in Meggen near Lucerne. Franz Füeg, 1960–1968.

and wanted to "build these back into the new church so that the sacred stones could become materials in a new work and the old resurrected in the new."[39] The image that explains the entire building "is defined by the huge perimeter wall, which surrounds the main nave on four sides and then wraps around as an edging to the glass wall, and by the space which it surrounds. This huge, protective form is like an open cloak [...] – a theological image".[40] Unlike the religious spaces that he had realized before the Second World War whose impact resulted from the interaction between a dynamically dramatic use of light and homogenous, abstract and brightly plastered surfaces, the spatial effects are now determined by the materiality of the wall surfaces. At the same time, the theme of the wall structure is the interweaving of inorganic layering and organic growth. Behind the altar, writes Schwarz, "the bond of the masonry arches into a tree of life, the symbol of the sacred life that grows there, rooted in the altar, and the congregation stands in the sight of this huge symbol. It is built of stone, with bright fruits which are made of alabaster, although it could just as well be painted [...]."[41] The image of the tree of life is interwoven with the image of sedimentation as two dimensions of time in keeping with his interpretation of the development of the earth as quoted above. [Figs. 3.22, 3.23] At St. Florian Parish Church in Vienna (1957–1963) Schwarz employs forms that can be associated with both the natural world of plants and the world of technology, forms whose affinity he had already demonstrated in the book *Wegweisung der Technik*. [Figs. 3.24, 3.25]

There is a relationship between Schwarz's St Anna's Church in Düren and the large pilgrimage church of Aránzazu (Spanish; Basque Arantzazu) which is located near Oñati in a valley in the Basque Region and was designed by Francisco Javier Sáenz de Oiza together with Luis Laorga Gutiérrez (1950–1954). Sáenz de Oiza was, like Schwarz, influenced by the church architect Dominikus Böhm (1880–1955). The church traces its name back to *arantza* (thorns) and the miraculous appearance of the Virgin in a thorn bush in the 16th century – a fact that explains the use of limestone blocks with pyramidal surfaces to clad the

3.32 Marble quarry near Carrara.
3.33 a Illustration from the book
Von der Bebauung der Erde by
Rudolf Schwarz, Heidelberg, 1949.
3.33 b The base of the altar of
the Church of St. Andreas in
Essen-Rüttenscheid, Rudolf
Schwarz, 1954–1957.

3.34 Destroyed by an earthquake in 1968, the town of Gibellina in Sicily was covered by a thick layer of white concrete between 1984 and 1989 as proposed by the artist Alberto Burri.

3.35 The Villa Malaparte in Capri, Curzio Malaparte with Adalberto Libera, 1938–1942.

towers. The vast nave dominates the huge altar wall in the center of which one finds the tiny gothic figure of the *Virgen de Aránzazu*, surrounded by images of the dramatic geological transformations in the depths of the Basque mountains as interpreted by the artist Lucio Muñoz (1962). [Figs. 3.26, 3.27]

Created by the pressure of the earth, the structure and silky-matt sheen of slate have inspired many artists and architects. Erdman Hall Dormitory at Bryn Mawr College in Pennsylvania (1960–1965) demonstrates Louis I. Kahn's fascination with Scottish castles built upon rocky outcrops. The cluster-like interlinking of three building volumes with square floor plans enables him to clearly accentuate the loadbearing structure: through pilasters of reinforced concrete which lend the volumes a faceted, crystalline character. The façade consists of dark slate panels mounted between the light concrete strips. In the interior spaces colorful carpets seek to alleviate this raw materiality which is perceived by today's residents as cool and unfriendly. [Fig. 3.28]

A no less poetic interpretation of geology is the Beinecke Rare Book Library at Yale University in New Haven by Gordon Bunshaft (architectural office Skidmore, Owings & Merrill, 1959–1963). The library's Vierendeel steel structure floats above an internal courtyard designed by Isamu Noguchi, supported at each of its four corners by pyramid shaped blocks. The structure is indicated on the façade by a grid of light Woodbury granite filled in with 32 mm thick, 2.44 × 2.44 m white marble slabs from Vermont. The marbled stone allows golden light to enter the interior, at the heart of which are located the shelves of valuable books. [Figs. 3.29, 3.30] Light also transforms the interior of St. Pius' Church in Meggen by Franz Füeg (1960–1968), filtering into the space through 28 mm thick slabs of Pentelic marble (out of which the Parthenon was built). [Fig. 3.31]

Landform building

In the images of the Austrian photographer Margherita Spiluttini today's alpine landscape appears like a technical product consisting of rocks and plants which provide thin layers of covering to sections of tunnel and solid concrete constructions. But the material interdependency of landscape and city has existed since the very dawn of architecture. The marble landscape of Carrara feels like an inverted city whose extracted caves and chasms have been inserted as built volumes into real cities. [Fig. 3.32] In contrast with this, Matera, in the southern Italian region of Basilicata, can be seen as a subtracted city, hollowed out of the cliffs of the valley of the River Gravina. The Sassi (cave dwellings), which descend into the ground in the form of a funnel, were compared by the writer Carlo Levi with Dante Alighieri's vision of hell.[42]

Between 1984 and 1989, the Italian artist Alberto Burri created a harsh cemeterial landscape when he laid a crust of white concrete over the Sicilian village of Gibellina which had been destroyed by an earthquake in 1968. This hides the ruins of the houses and is permeated with narrow streets whose monumentality is a result of the motionless weight and stillness. [Fig. 3.34]

The Italian writer Curzio Malaparte contributed an anecdote on the subject of the interdependency of buildings and landscape. In his autobiographical novel *The Skin* (1949) he reports on Erwin Rommel's 1942 visit to the villa on Capri that Malaparte had designed with Adalberto Libera in 1938. The Field Marshall asked him whether he had bought the house or built it himself: "I replied," recounts Malaparte, "that I had bought the house as it stood. And with a sweeping gesture, indicating the sheer cliff of Matromania, the three gigantic rocks of the Faraglioni, the peninsula of Sorrento, the islands of the sirens, the far-away blue coastline of Amalfi and the golden sands of Paestum shimmering in the distance, I said to him: 'I designed the scenery.' 'Ach so!' exclaimed General Rommel. And after shaking me by the hand he departed." [43] [Fig. 3.35] This story was used by the American architecture theorist Stan Allen as the introduction to the program for a new way of looking at the city, the landscape and ecology that he describes as *landform building*. The objective is to unravel *object buildings* and *landscape fields* and understand both as elements of a holistic dynamic ecological system. [44]

Globalization and the relationship with place

The example of the Villa Malaparte brings us to the issue of the object which is place-specific and yet whose relationship with its surroundings is abstract and not mimetic. As a program, *site-specificity* lends a place a unique identity which is capable of resisting the global homogenization and commercialization of space and the reproduction of such meaningless non-places as shopping centers and hotel chains. [45] In architectural theory, a relationship with a place was principally investigated in terms of the potential for an urban and formal relationship with the natural and built environment, [46] in the fine arts, on the other hand, and, more specifically, in Land Art and minimalism, the materiality of the environment played a determining role. Artists identify and present the materials that concretely constitute a place – earth, waste, rubble –, free from any idealization.

In the field of architecture the Basel office of Herzog & de Meuron is one of the first to have understood the notion of site-specificity in such a way. The stone house built by the office in the small town of Tavole in Liguria (1985–1988) is located amidst abandoned olive groves and consists of a thin concrete frame structure filled in with natural dry stone masonry work. The grid of the concrete frame corresponds with that of the archaeologist whose first task is to spatially locate the discoveries of the past: The place is a conglomeration of materials which have to be ordered (*ordo* and *ornare*, "order" and "ornament" are related terms). This work by Herzog & de Meuron was presented by Philip Ursprung in an exhibition in the Canadian Centre for Architecture in Montreal in 2004 entitled *Archaeology of the Mind*, which was accompanied by the publication of the collection of texts *Natural History*. [47] The choice of this title was not unexpected. In texts such as "The Hidden Geometry of Nature" that they had been writing since the 1980s the architects had long been demonstrating their interest in "the complexity of a system of relationships which exists in nature, in an un-researchable perfection [...] and whose analogy in the realm of art and society interests us. Our interest is thus the hidden geometry of nature, a spiritual principle and not primarily the outer appearance of nature." [48]

3.36 The Schaulager of the Laurenz Foundation in Basel. Herzog & de Meuron, 1998–2003.
3.37 The house *Il Girasole* in Rome by Luigi Moretti, 1947–1950.

Ursprung compares this agglomeration of the geological deposits of a location with the approach of the American artist Robert Smithson, in whose *non-sites* the removal of material from its original location plays a significant role. Smithson and the Land Art of the 1960s were amongst the first to address the ecological questions of the destruction and loss of the environment.[49] Admittedly, Herzog & de Meuron also want to destroy any suggestion of a link with the architecture of *Heimatstil* and regionalism: "The building volume should not imitate nature but serve as a sort of instrument for appreciating a place, a place as created by nature and a place as shaped by existing structures."[50]

The Schaulager of the Laurenz Foundation in Basel (1998–2003) by Herzog & de Meuron is a place where art is, above all, capital that doesn't need a public to survive, even if exhibitions can be held in the building. Like gold bars, the works of art have to be stored in a vault under optimum conditions. Like many of the works of art which are waiting for their value to increase the architecture also assimilates strategies for fetishizing the factual that is piled up here for show. Here, nature is not the creative principle – neither is the sublime –, but is simply the gravel from the construction pit, the soil, but not the ground in which Martin Heidegger's metaphysics is rooted. The seemingly porous mud-colored façades of Jurassic limestone excavated from a building site combine with the deep crevices of the strip windows to create a geological landscape. [Fig. 3.36]

The use of the materials of nature as elements of an elaborate assemblage has its antecedents in architectural history. Luigi Moretti's house Il Girasole in Rome (1947–1950) emphasizes its relationship with its location adjacent to the ancient city wall through the use of crudely cut limestone blocks. The collision of "untreated" pieces of stone with finely detailed façades was a baroque feat of strength quite worthy of the city of Borromini and Bernini. In his essay "Trasfigurazioni di strutture murarie" ("The Transfiguration of Wall Structures", 1951) Moretti addresses the historical development that led to this "overcoming" of the wall and its transformation into a strong pictorial presence. The architect writes that this result can be achieved through the appropriate use of materials that produce an expressive surface effect and emphasize the tectonics of the wall.[51] [Fig. 3.37]

Il Girasole – like Fallingwater, Baker House or St. Anna's church in Düren – present us with images that their architects create from nature. But this is not pure representation: In these buildings, nature is tangibly present through the choice of the materials. Unlike in literature or landscape painting the use of stone, brick, wood, metal or ceramic should infect the creation and the perception of the architectural image with the sensory tactile presence of the material. The question of whether the use of natural material in such cases should be understood as an attempt to address the transfigurative potential of architecture or as a criticism of such ambitions will continue to occupy us in the following chapters.

Notes

1   Marc-Antoine Laugier, *An Essay on Architecture*, transl. Wolfgang and Anni Herrmann, Los Angeles: Hennessey & Ingalls, 1977, p. 12.

2   William Chambers, *A Treatise on the Decorative Part of Civil Architecture*. 2nd Edition. London: J. Smeeton, 1791, Reprint Mineola: Dover Publications Inc., 2003, p. 26f.

3   Ibid., p. 24.

4   Giovan Battista Piranesi, "Parere sull'architettura", in: *Osservazioni sopra la lettre de Monsieur Mariette aux auteurs de la Gazette Littéraire de l'Europe* (1765). Newly printed, Naples: CLEAN, 1993; Comp. Giovan Battista Piranesi, Observations on the Letter of Monsieur Mariette with Opinions on Architecture, and a Preface to a New Treatise on the Introduction and Progress of the Fine Arts in Europe in Ancient Times. Los Angeles: Getty Research Institute, 2002.

5   Claude Nicolas Ledoux, *L'architecture considérée sous le rapport de l'art, des mœurs et de la législation*. Paris: Hermann, 1997, p. 48. Translation by R. H.

6   Mariana Griswold Van Rensselaer, *Henry Hobson Richardson and His Works*. New York, Boston: Houghton, Mifflin & Co. Reprint New York: Dover Publications, 1969, p. 72.

7   E[ugène Emmanuel] Viollet-le-Duc, *Dictionnaire raisonné de l'architecture française du XIe au XVIe siècle*. 10 Volumes. Paris: B. Bance, 1854–1868.

8   E[Emmanuel] Viollet-le-Duc *Dictionnaire raisonné de l'architecture française du XIe au XVIe siècle*, *Rational Dictionary of French Architecture*, Vol IX, transl. by N.C. Ricker, Urbana: University of Illinois Press, 1919, p. 220.

9   E[ugène Emmanuel] Viollet-le-Duc, *Dictionnaire raisonné de l'architecture française du XIe au XVIe siècle*. 10 Volumes. Paris: B. Bance, 1854–1868. Translation by R. H.

10   [Eugéne Emmanuel] Viollet-le-Duc, *Entretiens sur l'architecture*. Paris: A. Morel et Cie, Volume 1: 1863, Volume 2: 1872. English translation: *Lectures on Architecture*, transl. by Benjamin Bucknall. London: Sampson Low, Marston, Searle and Rivington, Vol. 1: 1877, Vol. 2: 1881, Reprint New York: Dover Publications, 1987.

11   This accusation was already formulated by John Summerson in his essay "Viollet-le-Duc and the Rational Point of View", in: Summerson *Heavenly Mansions and Other Essays on Architecture*. New York, London: W. W: Norton, 1963, pp. 135–158, here p. 156.

12   Michael Gnehm, *Stumme Poesie. Architektur und Sprache bei Gottfried Semper*. Zurich: gta Verlag, 2004.

13   Gottfried Semper, *Style in the Technical and Tectonic Arts; or, Practical Aesthetics*, transl. by Harry Francis Mallgrave and Michael Robinson. Los Angeles: Getty Research Institute, 2004, p. 219.

14   Ibid., p. 698.

15   Isidre Puig-Boada, *El pensament de Gaudí. Compilació de textos i comentaris*. Barcelona: Editorial La Gaya Ciència, 1981; Antoni Gaudí, *Manuscritos, artículos, conversaciones y dibujos*, ed. Marcià Codinachs. Murcia: Colegio Oficial de Aparejadores y Arquitectos Técnicos de la Región de Murcia, 2002.

16   Juan José Lahuerta (ed.), *GaudíUniverse*. Barcelona: CCCB, 2002.

17   Ibid., p. 125.

18   Ibid., p. 126.

19   Puig-Boada, *El pensament de Gaudí* (see note 15), p. 226.

20   Semper, *Style* (see note 13), p. 698.

21   Comp. Toni Kotnik, "Experiment as Design Method. Intergrating the Methodology of the Natural Sciences in Architecture", in: Ákos Moravánszky, Albert Kirchengast (eds.), *Experiments. Architektur zwischen Wissenschaft und Kunst / Architecture Between Sciences and the Arts*. Berlin: Jovis Verlag, 2011, pp. 25–53.

22   Donald Hoffmann, *Frank Lloyd Wright's Fallingwater. The House and Its History*. New York: Dover Publications, 1978, p. 52f.

23   László Moholy-Nagy, *The New Vision 1928 fourth revised edition 1947 and Abstract of an Artist,* New York: George Wittenborn, 1947, transl, by Daphne M. Hoffman, p. 25.

24   Ibid., p. 63.

25   Alvar Aalto, "The Influence of Construction and Material on Modern Architecture", in: Aalto *Synopsis. Painting Architecture Sculpture*. 2nd Edition. Basel, Boston, Stuttgart: Birkhäuser Verlag, 1980, pp. 12–14, here p. 13.

26   Ibid.

27 Alvar Aalto, "The Reconstruction of Europe is the key problem for the architecture of our time" [Lecture delivered at Swiss universities in 1941, First printed in: *Arkkitehti* 5, 1941], in: Göran Schildt, ed., *Alvar Aalto in His Own Words,* New York: Rizzoli, 1998, pp. 149–164, here p. 154.

28 Ibid.

29 Ákos Moravánszky, "In the Alchemist's Laboratory. Aalto and the Materials of Architecture", in: Mateo Kries, Jochen Eisenbrand (eds.), *Alvar Aalto. Second Nature.* Exhibition Catalogue. Vitra Design Museum. Weil am Rhein: Vitra Design Museum, 2014, pp. 208–239.

30 Karl Fleig (ed.), *Alvar Aalto.* Volume 1: 1922–1962, Zurich: Girsberger, 1963, p. 200.

31 Moravánszky, "In the Alchemist's Laboratory" (see note 29), p. 237f.

32 Eugéne Emmanuel Viollet-le-Duc, *Le massif du Mont Blanc. Étude sur sa constitution géodésique et géologique sur les transformations et sur l'état ancien et moderne de ses glaciers.* Paris: Librairie polytechnique J. Baudry, 1876.

33 Karl Blossfeldt, *Urformen der Kunst.* Berlin: Ernst Wasmuth Verlag, 1928. English edition: *Art Forms in Nature,* London: A. Zwemmer, 1929.

34 Rudolf Schwarz, *Wegweisung der Technik* (1928). New edition, ed. Maria Schwarz, Cologne: Verlag der Buchhandlung Walther König, 2008.

35 Rudolf Schwarz, *Von der Bebauung der Erde.* Heidelberg: Lambert Schneider, 1949, p. 22f.

36 Ibid., p. 23f.

37 Ibid., p. 25.

38 Ibid., p. 38f.

39 Rudolf Schwarz, *Kirchenbau. Welt vor der Schwelle.* Heidelberg: Kerle, 1960, p. 223.

40 Ibid., p. 233.

41 Ibid., pp. 232–233.

42 Carlo Levi, Christ Stopped at Eboli, transl. by Frances Frenaye. London: Penguin Modern Classics, 2000.

43 Curzio Malaparte, The Skin, transl. by David Moore. New York: NYRB Classics, 2013, pp. 204–205.

44 Stan Allen, Marc McQuade (eds.), *Landform Building: Architecture's New Terrain.* Baden: Lars Müller Publishers, 2011, pp. 33–37.

45 Marc Augé, *Non-Places: Introduction to an Anthropology of Supermodernity,* transl. by John Howe. London: Verso, 1995.

46 Tomás Valena, *Beziehungen. Über den Ortsbezug in der Architektur.* Berlin: Ernst & Sohn Verlag, 1994.

47 Philip Ursprung (ed.), *Herzog & de Meuron. Natural History.* Exhibition catalogue. Montreal, Canadian Centre for Architecture, Baden: Lars Müller Publishers, 2005.

48 Jacques Herzog, "The Hidden Geometry of Nature" (lecture 1988), in: Gerhard Mack, *Herzog & de Meuron 1978–1988. The Complete Works.* Volume 1. Basel, Boston, Berlin: Birkhäuser Verlag, 1997, pp. 207–211, here p. 210, transl. by Claire Bonney.

49 Ann Reynolds, *Robert Smithson. Learning from New Jersey and Elsewhere.* Cambridge, Mass.: The MIT Press, 2003.

50 Herzog, "The Hidden Geometry of Nature" (see note 48), p. 211. Translation by R. H.

51 Luigi Moretti, "Trasfigurazioni di strutture murarie", in: *Spazio 4* (January-February 1951), English "Transfiguration of Wall Structures", in: Federico Bucci, Marco Mulazzani (eds.), *Luigi Moretti. Works and Writings,* transl. by Marina de Conciliis. New York: Princeton Architectural Press, 2002, pp. 167–172, here p. 168.

4.
THE FOUR ELEMENTS OF ARCHITECTURE

Semper in the Crystal Palace

The *Exhibition of the Works of Industry of All Nations* opened on 1st May 1851 in London's Hyde Park. The *Great Exhibition*, as it was called, was housed in the Crystal Palace, designed by Joseph Paxton. The gigantic cabinet of curiosities containing technical machinery, natural objects, and works of art was, in the words of Henry Cole – who had organized the exhibition under the patronage of Prince Albert – "an unrivalled storehouse for the useful results of all human industry."[1] Inside the Palace the entire world was present, systematically classified into every form of natural, industrial, and handcrafted product, presented as objects of study and entertainment. The exhibits were organized in *courts* – which were generally named after stylistic periods (Romanesque, Renaissance) or places (Alhambra, Pompeii, Nineveh) while there were also sections such as natural history, ethnology, geology or zoology. The six million visitors to the exhibition included Charles Darwin, Lewis Carroll, Charlotte Brontë, and Charles Dickens, as well as Gottfried Semper, who visited the exhibition almost every day.[2] [Fig. 4.1]

The opening coincided with the second anniversary of the outbreak of the May Uprising in Dresden, during which Semper had been involved in the construction of barricades. After the defeat of the uprising he was accused of high treason and became the subject of an arrest warrant. He fled first to Paris with the intention of continuing on to New York via Great Britain but, in the hope of being offered work, he remained in London where Cole involved him in the design and coordination of some of the presentations of the *Great Exhibition*. Semper was working at the time on his text about the four elements of architecture and he first met Cole in December 1850 to ask for his support for the publication of his study of polychromy (see p. 217).[3] The ethnographic exhibits and, in particular, the textiles and everyday objects from Africa and Asia, but also the new industrial machines which Semper was able to study even before the exhibition opened, provided inspiration for his theoretical work. Most important to him, however, was the "Caribbean hut," the reconstruction of a fisherman's hut from the island of Trinidad. For Semper, the examination of this bamboo hut must have offered a confirmation of his system of the four elements of architecture similar to that which would have been provided to Johann Wolfgang von Goethe had he truly stumbled upon his theoretical reconstruction of the archetypal plant or *Urpflanze*, which contained all possible vegetable organs of a plant in embryonic form, during a walk in the woods. Just as the *Urpflanze* "simply embodied the type of flowering plant from which one could imagine all vegetable forms had emerged,"[4] Semper could describe his system of the four elements of architecture using the example of the architectural techniques and materials of the Caribbean hut.[5]

At the time of the exhibition Trinidad was a British colony. Slavery had been abolished on the island 17 years earlier but the living conditions of the plantation workers were barely distinguishable from those of the former slaves. The everyday objects of the "primitive" peoples and the modern products of the colonial powers sought to spectacularly impress upon visitors the supremacy of Western culture. For Semper, however, the aesthetic quality of the objects of the "half-barbaric nations" provided precise proof of the fact that "we, with our science [...] have until now accomplished very little in these areas."[6] "We have not become the intellectual masters of the material, and in this regard we allow ourselves to be put to shame by the Hindus and Iroquois," he added later.[7]

For many thinkers, the failings of the French Revolution of 1789 had revealed the powerlessness of enlightened reason which, while it leads to technical progress, is unable to prepare society for new ideas. It is for this reason that Friedrich von Schiller, in his letters discussing man's aesthetic education, demanded that this should foster "practical culture" - the "training of sensibility" – as a counterpart to "theoretical culture."[8] "Practical culture" is the tool that can teach freedom, even "under the influence of a barbarous constitution."[9] Semper already refers to this program in the title of his two-volume work *Style in the technical and tectonic arts or practical aesthetics*. His friend Richard Wagner, who had also had to flee as a result of his participation in the May Uprising in Dresden and who then convinced Semper to move to Zurich in 1854, used this as the basis for the development of his concept of the total work of art that would also come to occupy Semper.[10] On the one hand, the machines in the halls of the *Great Exhibition* made Semper aware of the success of capitalism in its striving for globalization and, hence, of the success of materialism and "theoretical culture". On the other hand, however, he interpreted the tools, textiles and handmade products of distant peoples as proof of the continuity and basic order behind the "Babylonian confusion of tongues" communicated by the exhibition.[11] In his report on the *Great Exhibition* he proposes the development of a pedagogic system which will teach *"the arts in their application to practical knowledge."*[12] The basis of this teaching concept is Semper's system of the four elements of architecture.

The theory of the elements

It was the Greek philosopher Empedocles (492–432) who first organized the four elements of fire, water, earth, and air as a tetrad. His aim in doing so was to bridge the contradiction between the dynamic teaching of Heraclitus with its notion of things in flux and the static Eleatic school and its conviction that stability is the basis of reality. Empedocles described the four elements as the *root of all things*, whose characteristics are determined by the precise relationship between the elements as they strive for equilibrium. He believed that we can only perceive the outside world because the human eye is an analogy of the earth, its fiery core sending out optical rays which scan its surroundings, surrounded by earth, air, and water. The result of this is a constant exchange,

4.1 View of the Crystal Palace in Hyde Park, London, 1851. Watercolor by Edmund Walker, Victoria & Albert Museum, London.

a material connection, between the perceiver and the perceived – a thesis that reemerged, albeit in a new, scientific psycho-physiological guise, in the empathy theories of the 19th century. The world expresses itself in images which are produced by the resonance of the elements in us and in the things around us. Aristotle explained the four elements as a combination of the four basic characteristics of warm, cold, dry, and wet: Water is cold and wet, fire is dry and warm, air is warm and wet, the earth is cold and dry.

Empedocles' tetrad and the doctrine of the four elements is not the only cosmological diagram to organize the materiality of the world. Far Eastern philosophy speaks of five elements: In Taoism, nature consists of the combination of wood, fire, metal, water, and earth, in Buddhism of earth, water, fire, air (wind), and void. In Western philosophy, however, it is the notion of the four elements that dominates and influences thinking in a wide range of disciplines including anthropology, medicine, art, and architecture. The doctrine of the elements regards man as being embedded in the cosmos. The doctrine of the humors takes this further by describing his sanguine, melancholic, choleric or phlegmatic character and combining these four characters with the materiality of the bodily fluids which cause them: blood, black and yellow bile, and mucus. The seasons, the points of the compass, and the winds are also arranged according to this matrix and form the broader cosmic framework for the building.

The scholastic natural sciences of the Middle Ages retained the doctrine of the four elements although metaphysics speculated about the existence of an even deeper layer of unformed *materia prima* behind this organization of matter. This system was, however, rejected by the Einsiedeln-born doctor, astrologer, and alchemist Theophrastus von Hohenheim, better known as Paracelsus. He suggested an anatomical concept that was based not on the isolation and dismembering of the parts but rather on the inner unity of the microcosm of the human being.[13] He spoke of higher – finer – elements such as air and fire as opposed to rougher ones such as earth and water. And he separated fire from the material elements and compared it with heaven or the firmament.[14]

Learning from the Caribbean hut

The "primitive huts" of architectural history are the visual manifestos of their inventors. For Enlightenment thinkers, the question of the first appearance of a social form – of a language, an item of clothing or a building – plays an important role. It was thought that if one could recall the origin or have the initial appearance of a building before one's eyes one would be able to understand the essence of the architecture – while also recognizing the folly of the later superfluous alterations and additions which deface the clear original structure. This quest was also directed against the exuberance of the then widespread Rococo and explains the efforts taken by Marc-Antoine Laugier and other 18th-century thinkers to recall the first house (see p. 61). This was less of a challenge to memory than to fantasy. In his book *On Adam's House in Paradise* (1971) Joseph Rykwert tells the long history of imaginary reconstructions of the primitive hut.[15] However, in his comments about his "discovery", Semper emphasizes that, for him, the Caribbean hut was "not a figment of the imagination" but "a highly realistic example of a wooden structure taken from ethnology" and that he would place "before the reader [...] the equivalent of the Vitruvian primitive hut in all its details."[16] For in the Caribbean hut one can find "all the elements of antique architecture in their pure and most original form: the *hearth* as the centerpoint, raised earth as a *terrace* surrounded by posts, the column-supported *roof*, and the mat enclosure as a *spatial termination* or *wall*."[17] [Fig. 4.2] However, the four elements named by Semper do not have the same status. For example, the hearth as centerpoint, unlike a wall or a roof, is not necessarily connected with materiality. When Semper used these elements as the starting point for the development of a system of manufacturing techniques and materials to propose a course of study and the concept of an ideal museum, he changed the sequence and, hence, the assessment of the individual elements. The removal of his discovery, the hut, from its meaningful context had already transformed it into more of a diagram than a house. From the viewpoint of the related observations, whether it really was a fisherman's hut at all is not important.[18]

276　　　　　　Achtes Hauptstück.

Nach diesem hegt der Verfasser die Zuversicht nicht miss-
verstanden zu werden, wenn er kein Phantasiebild, sondern ein
höchst realistisches Exemplar einer
Holzkonstruktion aus der Ethnologie
entlehnt und hier dem Leser als der
vitruvianischen Urhütte in allen ihren
Elementen entsprechend vor Augen
stellt.

Nämlich die Abbildung des Mo-
dells einer karaibischen Bambushütte,
welches zu London auf der grossen
Ausstellung von 1851 zu sehen war.
An ihr treten alle Elemente der an-
tiken Baukunst in höchst ursprüng-
licher Weise und unvermischt hervor:
der Heerd als Mittelpunkt, die durch
Pfahlwerk umschränkte Erderhöhung
als Terrasse, das säulengetragene
Dach und die Mattenumhegung als
Raumabschluss oder Wand.

Karaibische Hütte.

4.2 The Caribbean hut at the Great
Exhibition of 1851 in London.
Drawing in Gottfried Semper,
Style, Volume II, Munich 1863.

Semper's system

Semper provided the most comprehensive explanation of his system in the
second chapter of the first volume of his *Style*, "Classification of the Technical
Arts." He starts by describing "the four main categories into which raw materials can be classified according to their technical purpose."[19] These are firstly
defined by their characteristics:

"1) pliable, tough, highly resistant to tearing, of great absolute strength;

2) soft, malleable (plastic), capable of being hardened, easily shaped and
formed and retaining a given form when hardened;

3) stick-shaped, elastic, principally of *relative* strength, that is, resistant to
forces working vertically along the length;

4) strong, *densely aggregated*, resistant to crushing and compression, thus of
significant *reactive* strength. It is thus suited to being worked into any required
form by removing parts of the mass or by inserting regular pieces in strong
systems, constructed on principles of reactive strength."[20]

Following this description of the characteristics of the four material categories which are not related to concrete materials Semper then distinguishes the
four primitive techniques – the four "main artistic activities."[21] These are:

"1) textiles,

2) ceramics,

3) tectonics (carpentry),

4) stereotomy (masonry, and so on)."[22]

According to Semper each of these primitive techniques "has its own do-main of forms whose production is, so to speak, the technique's most natural and ancient task."[23] He points out that each technique has a certain material that "can be considered its primeval material which is the most convenient means for producing forms within its original domain."[24] As an example he mentions ceramics which is not just restricted to clay vessels but also includes the for-mally related "glassware, stoneware and metalware." Even wooden barrels and buckets or woven baskets "are stylistically related to ceramics in this respect."[25] On the other hand, there are objects which, though made of clay, must be placed "in a formal relationship with another domain."[26] These include "bricks, roof tiles, terra-cotta, and glazed tiles – used both for dressing walls and tiling floors."[27] Such ceramic products belong stylistically to either stereotomy (brick, roof tiles) or textiles (wall and floor tiles).

This flexible organization which was not based on fixed material catego-ries had already been proposed by Semper in *The Four Elements of Architec-ture* which he had finished in London and published in the year of the *Great Exhibition*.[28] This represents a further development of his contribution to the debate about polychromy and the idea of studying biological typologies. Even more important than these, however, is his politically motivated interest in the relationship between social development and the transformation of form. In his text, Semper shares Vitruvius' view of the "setting up of the fireplace and the lighting of the reviving, food-preparing flame" as the origin of "human set-tlement."[29] Grouped around the fireplace were the other three elements, "the *roof*, the *enclosure*, and the *mound*, the protecting negations or defenders of the hearth's flame against the three hostile elements of nature."[30] "Technical skills" are organized in terms of these elements: the "*ceramics* and afterwards metal works around the *hearth*, *water* and *masonry works* around the *mound*, *wood works* around the *roof*" and the art of the weavers of mats and carpets around the "*enclosure*".[31] Under the influence of the *Great Exhibition*, social factors play a lesser role in his later works and, in particular, in *Style*, while the importance of the technical arts other than architecture increases strongly.[32]

In 1852, during his exile in London, Semper carried out a short study in which he presented his proposal for an ideal museum.[33] In keeping with the ideality of the museum his layout is more a diagram than a floor plan. The four "roots or fundamental Motives of all human Works" – which are, at the same time, "identical with the first Elements of human Industry": textiles, ceram-ics, tectonics and stereotomy – are positioned at the centers of the sides of the square.[34] The corners are the "junction points, with other Collections which to-gether will mutually Complete themselves." [35] As an example, Semper mentions cast bronze doors, whose form is influenced by both ceramic and stereometric techniques. [Fig. 4.3]

Semper's diagram is not a rigid structure aimed at classifying the products of the decorative arts but rather a means of establishing relationships, con-necting artifacts with the possibilities presented by artifacts and giving these meaning. Materials can assume the role of another material. Semper had been commissioned to draw up a study of the metal products of the decorative arts. Ironically, however, he did not regard metal as one of the primeval materials, characterizing it as the material, "that unites all the properties of the raw mate-rials listed above."[36]

But did Semper's discovery of the Caribbean hut help him to understand his four elements as parts of a greater whole and provide a welcome example for an already developed theory or a projection screen for metaphysical speculations about the essence of architecture? Empirical research, metaphysical thinking, and fanciful associations are mutually dependent. For Semper, the hut was both an ethnographic object and a theoretical diagram. Observation, analysis, and fantasy should complement each other correctively – he writes that even archaeology can "scrutinize the past as keenly and shrewdly as it likes, but ultimately it is left to the divining sense of artists to reconstruct something whole [...]."[37]

4.3 Design for an ideal museum, pencil drawing by Gottfried Semper, 1852.

The spatial and decorative program for the museum ensemble for the imperial court in Vienna (Gottfried Semper and Carl von Hasenauer, 1871–1891) was drawn up in connection with Semper's diagram. The five-meter-high bronze figure of the sun god Helios on the dome of the Museum of Natural History is surrounded by allegorical figures of the four elements – Urania (air), Poseidon (water), Gaia (earth) and Hephaestus (fire) – while these allegories are pursued on the four façades.

Semper's systematization of the four elements is made particularly interesting by the reversal of direction of causality which can be traced back to his theory of *Stoffwechsel*. The analysis of the wall and its original textile-based constructional technique leads to the redetermination of one of the four elements, because the category of textiles that this creates becomes a producer of new artifacts made from a range of materials. Within the spaces of the ideal museum, point A may indicate textiles, but the group of objects assembled here is increasingly expanded through the addition of other objects which are similar, but not produced from textile fibers. In order to understand how the system works, the following sub-chapters will now examine the four elements individually.

The wall: Textile Art

According to Semper the first of the four elements is textiles, the technique of working with materials which are *"pliable, tough, highly resistant to tearing, of great absolute strength."*[38] The result is two-dimensional fabric, the material of the first spatial enclosures, the walls of houses. Later, craftsmen also formed or represented fabric patterns using other materials: "[...] textiles encompasses more than actual fabrics."[39] [Figs. 4.4 a–d] Semper criticized those architectural historians whose drawings of the tents of nomadic tribes paid special attention to the catenary curve of the tent roof. These overlooked "the general and less dubious influence that the carpet in its capacity as a *wall*, as a vertical means of protection, had on the evolution of certain architectural forms. Thus I seem to stand without the support of a single authority when I assert that the carpet wall plays a most important role in the general history of art."[40] Here, Semper is emphasizing the primary, space-dividing function of the textile wall and he

Flaggenstäbe, Schmuck der Aegyptischen Pylonen; von einem Wandgemälde am Tempel des Khons zu Theben.

4.4 Examples of textile art from Gottfried Semper's *Style*.
a. Flagpoles, decoration of Egyptian pylons; from a wall painting in the Temple of Chons at Thebes. *Style,* Volume I, Frankfurt am Main 1860.
b. Egyptian capital and ladies' hair decoration. *Style,* Volume I.
c. Assyrian wall paintings. *Style,* Volume I, Plate XII
d. Section, view from below, and details of a truss of the paneled ceiling of the Theseus Temple in Athens. *Style,* Volume I, Plate VI.

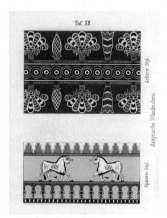

regards the load-bearing structure of the tent as secondary. The basic technical motif of textiles, the knot, and the principle of dressing which is developed from this starting point will be addressed in Chapter 8.

It is astonishing that Semper connects the most important element in architecture with a light, inherently instable material which is not firmly anchored to the ground. He associates this architecture – which 'flutters' like the clothes, carpet walls, and flags that illustrate his book - not with the earth but with the element of air. The architectural history of the 20th century sees such floating architectures as a manifestation of the revolutionary spirit, as utopias and designs for a coming architecture which has yet to find solid ground. This lightness became topical again after 1968 and found its expression in the pneumatic, inflatable architecture of the French group Utopie or the Austrian group Haus-Rucker-Co.[41] In terms of Semper's theory of *Stoffwechsel* we can understand this tying down and petrification of the originally labile and mobile as a gesture of localization.

The forms of nomadic tents and their transformation or translation into solid materials in the architecture of tribes as they settle down was the subject of an elective at ETH Zurich in 2013. Having investigated the architecture of the refugee camps of the Western Sahara, Jonas Wirth arrived at the conclusion that the tents, whose residents had originally still held out hope of a speedy return to their homelands, were replaced over time by buildings constructed of mud or cement stone. These, however, retained details which were characteristic of the tents. Of particular interest are the huts built of colorful metal drums

4.5 Metal tents made from unrolled oil drums in the refugee camp at Tindouf (Algeria) in the Western Sahara, 2011.
4.6 Copper tent in Haga Park, Stockholm. Designed by the architect Louis Jean Desprez for King Gustav III, 1787–1790.

4.7 "Knitting-on" using the marble of an ancient temple: The wall of the 13th century Franconian fortress in Parikia on the island of Paros.

4.8 The design of the footpath on Philopappos hill in Athens. Dimitris Pikionis, 1951–1958.
4.9 Sketch of a house by Dimitris Pikionis, from Dimitris Pikionis, *Architectural Sketches 1940–1955*, ed. Agni Pikionis, Athens, 1994.

which have been rolled flat and lined on the interior with cotton in order to reduce heat radiation.[42] [Fig. 4.5] Tents were often built of solid materials as a way of commemorating military campaigns, as exemplified by the *Koppartälten*, the copper tents that the architect Louis Jean Desprez built for King Gustav III in Haga Park in Stockholm (1787–1790), [Fig. 4.6] or Karl Friedrich Schinkel's tent room in Charlottenhof Palace in Potsdam (1826–1829), the summer residence of Crown Prince Friedrich Wilhelm.

The textile analogy of knitting-on was already mentioned in Chapter One. Further examples include wall constructions that have a special relationship with a place due to the integration of such *objets trouvés* as fragments of stone from a building site as demonstrated by the use of marble from an ancient temple in the construction of a 13th-century Franconian fortress in Parikia

4.10 Wall texture of St. Mark's Church in Björkhagen near Stockholm by Sigurd Lewerentz, 1958–1963.
4.11 Examples of ceramics from Gottfried Semper's *Style*.
a. Basic forms of pottery after Ziegler. *Style,* Volume II.
b. Candelabra capital (Pompeii). *Style,* Volume II.

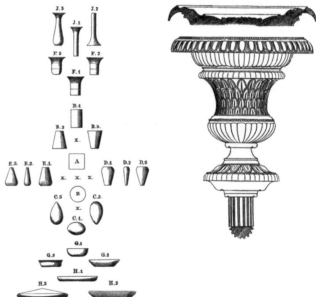

on the Greek island of Paros. [Fig. 4.7] The Greek architect Dimitris Pikionis designed the public footpath on Philopappos Hill in Athens in a similar way, interweaving ancient fragments of stone from the ground with the bedrock and constructional elements that he had developed himself with a highly precise level of detail. His architectural sketches of residential buildings also demonstrate a playful approach to richly textured fabric walls and light textile curtains. [Figs. 4.8, 4.9] And here we should also not forget Sigurd Lewerentz's

Künstliche verzeichnung wie man sich vermlt/die aller ersten Menschē gelebt/vnd durch erfindung des feures in gemeinschafft vnd freundliche beywonung kome/vnd die spraach der rede sich vnter jnen erhaben haf. LXI

Künstliche fürmalung wie die ersten Menschen/das Bawwerck durch mancherley hütten vnd wonungen erfunden haben. LXII

Künstliche fürmalung der alten Scholchier erste hültzene Gebew/ mit warhafftiger Contrafactur solcher Häuser/wie sie in Schweiß vnd Schweden/Nortweden vñ dergleichen Landtschafft im brauch sind.

4.12 a, b, c Illustrations from the Vitruvius edition *Vitruvius teutsch* by Walther Hermann Ryff, Nuremberg, 1548.
a. The discovery of fire, Plate LXI.
b. The construction of the first hut, Plate LXII.
c. The first timber houses, Plate LXIII.

experimental investigations of the textile effect of bricks and joints which involved the experimental use of different types of sand (e.g. from ground slate) for the mortar. [Fig. 4.10]

4.13 Fireplace in the Villa Karma in Clarens near Montreux by Adolf Loos, 1903–1906 (completed by Hugo Ehrlich).

Fire: Ceramics

Semper's second category, ceramics, is dedicated to materials that are *"soft, malleable (plastic), capable of being hardened, easily shaped and formed and retaining a given form when hardened."*[43] Plasticity, homogeneity, and the ability to harden are the three basic characteristics of all plastic matter. The word "pottery" fails to embody the enormous cultural significance of ceramics: Ceramic vessels are "symbols of faith" that were "preserved in the protecting womb of the earth because of their use as objects in funeral rites."[44] They are the "oldest and most eloquent of historical documents. If one examines the pots produced by a given group of people, it is usually possible to say what they were like and what stage of development they had reached!"[45] This fact is also related to the durability of ceramic, terracotta and the fossilized remains of animals and plants: "Apart from these two artifacts of the past, everything is formless and silent."[46] In the "technical-historical" part of the chapter on ceramics Semper uses examples such as pots and vases to substantiate this interrelationship between the history of ceramics and geology.[47] [Figs. 4.11 a, b]

The Greek word for "sculpture" signifies pictorial representations but doesn't include pottery. The term "pottery", on the other hand, is limited to the production of pots. Semper allotted potter's clay a general significance as a sculptural material: He speaks of a "primeval material." The "plastic, soft paste" is given a form which assumes a fixed shape through hardening.[48] This description alone is enough to suggest the transferability of this technique to other materials such as glass or iron (or concrete, although this was not yet an issue for Semper). The examples of ceramics presented by Semper are principally clay pots, beginning with the *dolium,* the large ceramic cask which was home to the Cynic philosopher Diogenes of Sinope. Semper presents, on the one hand, ceramic vessels and capitals with wickerwork-like decoration and, on the other hand,

4.14 Altar in the Church of
St. Francis, Ljubljana. Jože Plečnik,
1925–1927, decorated according to
the original plans until the 1970s.
4.15 Boiler house of the
Goetheanum in Dornach, Rudolf
Steiner, 1914.

pots, bowls, and goblets of blown glass and metal in order to prove that technical forms can be transferred to other materials.

The "*ceramics* and afterwards metal works" arranged themselves around the hearth, writes Semper.[49] The heat of the fire is necessary for hardening the clay paste – or melting the metal. However, more important than the technical process is the myth which sees the hearth as the birthplace of human society. Vitruvius follows on from Lucretius in describing the first gathering of people around the warming fire as the origin of human civilization: In prehistory, people lived like animals, alone in forests, caves, and copses. But on one occasion, as if by chance, some trees "caught fire and so the inhabitants of the place were put to flight, being terrified by the furious flame. After it subsided, they drew near, and observing that they were very comfortable standing before the warm fire, they put logs on and, while thus keeping it alive, brought up other people to it, showing them by signs how much comfort they got from it. In that gathering of men, at a time when utterance of sound was purely individual, from daily habits they fixed upon articulate words just as these happened to come; then, from indicating by name things in common use, the result was that in this chance way they began to talk, and this originated conversation with one another."[50] The emergence of language was followed by learning to walk upright which also opened up the view of the "splendour of the starry firmament" as well as making it possible to build the first houses – initially as imitations of birds' nests and then as discrete buildings which are as logical as the first social artifact – language itself. According to the philosopher Peter Sloterdijk one can develop Vitruvius' ideas into a theory of 'thermic socialism'. He cites the Vitruvian notion that people were first motivated to come together in groups by the irresistible twin comforts of the welcoming warmth of the fire itself and the pleasure of conversing about such a pleasurable phenomenon. [Figs. 4.12 a, b, c]

Like Vitruvius, Semper also refers to the ancient legends by describing how fire brought people together: "The first sign of human settlement and rest after the hunt, the battle, and wandering in the desert is today, as when the first men lost paradise, the setting up of the fireplace and the lighting of the reviving, warming and food-preparing flame. Around the hearth the first groups assembled; around it the first alliances formed; around it the first rude religious concepts were put into the customs of a cult. Throughout all phases of society the hearth formed that sacred focus around which the whole took order and shape. It is the first and most important, the *moral* element of architecture."[51] Semper also describes the hearth as the "embryo of the form of society in general and as a symbol of settlement and unification,"[52] a formulation that he repeated in his lecture "On Architectural Symbols."[53]

The status of fire is unlike that of the other three elements. The Flemish naturalist, doctor, and alchemist Johan Baptista van Helmont argued that fire was not a substance but a force, an energy that unites but also destroys. Vitruvius' narrative also expresses the way in which the power of fire both destroys the forest and opens a window onto the "firmament". Leon Battista Alberti's description of the dangers associated with fire was even more comprehensive: sudden conflagrations, lightning, earthquakes and floods, "and so many irregular, improbable, and credible things that the prodigious force of nature can produce, which will mar and upset even the most carefully conceived plan of an architect."[54] Fire both establishes and threatens human civilization, separating it from and at the same time connecting it with nature. The key is the precise calibration of thermal comfort and the danger of being burnt and this is determined by distance. Sloterdijk notes that architectural forms reflect the projections of the "sphere-forming potential" of fire.[55] The spatial compositions of Frank Lloyd Wright's private houses grow outwards from the center, the location of the fireplace. The motto "Good friend, around these *hearth*-stones speak no evil word of any creature" is inscribed in the room containing the fireplace in his own house and studio in Oak Park, Chicago (1889). In Wright's living spaces the fire is usually framed by a monumental stone or brick chimneypiece which is often symbolically decorated; the colored glass of the windows cuts off the view of the outside.

Many architects mention the role of fire in the production of building materials. In his book *Philosophy of Structures* the Spanish structural engineer Eduardo Torroja interprets brick in the context of the theory of the four elements. He writes that it is the first building material, "created by human intelligence from the four elements: earth, air, water, and fire."[56] This plastic and human material, "being laboriously assembled, cast with skill, dried with patience, and transformed into stone in the heat of fire grievously kindled, presents characteristics and morphology in its manufacture which are genuinely specific and totally different from those of natural stones."[57] But brick is not the only building material that can be associated with fire. Speaking about his steel church at the *PRESSA* exhibition in Cologne (1928), Otto Bartning commented that "steel, copper and leaded, stained glass are products of the melting of ore and quartz and, hence, have shared a baptism of fire."[58]

In his apartments Adolf Loos built fireplaces based on English and American models. [Fig. 4.13] In such public buildings as the libraries of Frank Furness, Henry Hobson Richardson or Louis I. Kahn the monumental fireplace provides a communal centerpiece for the reader as he loses himself in his books. The form of the chimneypiece can provide a contrast with the formal architectural language of the building. In the farmhouses of Central Europe fireplaces and ovens with niches and benches for sitting and lying become small thermal architectures in their own right. In Gunnar Asplund's summer house in Stennäs in Sweden the fireplace also displays a plastic, soft, "ceramic" form.

In sub-chapter §162 of *Style*, which he devotes to stereotomic stone construction, Semper returns to the subject of the hearth. He describes it as the oldest and noblest symbol of society and civilization which is then transferred to the altar as the place of burnt offerings, which is the highest expression of the same cultural idea.[59] Baroque altars – or modern ones such as those of Le Corbusier's chapels – are examples of the

Die Kunst soll diesen Mängeln begegnen, sie ausbeuten und aus der Noth eine Tugend machen; nichts affektiren und erkünsteln, was der Natur des Holzes widerspricht; z. B. scheinbar aus einem einzigen kolossalen Stamm geschnittene Bretter künstlich zusammenleimen, sondern lieber die Einheiten noch verkleinern; durch absichtliche Trennung dem natürlichen Getrenntwerden vorbeugen, es unschädlich und unwahrnehmbar machen. Die bezeichneten Unzulänglichkeiten des Stoffes sind die reichhaltigste Quelle immer neuer formaler

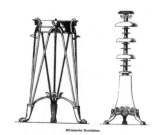

Etruskische Kandelaber.

Inneres der Kirche zu Borgund nach Nikolaisen.

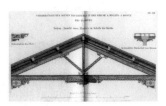

4.16 Examples of tectonics from Gottfried Semper's *Style*.
a. The plank construction of Egyptian furniture. *Style*, Volume II.
b. Etruscan candelabras. *Style*, Volume II.
c. Interior of Borgund Stave Church after Nikolaisen [sic!]. *Style*, Volume II.
d. Decoration of the open roof structure of the church of San Miniato al Monte in Florence. *Style*, Volume II, Plate XVII–XVIII.

4.17 The house of the Schmidt Brothers in Büelisacher, from Ernst
Gladbach, *Der Schweizer Holzstyl*, Zurich, 1882, Plate 5.

transcendentalization of the burnt offering through the orchestration of light.
In his church buildings in Prague and Slovenia Jože Plečnik designed not only
the altars but also liturgical vessels. Here he was again influenced by Semper's
theory. [Fig. 4.14] In his extension to the village church in Bogojina (1925–1954)
he interpreted the proximity of ceramics and devotional fire literally by positioning ceramic plates and jugs next to the altar as symbols of faith.

While the anthroposophist Rudolf Steiner referred to the theory of the elements of antiquity he still attributed a special quality to fire which differed from
the other three elements: As a result of its very delicate substantiality it could
permeate, heat, and transform air, water and earth. Steiner took this idea further in the boiler house of the Goetheanum in Dornach (1914) which represents
the flow of heat rising from a fire. [Fig. 4.15]

Fire also plays a special role in Sigfried Giedion's concept of a new modern
monumentality. In order to distance this program which he formulated in the
final years of the Second World War from Speerian "Pseudo-Monumentality"
Giedion described fireworks as the paradigm of that which is short-lived but
remains long in the memory. Vitruvius' fire remains a force for bringing people
together but as spectacle rather than thermal radiation.[60]

4.18 The Bridge Building of the Art Center College of Design in Pasadena, Craig Ellwood, 1970–1975.
4.19 The Pavilion of Reflections at the Manifesta 2016 in Zurich, Studio Tom Emerson, ETH Zurich.

The roof: Tectonics

The third category in Semper's system of techniques is tectonics. The term is often used to describe a general principle of architecture that distinguishes it from such non-constructive arts as painting. The art historian Heinrich Wölf-flin even used "tectonic" as the counter term to picturesque: In his book *Principles of Art History* (1915) he writes that "Painting *can* be tectonic, architec-

4.20, 4.21 House in Bernheimbeuk, architecten de vylder vinck taillieu, 2011.

ture *must* be. [...] For architecture, abolishing the tectonic framework would be tantamount to self-destruction."[61] In his book *Studies in Tectonic Culture. The Poetics of Construction in Nineteenth and Twentieth Century Architecture* Kenneth Frampton transformed this warning into a call for order. With his program for a tectonic architecture he is seeking to resist the threat of the scenographic.[62]

In contrast, Semper uses the term "tectonic" in a much more specific sense. In *Style* he writes that tectonics is the "art of assembling stiff, planklike elements into a rigid system."[63] These elements are "principally of *relative* strength, that is, resistant to forces working vertically along the length."[64] He begins by presenting the root forms of tectonics which is "*much older than architecture.*"[65] These tectonic root forms "had already in premonumental times – even before the sacred hut, the house of God, acquired the *monumental* framework of *its* art-form – achieved their fullest and most marked development in *movable domestic furnishings.*"[66] He is concerned with rigid frameworks and stands, metal tripods which meet the ideal of a stable yet transportable system. Only a quarter of the 40 illustrations in Semper's chapter on tectonics feature buildings – mostly timber-framed buildings –, all the others show furniture. It appears that Semper was principally interested in timber structures which would permit him to demonstrate the transfer of characteristic forms from other materials, such as the "stylistic relation" between old Scandinavian woodcarving and the "luxury of tapestries [...] in houses and sacred places"[67] or timber paneling that resembles barrel vaults. He asserts that this corresponds with "the antique principle" in monumental building "of concealing the artificial elements of a structure and exploiting them decoratively only in light movable supports and in the design of furniture."[68] [Fig. 4.16 a–d]

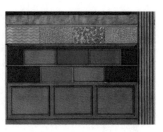

4.22 Examples of stereotomy from Gottfried Semper's *Style*.
a. Rustication of the Palazzo Pitti in Florence. *Style*, Volume II.
b. Rustication of the Palazzo Pitti in Florence. *Style*, Volume II.
c. Wall of the Casa di Sallustio in Pompeii. *Style*, Volume II, Plate XV.
4.23 Foundation wall of Kumamoto Castle, Japan, 1601–1607.

A tectonic structure is always a *pegma*, a framework, that frames a filling, writes Semper. Higher levels of tectonics are the lattice, the supports (e.g. tripods, candelabra), and the structure (e.g. roof trusses) [Fig. 4.17].[69] The filling has textile origins: "The energetic contrast in the framed filling between its two components – the frame and the filling – soon led artistic sensibility to utilize it and make it clear in an ideal way by expressing it symbolically."[70] Semper symbolically interprets the dialectic of active framing and passive filling. He draws an analogy with the growth of wood in describing the

4.24 Foundation wall of the Theatre of Marcellus in Rome, in Giovanni Battista Piranesi, *Le antichità romane*, Volume IV, Rome, 1784.

way in which the ornamentation stretches and the flat filling contracts as if expressing an inner life.

The frame can be seen not only as an image of movement but also as a boundary. The appeal of active design largely developed from the contradiction between the rigid and the mobile. In this sense, tectonics and textiles can be understood as a bipolarity. However, in contrast with theories which only identify architecture one-sidedly with tectonics, Semper regards texture (the textile components) and structure (the tectonic components) as inseparable.

In the "technical-historical" part of his explanation of tectonics Semper describes "the protective roof supported by tree trunks, covered with straw or reeds, and enclosed with woven mats" as the "mystical-poetic and artistic *motive* for the temple" but "**not** its material *model* or scheme."[71] The fact that hardly any other words in the book are set in bold type leaves us in no doubt about Semper's intention of distancing himself from those historians for whom the marble temple is "*in fact* nothing more than a petrified primitive hut whose whole and parts materially arose or were directly derived from the

4.25 Façade detail of the Palazzo dei Diamanti in Ferrara. Biagio Rossetti (?), 1492–1567.

basic elements of a wooden hut."[72] It is possible to be surprised by Semper's rejection of the wood-based origins of temple building as potential confirmation of his theory of *Stoffwechsel* but the Caribbean hut corresponded much more closely than the Vitruvian primitive hut with his notion of a woven rather than a tectonically jointed primeval building. The symbolic meaning of the roof as a mythical-poetic motif was often evoked during the course of the 20th century, not only by representatives of the domestic revival and critical (or uncritical) regionalism. For Otto Wagner, the modern metropolis also required the visible presence of the protective roof, which was embodied by the broad overhanging roofs of the rows of houses that were derived from the crowning cornices of Florentine palazzi. These not only emphasize the individuality of each building and the broad perspective sweep of the street but also provide the buildings with a clear upper limit (see Fig. 7.10).

When discussing fully tectonic structures Semper primarily refers to framework-based structures: half-timber buildings, roof trusses, and Norwegian stave churches. These are all monumental frames – articulated, bound and understood by Semper as symbols of plurality, in contrast with the closed, enveloped, covered spaces that uniformly present themselves as "collectivity". Semper also links the element of water with tectonics, describing Norman-English

4.26 Terrace of the Eidgenössisches Polytechnikum in Zurich, Gottfried Semper, 1858–1863.

and ancient Scandinavian roof construction as "a kind of ship construction applied to the roof in reverse."[73] [Fig. 4.16 c] In its role as the spatial boundary the texture is decisive while the tectonic structure is a supporting element. Loos went on to add that "Both the carpet on the floor and the tapestry on the wall require a structural frame to hold them in the correct place. To invent this frame is the architect's second task. [...] In the beginning was cladding."[74]

Semper's principal examples of tectonic architecture were medieval timber-framed buildings and he dedicated sub-chapter §155 of the second volume of his *Style* to the Swiss house, making use of, amongst other things, hitherto unpublished material from his fellow Zurich professor Ernst Gladbach.[75] However, it is unmistakable that, for Semper, tectonic frameworks, in contrast with textile surfaces, carry connotations of order and a lack of freedom. This is clearly exemplified in his above-mentioned criticism of Late Gothic. The "ossification into schematism and tediousness" embodies the inglorious end of Gothic as a strict tectonic system, and he ends his observations on the architecture of the Middle Ages with the lament "Requiescat in pace!"[76] He also cannot resist a small dig at Viollet-le-Duc in his comments on the roof structure of Westminster Hall in London which is presented in detail in the *Dictionnaire*: The exaggerated tracery, notches, and crockets which weaken the timber cross-sections are "merely *external* symptoms of the decline of these splendid decorative tectonics. Gothic increasingly alienated itself from its own *principle* and ended up by sacrificing itself entirely to mere surface ornament."[77] Semper's criticism of an over-exuberant tectonics and of its transition from being just one of the four elements of architecture into monumental ornament masquerading as the expression of an all-determining logic, has a new topicality given the possibilities offered by digital design and production technologies. But even without these new possibilities tectonics allows a range of playful liberties to be taken with its constructional principles. Strict tectonic effects were revealed earlier as pure orchestration, of which the façade of Peter Behrens' AEG Turbine Factory in Berlin (1908/09) provides a well-known example (see Fig. 8.47). Ludwig Mies van der Rohe welded double T mullions to the steel frame of his apartment tower at 860–880 Lake Shore Drive in Chicago (1947–1951) in order to emphasize the slenderness of the structure. During the period of steel-frame euphoria in post-war California which was fuelled by the capacity freed up by the decline in military production the American architect Craig Ellwood created homes that were supported and built like bridges. A late and impressive example of this is his Art Center College of Design in Pasadena (1970–1975). [Fig. 4.18] When architecture schools want to introduce their students to the craft of building at a scale of 1:1, tectonics tends to be the "primitive technique" of choice. For the European art biennale Manifesta Tom Emerson designed and built the floating Pavilion of Reflections (2016) together with his students at the ETH Zürich. [Fig. 4.19] The Belgian architectural office architecten de vylder vinck taillieu also works with the outward appearance of a tectonic system based on the interconnection of stick-shaped elements while challenging the classic rules of tectonics. The office's Haus in Bernheimbeuk (2011) is a primitive hut borne of a *pensée sauvage* with a tree bursting through the roof. [Figs. 4.20, 4.21]

The terrace: Stereotomy

The fourth and final category of primitive techniques in Semper's *Style* is stereotomy: the work with "hard, thick, and homogenous" materials which perform well under pressure.[78] In his system of primitive techniques stereotomy is an archaic element. Lacking the anthropomorphic, organic qualities of the other components of a building, mighty mounds of earth and terraces have a lifeless, mineral surface that is, at best, rhythmically subdivided. Stereotomy works with materials "that strongly resist crushing and cracking because of their hard, thick, and homogenous aggregate composition and thus have significant compressive strength. When parts of their mass are removed, what remains can be worked into any required shape and then reassembled – they come to serve as regular pieces in strong systems relying on compressive strength as the most critical constructional principle."[79] [Figs. 4.22 a–c]

For Semper, "the raised earthen plateau of the hearth" is the model for that elevation of the ground that people carry out everywhere in order to "*detach something from the earth and the world as a whole: a consecrated place* dedicated to some entity."[80] This raising of the ground for the altar is an image "of

4.27 Retaining wall in the Woodland Cemetery in Stockholm. Sigurd Lewerentz, 1915–1961.
4.28 Façade of the Church of Gesù Nuovo, Naples by Giuseppe Valeriano and Pietro Provedi, completed in 1601.

the *strong ashlar of the earth*", which represents "the *whole world*", in that it, on the one hand, contrasts with the consecrated object placed upon it with which it, on the other hand, creates a unity.[81] Unlike the organic it is the "lifeless, crystalline-mineral quality", that characterizes the mighty stone wall while also corresponding with that which is placed upon it, "the two combine to form a self-contained whole, what one might call a representative of a crystalline *universe*. Stone turns eurythmically inward on all sides and denies any external

119

4.29 South façade of the Swedish National Bank (*Rijksbanken*), Stockholm. Peter Celsing, 1965–1976.

existence."[82] The contrast between shell and filling can already be seen in the "simplest, most ancient structures – for example, the earth mound dressed with grass to lend strength to it."[83] Hence, the examples here are earth mounds, stone shells or cell structures. Semper emphasizes that the root of the word "construct", *struere*, signifies the filling of hollow spaces.[84] Stereotomy is in reality a monumental technique because its heavy, resistant materials "give the greatest possible guarantee of *durability* and because it offers a means for the creation of large works especially *large and spacious buildings*. This field is almost limitless as ultimately these materials [...] preserve the dimensions of their structural parts to ensure proper statics and mass resistance. These dimensions also correspond to the laws of absolute stability, which affect the *monumentality* of a work."[85]

Semper differentiates between the sub-division of the surfaces of stereotomic systems and the constructional organization of tectonics. He mentions the "massive ashlar mountains" of the pyramids, which "were covered with a carpetlike crust of polished stone."[86] Both ashlar and polygonal techniques involve the joining together of elements according to specific rules. The structural functionality of such constructions is based on pressure and counter-pressure. This differentiates them from tectonic structures, "whose supporting elements become organisms and frame and roof supports are expressed collectively and purely mechanically: they are the load needed to activate the life inherent in the columns. At the same time the frame and its supports are in themselves variously articulated and seem to be striving and essentially alive in their individual parts."[87] Stereometric surfaces are, on the other hand, determined by "the *eurhythmic law*."[88]

The architectural element that serves as an example is rustication, masonry which has a coarse "natural" appearance due to the use of roughly cut embossed blocks. Rustication is applied to city gates, battlements, and palaces. Japanese castles of the Edo period such as Kumamoto Castle (1601–1607) are built on bases with steep walls. These are also known as "rat walls" because the huge stone blocks are laid so precisely that not even a rat can climb them. [Fig. 4.23] In European architecture rustication is associated with "rusticity" or "naturalness". The architectural theorist Leonhard Christoph Sturm (1669–1719) proposed the use of a "coarse technique" – rustication – for the creation of the external wall to a city gate. Sebastiano Serlio (1475–1554), the author of one of the most important architectural treatises of the first half of the 16th century writes: "The columns banded by Rustic stones, and also the architrave and frieze interrupted by the voussoirs, represent the work of Nature, but the capitals, part of the columns and the cornice with the pediment represent the work of the human hand."[89] Giovanni Battista Piranesi's engravings of Roman masonry walls which combine technical achievement with the sublime effect of huge rocky formations added a new, dramatic dimension to a European notion of antiquity that had long been focused on Athens. [Fig. 4.24]

Principal examples of expressive rusticated design include such Florentine Renaissance palaces as Alberti's Palazzo Rucellai (1446–1451), Michelozzo's Palazzo Medici Riccardi (1444–1460), Giuliano da Sangallo's Palazzo Strozzi (1489–1539) and the Palazzo Pitti (1458–1764), which was started by Filippo Brunelleschi and completed by Bartolomeo Ammanati and whose robust base of huge, roughly cut blocks, which resemble rocky fragments, has inspired

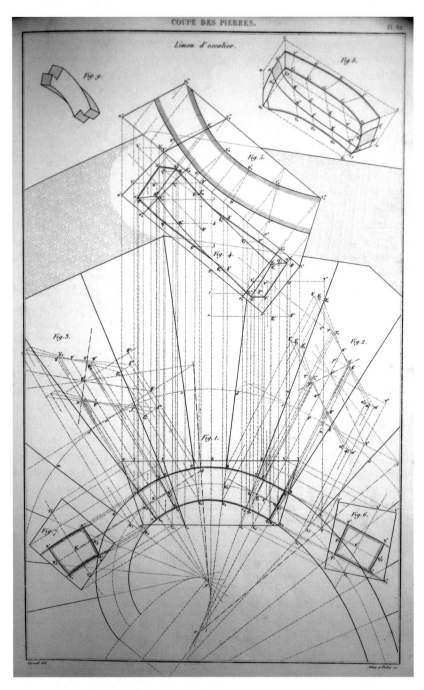

4.30 Projection of a stair stringer. Illustration from the *Traité de stéréotomie* by Charles-François-Antoine Leroy, 1870.

4.31 Vault of the vestibule of Arles Town Hall. Jules Hardouin-Mansart, 1673–1676.
4.32 Vestibule of Palais Rohan (since 1835 the City Hall) in Bordeaux. Richard-François Bonfin, 1778–1784.

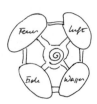

4.34 Museum der Obsessionen, sketch by Harald Szeemann, from Harald Szeemann, *Individuelle Mythologien*, Berlin, 1985.

4.33 Translucent glass panels form the façade of the Kunsthaus in Bregenz. Peter Zumthor, 1990–1997.

4.35 Detail of the façade of the
Bruder Klaus Field Chapel in
Wachendorf. Peter Zumthor,
2005–2007.

generations of architects – including Semper himself, for example, in the design of the terrace of the Polytechnikum (ETH) in Zurich. [Figs. 4.25, 4.26] Lewerentz also made use of such references for the *"strong ashlar of the earth"* in the design of the retaining wall of his Woodland Cemetery in Stockholm (1915–1961). [Fig. 4.27] The brick sculptures of the Danish artist Per Kirkeby, who is also a geology graduate, are stereometric structures in the spirit of Rudolf Schwarz's *Bebauung der Erde* (*Of the Development of the Earth*) (see p. 80–85).

An outstanding example of the covering of a façade with a rusticated dressing is Trinità Maggiore, the Jesuit church in Naples known as Gesù Nuovo (Giuseppe Valeriano, Pietro Provedi, 1584). The façade structure of the 15th-century Palazzo Sanseverino (architect Novello da San Lucano), with its pyramidal embossed blocks of hard volcanic Piperno stone, was retained and continued for the façade of the church. [Fig. 4.28] A modern variant of the Scandinavian granite architecture of National Romanticism is the Swedish National Bank building in Stockholm by Peter Celsing (1965–1976) a façade of which is built in two layers. The external grid is clad with roughly textured black Gylsboda granite slabs from the South of Sweden while smoother granite is used for the deep window niches. [Fig. 4.29]

Semper hardly mentions stone vaults as an important area for stereotomy. In the technical-historical section he writes that the "Roman work proper" that "expressed in stone" this people's idea of world domination was the vault. The Romans had transferred *"the concameration, the vaulted cell system that had been known since ancient times but had been used only for substructures"* to above-ground construction.[90] But his system, being determined by the textile metaphor, apparently didn't permit him to seriously address the "Roman work" in the same way that he had examined other constructional techniques.

In architecture it is primarily the cutting of the stone, the determination of the form of the stones of an arch or of the elements of a stone vault that are regarded as stereotomy which, in turn, is a branch of stereometry. The technique of representative geometry was used in the development of a system of projection that facilitated the production of working drawings of those individual stones which a craftsman could not simply cut by eye. The foundations for the system were laid by the French architect Philibert de l'Orme in his *Traité d'architecture* (1576). The widely used handbook for stereotomy in the 19th century is the *Traité de stéréotomie* by Charles-François-Antoine Leroy (1870). [Fig. 4.30] The science of stereotomy developed further in the 17th and 18th centuries and enabled the construction of such extraordinarily virtuoso examples of vaults with complex spatial forms as the vestibule of the town hall in Arles (Jules Hardouin-Mansart, 1673–1676) or the former Palais Rohan (since 1835 the City Hall) in Bordeaux (Richard-François Bonfin, 1778–1784).[91] [Figs. 4.31, 4.32]

Semper stated that stereotomy permitted a particularly large number of processes of Stoffwechsel. It includes "the art not only of masons and excavators but also of mosaicists, wood and ivory carvers and metalworkers. Even jewelers derive some of their stylistic principles from this technique."[92] As a *"secondary technique"* stereotomy generally no longer works with those materials "in which the pure functional-formal theme was originally and primarily embodied."[93] The fact that even glass can be used stereometrically can be seen in the façade of Peter Zumthor's Kunsthaus in Bregenz (1990–1997). Generally regarded as a weightless, transparent "non-material", these translucent panels of etched glass lean heavily on the substructure and are held in position by steel clips – a solution that accentuates the weight of the material. [Fig. 4.33]

The four elements and postmodernity

In October 1976 the exhibition *MAN transFORMS,* which was curated by Hans Hollein, opened in the Cooper-Hewitt Smithsonian Design Museum in New York. Mirroring the way in which Semper's diachronic presentation of the objects in his work *Style* sauntered its way through various historic periods, Hollein and the invited architects and designers also wanted to primarily demonstrate the formal transformation of everyday objects. The aim was not to document an evolutionary process of selection in which, like in the search for the "good form", one moved towards an ever better product but, rather, to illustrate associations and moods. Part of the exhibition was dedicated to the four elements. The quantity of water necessary for building an igloo was exhibited in 84 buckets while edited sequences of images on a monitor demonstrated the beneficial and destructive energy of fire.[94]

There is a striking similarity between Semper's plan for an ideal museum and the plan of Harald Szeemann's "Museum der Obsessionen" *(Museum of Obsessions).*[95] The latter is an imaginary place, a matrix of elements. For the curator, the term "obsession" was free of negative connotations. Rather, it was a "happily recognized, even anticipatory source of energy which didn't care whether, in the view of society […] it expressed itself or allowed itself to be used in a dangerous or beneficial way."[96] The Museum of Obsessions is an imaginary but still accessible world, in that it addresses much more complex relationships than real museums. [Fig. 4.34]

Given that elemental theory is considered a product of the mythical consciousness which is associated with alchemy and is taken most seriously by psychologists such as Carl Gustav Jung, Gernot Böhme talks today of a "return of the elements" which is a consequence of a new environmental consciousness.[97] However, the theory of the four elements, whose geometrical discipline and potential for transformation offers a "cosmological" basis for the interpretation of materials, production techniques, and structural forms, is deconstructed by those architects who reject this basis. Rem Koolhaas, for example, selected *Fundamentals* as the theme of the 14th Architecture Biennale in Venice, the main exhibition of which was entitled *Elements.* 15 elements of architecture were documented and discussed in separate catalogues: floor, wall, ceiling, roof, door, window, façade, balcony, corridor, fireplace, toilet, stair, escalator, elevator and ramp. Rather than forming a system these terms are more like headings in an encyclopedia. In contrast with Semper's elements, which refer to an archaeology of technical knowledge and the work of the craftsman or the architect, the elements of Koolhaas and his colleagues belong more to the world of industrial products which are selected and used, but not created by architects.

Semper's typology of the primitive techniques was the starting point for the exhibition *Sempering* at the 2016 Milan Triennale. The curators used Semper's system of the four elements as a pretext for placing his *Style,* open at the page with the image of the Caribbean hut, next to the entrance to the exhibition. However, they also extended his system and presented eight rather than four production techniques: stacking, weaving, folding, connecting, molding, blowing, engraving and tiling.[98] The decoration of surfaces, whether by painting, engraving or laying tiles, cannot represent a separate category in Semper's system of constructions. And yet the attempt to do so reveals these curators' intentions of challenging the unity of a comprehensive system which is based on an underlying metaphysical concept. The result is that the ambitious idea – despite the XXXL-scope of the publications on *Elements* and *Fundamentals* – loses itself in the encyclopedic and anecdotal without contributing substantially to our knowledge about architecture and its possibilities in a way comparable with Semper's *Style.* The field where the four elements come together again is architecture. Zumthor's Bruder Klaus Field Chapel in Wachendorf (2005–2007) is the result of a process of material transformation. First, a tent-shaped "primitive hut" of spruce trunks was created and this was then shrouded in a tower-like shell of rammed concrete, poured in 50 cm layers. A fire was then allowed to burn inside the shell for three weeks during which the tree trunks turned to charcoal and, as they were removed, they left behind a grooved black surface. The openings required for fixing the formwork were filled with glass plugs while rainwater enters through the oculus, collecting on the floor. This is covered with zinc lead produced by the melting and pouring of old metal cans. The small wheel on the inside wall represents Bruder Klaus, Switzerland's patron saint, the mystic Nicholas of Flüe, whose visions are interpreted by the Swiss School of Psychoanalysis, the teachings of Carl Gustav Jung, as alchemistic symbols.[99] [Fig. 4.35] While theorists, historians, and curators strive to address the question of materiality at the interface between physical/sensory presence and meaning, it is once again architecture that succeeds, with great precision and poetry, to shed light on the connections between work and material, culture and religion.

Notes

1   Marie Louise von Plessen, Julius Bryant (eds.), *Art and Design for All. The Victoria and Albert Museum. Die Entstehungsgeschichte des weltweit führenden Museums für Kunst und Design.* Munich, London, New York: Prestel, 2011, p. 115.

2   Comp. Harry Francis Mallgrave, *Gottfried Semper. Architect of the Nineteenth Century*, New Haven, Connecticut: Yale University Press, 2001. p. 197.

3   Ibid.

4   Johann Wolfgang von Goethe, *Aufsätze, Fragmente, Studien zur Morphologie,* ed. Dorothea Kuhn, Wilhelm Troll, Karl Lothar Wolf. Weimar: Böhlau, 1964. p. 334. Translation by R. H.

5   Gottfried Semper, *Style in the Technical and Tectonic Arts; or, Practical Aesthetics,* transl. by Harry Francis Mallgrave and Michael Robinson. Los Angeles: Getty Research Institute, 2004, p. 666.

6   Gottfried Semper, "Science, Industry and Art. Proposals for the Development of a National Taste in Art at the Closing of the London Industrial Exhibition (1852)", in: Semper, *The Four Elements of Architecture and Other Writings,* transl. by Harry Francis Mallgrave and Wolfgang Herrmann. Cambridge: Cambridge University Press, 1989, pp. 130–167, here p. 134.

7   Semper, *Style,* (see note 5), p. 119.

8   Friedrich Schiller, "Über die ästhetische Erziehung des Menschen in einer Reihe von Briefen" (1793/94), in: Volume 12: *Schillers sämtliche Werke*. Stuttgart, Berlin: J. G. Cotta'sche Buchhandlung, without date [around 1905], pp. 3–120, here p. 29. Translation by R. H.

9   Ibid.

10   Richard Wagner, "The Artwork of the Future", in: Wagner, *Richard Wagner's Prose Works*, Volume 1, transl. by William Ashton Ellis. London: Kegan Paul, Trench, Trübner & Co., Ltd, 1895.

11   Gottfried Semper, "Science, Industry and Art" (see note 6), p. 130.

12   Ibid., p. 163.

13   Comp. Walter Pagel, "Paracelsus als 'Naturmystiker'", in: Udo Benzenhöfer, *Paracelsus*. Darmstadt: Wissenschaftliche Buchgesellschaft, 1993, pp. 24–97.

14   Ibid., p. 44.

15   Joseph Rykwert, *On Adam's House in Paradise. The Idea of the primitive Hut in Architectural History*. New York: The Museum of Modern Art, 1971.

16   Semper, *Style* (see note 5), p. 666.

17   Ibid.

18   It is astonishing how little we know of this hut in its role as an exhibit in the exhibition. The Caribbean hut cannot be seen in any of the hundreds of images of the interiors and objects in the exhibition and it is also not mentioned in the catalogue of the ethnography section.

19   Semper, *Style,* (see note 5), p. 109.

20   Ibid.

21   Ibid.

22   Ibid.

23   Ibid.

24   Ibid.

25   Ibid., p. 110.

26   Ibid.

27   Ibid.

28   Gottfried Semper, "The Four Elements of Architecture. A Contribution to the Comparative Study of Architecture (1851)", in: Semper, *The Four Elements of Architecture and Other Writings,* transl. by Harry Francis Mallgrave and Wolfgang Herrmann, Cambridge: Cambridge University Press, 1989, pp. 74–129.

29   Ibid., p. 102.

30   Ibid.

31   Ibid., p. 103.

32   Comp. Heiz Quitsch, *Gottfried Semper – Praktische Ästhetik und politischer Kampf*. Braunschweig, Wiesbaden: Friedr. Vieweg & Sohn, 1962.

33   Gottfried Semper, *The Ideal Museum. Practical Art in Metals and Hard Materials*, ed. Peter Noever, Vienna: Schlebrügge Editor, 2007.

34   Ibid., p. 56.

35   Ibid., p. 57.

36   Semper, *Style,* (see note 5), p. 110.

37   Ibid., p. 79.

38   Ibid., p. 109.

39   Ibid., p. 110.

40   Semper, "The Four Elements" (see note 28), p. 103.

41   Marc Dessauce (ed.), *The Inflatable Moment: Pneumatics and Protest in '68*. New York: Princeton Architectural Press, 1999.

42   Jonas Wirth, *Zwischen Stoffen. Eine theoretische Untersuchung der Bauformen in den Flüchtlingslagern der Westsahara unter den Aspekten des Stoffwechsels und dem Prinzip der Bekleidung*, Elective paper ETH Zürich, Institut gta, unpublished manuscript, 2013.

43   Semper, *Style* (see note 5), p. 109.

44   Ibid., p. 468.

45   Ibid.

46   Ibid., p. 554, note 1, here Semper is quoting the French naturalist Alexandre Brongniart.

47   Ibid., p. 559ff.

48   Ibid., p. 467.

49   Semper, *The Four Elements* (see note 28), p. 103.

50   Vitruvius, *Ten Books on Architecture*, transl. by Morris Hicky Morgan. Cambridge, Mass.: *Harvard University Press, 1914*, p. 60.

51   Semper, *The Four Elements* (see note 28), p. 102.

52 Gottfried Semper, "Ueber den Zusammenhang der architektonischen Systeme mit allgemeinen Kulturzuständen" (1853), in: Semper., *Kleine Schriften,* ed. Hans and Manfred Semper. Berlin, Stuttgart, 1884. Reprint Mittenwald: Mäander Kunstverlag, 1979, pp. 351–368, here p. 352. Translation by R. H.

53 Gottfried Semper, "On Architectural Symbols" Lecture, held in London, 1854, ed. Henry Francis Mallgrave in: *Res 9,* Spring 1985 (theme issue *Anthropology and Aesthetics*), pp. 61–67.

54 Leon Battista Alberti, *De re aedificatoria* (Florence 1486), *On the Art of Building in Ten Books,* transl. by Joseph Rykwert, Neil Leach, Robert Tavernor. Cambridge, Mass.: The MIT Press, 1988, p. 320.

55 Peter Sloterdijk, *Spheres. Macrospherology,* transl. by Wieland Hoban. Volume 2: Globes. Cambridge, Mass.: MIT Press, 2014, p. 242.

56 Eduardo Torroja, *Philosophy of Structures.* English version by J. J. Polivka and Milos Polivka. Berkeley and Los Angeles: University of California Press, 1967, p. 28.

57 Ibid.

58 From Otto Bartning's speech marking the consecration of the Steel Church in Cologne on 31st March 1928, quoted in: Hans K. F. Mayer, *Der Baumeister Otto Bartning und die Wiederentdeckung des Raumes.* Heidelberg: Verlag Lambert Schneider, 1951, p. 48. Translation by R. H.

59 Semper, *Style,* (see note 5), p. 726.

60 Ákos Moravánszky, "Das Monumentale als symbolische Form. Zum öffentlichen Auftritt der Moderne in den Vereinigten Staaten", in: Carsten Ruhl (ed.), *Mythos Monument. Urbane Strategien in Architektur und Kunst seit 1945.* Bielefeld: transcript Verlag, 2011, pp. 37–61.

61 Heinrich Wölfflin, *Principles of Art History: The Problem of the Development of Style in Early Modern Art,* transl. by Jonathan Blower. Los Angeles: Getty Publications, 2015, p. 228.

62 Kenneth Frampton, *Studies in Tectonic Culture. The Poetics of Construction in Nineteenth and Twentieth Century Architecture,* Cambridge, Mass.: The MIT Press, 1995.

63 Semper, *Style,* (see note 5), p. 623.

64 Ibid., p. 109.

65 Ibid., p. 623.

66 Ibid.

67 Ibid., p. 678.

68 Ibid., p. 693.

69 Ibid., p. 624.

70 Ibid., p. 625.

71 Ibid., p. 665.

72 Ibid.

73 Ibid., p. 694.

74 Adolf Loos, "The Principle of Cladding (1898)" in: Loos, *Spoken into the Void: Collected Essays 1897–1900,* transl. by Jane Newman and John Smith. Cambridge, Mass.: MIT Press, 1983, p. 66.

75 Gottfried Semper, "Log Construction. The Swiss House", in *Style,* (see note 5), pp. 689–692.

76 Ibid., p. 698.

77 Ibid., p. 696.

78 Ibid., p. 725.

79 Ibid.

80 Ibid., p. 726.

81 Ibid.

82 Ibid., p. 728.

83 Ibid., p. 740.

84 Ibid., p. 751, note 1.

85 Ibid., p. 725.

86 Ibid., p. 726f.

87 Ibid., p. 728.

88 Ibid., p. 86.

89 *Sebastiano Serlio On Architecture. Volume One: Books I–V of "Tutte l'opere d'architettura et prospetiva" by Sebastiano Serlio,* transl. by Vaughan Hart and Peter Hicks, New Haven and London: Yale University Press, 1996, p. 270.

90 Semper, *Style,* (see note 5), p. 756.

91 C[harles]-F[rançois]-A[ntoine] Leroy, *Traité de stéréotomie comprenant les applications de la géométrie descriptive à la théorie des ombres, la perspective linéaire, la gnomonique, la coupe des pierres et la charpente.* Paris: Gauthier-Villars, 1870.

92   Semper, *Style,* (see note 5), p. 110.

93   Ibid., p. 725.

94   Hans Hollein, *Design, MAN transFORMS. Konzepte einer Ausstellung. Concepts of an Exhibition,* ed. University of Applied Arts, Vienna. Vienna: Löcker Verlag, 1989, p. 96.

95   Harald Szeemann, *Individuelle Mythologien.* Berlin: Merve, 1985, p. Inside front cover.

96   Harald Szeemann, *Museum der Obsessionen.* Berlin: Merve 1981, p. 125f. Translation by R. H.

97   Gernot Böhme, Hartmut Böhme, *Feuer Wasser Erde Luft. Eine Kulturgeschichte der Elemente.* Munich: Verlag C. H. Beck, 1996, p. 299f.

98   Luisa Collina, Cino Zucchi (eds.), *Sempering. Process and Pattern in Architecture and Design.* Milan: Silvana Editoriale, 2016.

99   Marie-Louise von Franz, *Die Visionen des Niklaus von Flüe, Studien aus dem C. G. Jung-Institut Zürich.* Volume IX. Zurich: Rascher, 1959.

5.
THE NATURE OF MATTER

I Rigoristi

The birth of the idea of truth to materials in architecture is associated with the name of the Venetian Franciscan priest Carlo Lodoli (1690–1761). Lodoli did not publish his teachings himself. His theories were disseminated by his pupils Francesco Algarotti and Andrea Memmo, who idolized him as the Socrates of architecture, an uncompromising and radical seeker after truth. Like the Greek thinker, who "sought to cleanse philosophy of the babble and errors of the Sophists," Lodoli, according to Algarotti, wanted to return architecture to its true fundamentals.[1] *Rappresentazione* (representation) is a key word in this theory: Nothing should be visible in architecture that fails to correspond with the truth. In his *Saggio sopra l'architettura* (*Essay on Architecture*) Algarotti quoted Lodoli's conclusion: "[...] one wouldn't only have to completely destroy the one or the other part, but every old and new building, especially those that are regarded as beautiful and as artistic models."[2] These buildings are "built of stone and appear to be of wood," which means, for Lodoli and Algarotti, that "practice" and "theory" have become a contradiction. "Why should stone not be stone? Wood not be wood? Why shouldn't everything be that which it is and not something else? Architecture must be exactly the opposite of everything that one teaches and does in these buildings – it should be in keeping with the characteristic texture, suppleness or stiffness of the material, with its varying resisting force, in a word, with its very essence and nature. And given that the nature of wood is so utterly different from the nature of stone, so must the form that one gives to buildings of wood be different from the form that one gives to buildings of stone. Nothing is more vulgar, he [Lodoli, Á. M.] adds, than striving to ensure that a material appears not to be itself but something different. This is a constant masquerade, a permanent deception."[3]

Only if form, construction and decoration are derived "from the nature and essence of the material" can one build in an "architecturally rational" manner.[4] "This is the main argument and, so to say, the battering ram of our philosopher, with which he lashes out violently, as if he intends to get rid of all old and new buildings and present us with his own architecture which is at one with its materials, an architecture without deceit, based on the essential [...]."[5] Algarotti describes Lodoli's demands as "terrible", because his radical rationalism would have undermined the authority of Vitruvius' theory by showing that the Roman author violated the doctrine of truth to materials with his notion of the timber origins of the Greek temple. In retrospect, it appears to us that the teachings of the Franciscan priest were perceived as "shocking" more because of his desire to be one of the first to decide what was allowed be visible on a façade and what should be hidden. Lodoli's linking of truth and the visibility of building materials meant that reason and architectural morality had finally become inseparable from the question of the relationship between structure and surface.[6]

Christian art and truth to materials

Architectural historians of the modern era associate the rationalism of Lodoli and his followers with the French classicism of Marc-Antoine Laugier, the material ethic of John Ruskin and – in the case of Alberto Sartoris – even with 20th-century functionalism.[7] Not only the theory of truth to materials but also concepts and terms such as "function" or "organism" have been employed to justify the notion that the *rigoristi* (rigorists) were "the first moderns" (Joseph Rykwert).[8] These artificial genealogies enabled much modernist ideology to be projected back onto historic material: Even Memmo's and Algarotti's interpretation of the thoughts of their master were influenced by other received ideas. The diverse statements about truth to materials never speak for themselves and the message of modern texts is no easier to decipher than Algarotti's archaic language, despite being much more recent.

It was the respected professor of the École Polytechnique in Paris, Jean-Nicolas-Louis Durand (1760–1834), who highlighted correctly applied materials as being the source of beauty in architecture. Aesthetic proportions and forms are derived from the nature of the materials and the meeting of intended purpose.[9] In his work *Précis des leçons d'architecture* (*Précis of the Lectures on Architecture*, 1819) Durand cites brickwork as proof of the fact that this material was already used uncovered in antiquity: "To be sure of this, we have only to look at the imposing remains of the buildings of antiquity; at the splendid fabrics, in every part of Italy, in which stone, brick, marble and so on, show themselves as they are, and where they should be […]."[10] He illustrates this by showing four façades as options for executing the same floor plan in ways which use materials appropriately: as brickwork, stone, plaster, or with a timber frame.[11] [Fig. 5.1] However, examples such as brick-built and iron-reinforced beams which are clad to imitate stone construction contradict Durand's claims that the architecture of antiquity was the embodiment of the appropriate use of materials. [Fig. 5.2]

More than a century later the architect Paul Schmitthenner was working on his textbook *Gebaute Form* (*Built Form*, 1943–1949), in which he, like Durand, illustrated the original typology of the dwelling house (which, hardly coincidentally, evokes memories of Goethe's garden house) in its various material incarnations: with a timber frame in-filled with rubble, in rough masonry, in brick or – characterized physiognomically– as "the house with cool noblesse" or "the house with the first face" etc. Schmitthenner describes the original typology as a "theme", which brings us close to Semper's theory of transformation. This decision to label the original typology "the subject" was a rigorous but "impractical" decision, because it involves the immaterial idea, which can only appear in its various materializations. However, the architect shied away from accepting the principle of dressing as the lesson from his own sequence of images because, in the 1940s, this would still have been anathema. Hence, Schmitthenner proposed another relationship between material and form: "The laws governing the relationship between material and form are immutable, natural laws. Material and form are like body and soul. The soul, the spirit is transformed but the material remains. Perfection is found in the combination. Perfection, when material and form have become an indivisible unity. That is the essence of synthesis."[12] [Figs. 5.3 a–d]

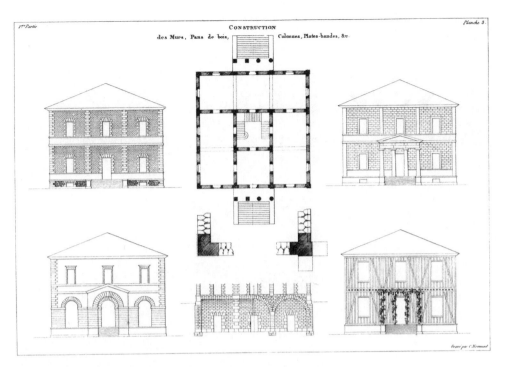

5.1 Structures built of various materials, plate from Jean-Nicolas-Louis Durand, *Précis des leçons d'architecture*, Volume 1, Paris, 1819.
5.2 Architectural detail from the audience chamber of Hadrian's Villa at Tivoli, around 118–130.

In his book *True Principles* (1841) the English architect Augustus Welby Pugin sharply attacked the dishonesty of the architecture of his time.[13] The use and treatment of such structural elements as beams in classicist architecture reveal the origin of the model in timber architecture and this, writes Pugin, is a violation of the true principles of building. The Gothic, on the other hand, uses stone in line with its properties. Pugin criticized render as an expression of falsehood and of the moral decay of his time. He believed, however, that the moral world of Christendom, "the ancient feelings and sentiments," could be restored.[14] In his earlier book *Contrasts* (1836) Pugin had been the first to work

5.3 Illustrations from Paul Schmitthenner, *Gebaute Form* (1943–1949, published 1984).
a. The subject: The longitudinal side shown without materials.
b. The house with a timber frame filled-in with rubble.
c. The house with rough masonry.
d. The house with pilasters.

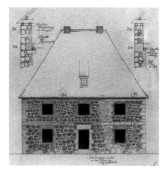
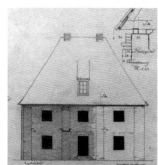

with comparative tables of illustrations as a means of demonstrating the moral degeneracy of contemporary architecture.[15] Architectural details previously executed by craftsmen had become cheap surrogates, carved timber or stone decoration replaced by painted wallpaper.[16] [Fig. 5.4]

The supporters of the movement for liturgical reform who belonged to Cambridge's Camden Society picked up on and popularized Pugin's ideas in the journal *The Ecclesiologist* which they founded in 1841.[17] It is this publication that best documents the shift in attitudes to fair-faced brick architecture from initial rejection to complete support. The ideal which the ecclesiologists initially had in mind was the rough stone façade, the irregularity of which best embodied the pictorial aesthetic of the *picturesque*. This illustrates the close interrelationship between this aesthetic and a concept which was soon to develop the outlines of a firm principle in the shape of the theory of truth to materials. Brickwork initially failed to meet the requirements of this concept unless the fair-faced brick façade had been enhanced with artistic devices in order to create a picturesque effect. Such devices included colored majolica inlay or the use of bricks of a range of hues and finishes.

The ideas disseminated by *The Ecclesiologist* soon found an audience on the continent in such publications as the *Kölner Domblatt* or the *Annales archéologiques*, journals between whose editors there was an intense exchange of ideas.[18] August Reichensperger, who edited the *Kölner Domblatt* between 1842 and 1844 and after 1849, reproduced Pugin's arguments almost verbatim. In his book *Die christlich-germanische Baukunst* (*Christian-Germanic Architecture*, 1845) he confirms that: "Today we know how to make everything out of anything using mortar and whitewash [...] gypsum magically transforms every wall and beam into a brilliant marble and porphyry surface or column [...].

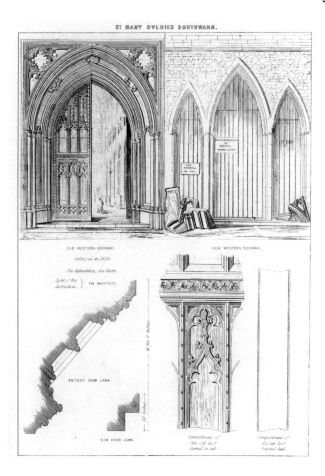

5.4 Comparison between the old and new western doorways and details of the Church of St Mary Overie, Southwark from the book by Augustus Welby Pugin, *Contrasts*, London, 1841.

such play-acting, flirting and cheating, such papering, patching and hammering, such empty beggarly pride, which is swelling up everywhere, even in the mortar palaces of our capitals, in *one* word, such *deceitful* fiddling was far below the dignity of those great masters of the Middle Ages whose innermost beings were characterized more than anything by *truthfulness* and *lawfulness* and who [...] expressed this in all their creations."[19]

Representatives of the Gothic Revival such as Reichensperger, the architect Georg Gottlob Ungewitter or Conrad Wilhelm Hase, the founder of the Hanover School of architecture, helped the theory of truth to materials to become generally accepted as a basic architectural principle in the final years of the 19th century. "At a time in which architecture in Germany has predominantly been exercised by dilettantes playing tentative games with randomly borrowed and purely externally used forms" Hase has "courageously unfurled his banner and spoken up for the basic principle that states that the highest imperatives of architecture are truth and authenticity and that artistic form must correlate with the construction and the material," eulogized the *Deutsche Bauzeitung* in 1898.[20]

The doctrine of truth to materials became a basic theoretical principle of Protestant church building. The Congress of the German Evangelical Church

5.5 Round arches in the Cathedral of Murano. Illustration in John Ruskin, *The Stones of Venice*, Volume II, London 1907, Plate V.

Archivolt in the Duomo of Murano.

in Barmen in 1860 resolved that the dignity of church building "forbids the mere pretense of solidity and permanence" and demands "solid material."[21] The *Eisenacher Regulativ* of 1861 formulated rules for the construction and aesthetics of evangelical church buildings. This, too, emphasized that the building of churches required "durable material and solid construction free of deceptive plasterwork or paint."[22]

The lamps of truth

The most influential representative of truth to materials was John Ruskin (1819–1900), the "Luther of the arts" as he was described by his friend, the painter and pre-Raphaelite Edward Burne-Jones.[23] Ruskin denied having been influenced by Pugin, although Patrick Conner has shown that he had carefully studied the *True Principles*.[24] In *The Seven Lamps of Architecture* (1849) and, in particular, in the chapter "The Lamp of Truth" Ruskin rejects all forms of "architectural deceits". Deceits are a result of the simulation of a false construction via the "painting of surfaces to represent some other material than that of which they actually consist (as in the marbling of wood)" or through the use of cast or machine-made ornaments.[25] He sanctioned the cladding of façades with marble as long as these did not imitate the appearance of a more valuable, solid stone façade.

Ruskin claims that as soon as iron "takes the place of the stone" and replaces the stone buttresses that "would have done as well; that instant the building ceases […] to be true architecture."[26] He regarded deliberate deception as the criterion for dishonesty in architecture; if it is clear that architectural elements are merely painted, one cannot speak of lies. On the other hand, Ruskin sharply condemned the use of cast iron ornamentation, which he held responsible for the "degradation of our national feeling for beauty."[27] No other ornaments are "so cold, clumsy, and vulgar, so essentially incapable of a fine line or shadow, as those of cast iron."[28] He accepted plaster as a support for paint: plaster is

5.6 Garden building of St Hilda's College in Oxford. Alison and Peter Smithson, 1968–1970.

applied to the brick wall like a gesso ground is applied to the canvas. But he rejected the use of plasterwork to imitate stone.

More bricks were used in the Victorian and Edwardian periods (1837–1914) in Great Britain than ever before. This development was encouraged not only by the reduction in the brick tax in 1850 but also by the works of Ruskin and, in particular, *The Stones of Venice* (first published 1851–1853) with its celebrated chapter "The Nature of Gothic." Polychrome, labor-intensive brick architecture appealed to Ruskin, who regarded the craftsman's satisfaction in his work as one of the main criteria of good architecture. This was why he strictly rejected the painstaking, mechanical imitation of Gothic. The architecture that he propagated in his books and lectures appeared – in particular in comparison with the classical tradition – as naive, coarse and even ugly. [Fig. 5.5]

John Summerson opens his 1948 essay about William Butterfield, a pioneer of the brick architecture inspired by Ruskin, with the comment that people with taste would find his buildings ugly today. According to Summerson, the vicars of churches designed by Butterfield would willingly whitewash their façades. The essay is entitled "William Butterfield; or, the Glory of Ugliness" but, for the English architectural historian, *ugliness* did not necessarily have negative connotations.[29] In the 1930s the important architecture journal *The Architectural Review* had already launched a campaign which was influenced by surrealism and whose aim was to recognize "beauty, ugliness and the power to disquiet" in

5.7 Red House, William Morris' home in Upton, Bexleyheath by Philip Webb, 1858/59.
5.8 All Saints' Church in London, William Butterfield, 1850–1859.

5.9, 5.10 Oxford University Museum of Physical Sciences, Thomas Deane and Benjamin Woodward, 1855–1861 (decorative details completed in 1911).

5.11 Trinity Church in Boston.
Henry H. Richardson, 1872–1877.
5.12 Marshall Field Wholesale
Store, Chicago. Henry H.
Richardson, 1885–1887,
demolished 1930.

everyday spaces.[30] At the time at which Summerson's essay appeared, ugliness
had become a critical concept in British architecture that was soon offering historical legitimation to architects such as Alison and Peter Smithson and their
program of "New Brutalism". Their garden building for Saint Hilda's College

5.13, 5.14 Allegheny County
Courthouse and Jail, Pittsburgh.
Henry H. Richardson, 1883–1888.

Oxford (1968) presents prefabricated concrete columns and the oak frame that is attached to them as the load-bearing structure whereas it is actually the brick wall behind this orchestrated façade that is carrying the load. The architects justified this solution on the basis of the need to shield the student residence more strongly from the outside world. Their search was for expressive material effects rather than the cultivated tedium which had been propagated by Geoffrey Scott in 1914 as the "Architecture of Humanism."[31] [Fig. 5.6]

Although it appears today to contradict the general image of English architecture, brick was scarcely used as a façade material in the first half of the 19th century. The visible brick contradicted the white, neo-classical ideal and, initially, even its mere redness was arguably too much for English taste. It is thus no surprise that William Morris gave the name Red House to the home that Philip Webb designed for him in Upton, Bexleyheath (1859/60) – this was intended as a provocation. Morris wanted a house "very mediaeval in spirit" which was built in the style of the 13th century and far removed from contemporary taste.[32] [Fig. 5.7]

Butterfield was convinced that he had a "mission to give dignity to brick."[33] The material's resistance to fire was without doubt a very strong argument in industrial cities like London or Manchester but his first programmatic buildings such as All Saints' Church in London (1850–1859) were heavily criticized, even by his friends. [Fig. 5.8] The façade is clad with soft pink bricks and decoratively structured with the use of horizontal bands of tarred bricks. This façade texture was known in Victorian England as *constructional colour* as a means of emphasizing the contrast with an opaque color treatment (such as, for example, the use of colored plaster). Butterfield rejected cheaper, machine-produced and surface-colored bricks, preferring to use thin bricks with fine joints laid in Flemish bond. Ruskin praised Butterfield's All Saints' Church; George Hersey even suggested that it was under the influence of this church that Ruskin developed his position on polychromy.[34]

The stylistic direction described as "Ruskinian Gothic" took after Italian models in the areas of incrustation and the use of contrasting colors. The Oxford University Museum of Physical Sciences (today Oxford University Museum of Natural History) by Thomas Deane and Benjamin Woodward (1855–1861, decorative details first completed 1911) is a leading work of Ruskinian Gothic. It follows Ruskin's advice to "adopt the pure and perfect forms of Northern Gothic, and work them out with Italian refinement."[35] A gothicizing iron structure supports the huge glass roof of the exhibition space; the shafts of the columns are of cast iron and the arches of forged iron. The secondary decoration fixed to the load-bearing structure transforms the iron beams into images of trees and plants. [Figs. 5.9, 5.10] At first glance, this use of iron appears to contradict Ruskin's principles; However, in his book *The Seven Lamps of Architecture* he had already noted that: "Abstractedly there appears no reason why iron should not be used as well as wood; and the time is probably near when a new system of architectural laws will be developed, adapted entirely to metallic construction."[36] Having said this, he speaks in a footnote about: "the ferruginous temper which I saw rapidly developing itself, and which, since that day, has changed our merry England into the Man in the Iron Mask."[37]

5.15 Crane Memorial Library in Quincy, Massachusetts. Henry H. Richardson, 1880–1882.
5.16 Glessner House, Chicago. Henry H. Richardson, 1885–1887.

Truth to materials as a national style in the United States

The North American fascination with nature and the link between nature and the political and cultural identity of the young nation was first philosophically formulated in the transcendentalism of Ralph Waldo Emerson. The aesthetic of the picturesque and the sublime which was closely associated with the observation of the beauty of nature strongly influenced art and architecture in the 19th century. The architecture of Henry Hobson Richardson (1838–1886) combines elements of the picturesque such as irregularity, contrast, and color with components of the sublime such as the awesome, the overwhelming, and the monumental. Richardson left his home town for Boston in order to study at Harvard University in 1857 at around the same time that Andrew Jackson Downing and Alexander Jackson Davis were disseminating the aesthetic of the picturesque in their writings and projects. This aesthetic later became a decisive influence on the appearance of many American cities due to the work of Frederick Law Olmsted, who subsequently became a friend of Richardson. In the early 1860s Richardson studied architecture at the École des Beaux-Arts in Paris, but none of the opposing stylistic directions propagated there by the students loyal to Rome and the Gothicists interested him. Richardson, in contrast, was fascinated by Romanesque architecture, perhaps inspired by the debate about the round arched style that, having been initiated by Heinrich Hübsch in 1828, was still raging in Germany.[38] Richardson visited the early medieval cathedrals of France and Spain and became one of the first architects to compile a large collection of photographs. He returned from Paris to North America in 1865. His early buildings already demonstrate the influence of the Southern French and Iberian Romanesque. Trinity Church in Boston (1872–1877) was his first major triumph. The compact building with the mighty crossing tower appears friendly due to the warm colors of the façade in which the texture of the wall is structured by granite blocks with red sandstone surrounds. [Fig. 5.11] The libraries that Richardson built in North Easton and some of Boston's other small industrial satellites demonstrate his interest in picturesque effects.[39] Such later buildings as the subsequently demolished Marshall Field Wholesale Store in Chicago (1885–1887) [Fig. 5.12] or his perhaps most important work, Allegheny County Courthouse and Jail in Pittsburgh (1883–1888), [Figs. 5.13, 5.14] embody the aesthetic of the sublime which in this latter example – quite in keeping with the program – is quite capable of becoming threatening. Richardson's early use of color has been replaced by the homogenous silver gray of the monolithic building volume; the weight of the granite blocks and huge stones of the arches dominate the overall effect. Crane Memorial Library in Quincy, Massachusetts (1880–1882) represents a revision of his early picturesque style in the direction of increasing severity with a finely calibrated asymmetry. [Fig. 5.15] Like Richardson's post-1880 public buildings, the Glessner House in Chicago (1885–1887) has a monolithic effect with equally forbidding results. [Fig. 5.16] The lessons from the architecture of the Middle Ages can no longer be traced back to concrete models, as had been the case with Trinity Church. The vocabulary of "Richardsonian Romanesque" is complete and its influence is spreading – not least due to the high-quality photographs that Richardson very consciously uses in order to win new clients.

Louis Henry Sullivan (1856–1924) initially continued resolutely along the path carved out by Richardson. Influenced by the Marshall Field Wholesale Store Sullivan designed the Auditorium Building in Chicago (1886–1889), a massive block with a granite-clad lower façade zone. According to Rudolph M. Schindler the building struck Sullivan's contemporaries like a meteor from another planet. [Fig. 5.17] In Sullivan's work the weight of Richardsonian Romanesque (or Modern Romanesque) then gave way to façade designs which appeared increasingly lighter, an effect that was made possible by, amongst other

5.17 Auditorium Building, Chicago. Louis H. Sullivan, 1886–1889.
5.18 The northern block of the Monadnock Building, Chicago. Burnham and Root, 1889–1892.

5.19 The First Presbyterian Church, Detroit. Mason and Rice, 1890/91. Illustration from Paul Graef, ed., *Neubauten in Nordamerika*, Berlin, 1897, Plate 88.

things, their separation from the load-bearing structural frame. The last major high-rise building in Chicago with a load-bearing masonry façade, a mammoth of brick architecture, was the Monadnock Building by Burnham and Root (1889–1892). [Fig. 5.18] The bulky "material style" of Sullivan's Auditorium Building effortlessly became an aesthetic of dressing (see p. 248–251) a fact that must at least raise doubts about the incompatibility of the two positions.

Richardson's impact in Europe

Growing dissatisfaction with the "masked ball" of historicism and its inability to create something new encouraged the search for alternatives in the final decades of the 19th century. The new images from the USA stimulated the architectural debate and the influence of America is clearly recognizable in the efforts of many European countries from Finland to Hungary or Switzerland to establish what became known as a "national style." During this period the principle of the appropriate use of materials appeared to be the one architectural rule which was immune to the infighting of the representatives of the various styles of historicism. "A Principle and no Parties!" was the consequently fitting title of Johann Heinrich Wolff's lecture in 1846. He demanded that "the nature of the materials that are at our disposal and their resulting compositions and structures" should be "the underlying basis of the design."[40] In his lecture – as in his earlier writings – Wolff acknowledged Schinkel's brick buildings as exemplars of truth to materials.[41]

One of the first essays about the truth to materials of North American architecture to appear in the German-speaking professional press was Ludwig Gruner's "Der Yankee-Styl," which appeared in Ludwig Förster's *Allgemeine Bauzeitung* in 1874.[42] Gruner underlined that the use of such durable façade materials as granite, brick, brownstone, and marble was the most important characteristic of the architecture of New York. "Blessed with such a wealth of

5.20 Monument to the Battle of the Nations in Leipzig by Bruno Schmitz, 1897–1913.
5.21 Main Railway Station in Stuttgart, Paul Bonatz and F.E. Scholer, 1914–1928.

materials" the Americans can dispense with the use of surrogates: "[…] the American public must have abhorred deceit or, at least, gleaming forgeries. And the same is true apropos that article which is so popular for imitations in Northern Germany: Cement, because it rarely appears, if ever, to be used as the external layer or means of decoration."[43]

Richardsonian Romanesque owes much of its influence in Germany to the intermediary role of Karl Hinckeldeyn who was Technical Attaché at the German Embassy in Washington between 1884 and 1887 before occupying influential positions back home as a government and building official and then, from 1902, as Rector of Berlin's Academy of Architecture. In 1897 he published, together with Paul Graef, the book *Neubauten in Nordamerika* (*New Buildings in North America*), which was illustrated with 100 exquisite heliotype plates.[44] [Fig. 5.19] The high-resolution prints which Richardson had already admired and made use of had an impact in Germany and Central Europe. No less important was the role of the architect Rudolf Vogel, who worked in Richardson's office. Vogel's book *Das amerikanische Haus* (*The American House*) was published by Berlin's Wasmuth Verlag in 1910.[45]

"There are two things […] that meet the eye of the European and, especially, the German architect on his first visit to American cities: the tremendous

5.22 St. Anton's Church in Zurich-Hottingen. Karl Moser, 1906–1908.
5.23 Reformed church in Városliget Avenue in Budapest. Aladár Árkay, 1911–1913.

height of the buildings and the absolute domination of authentic building materials", reports the architect Leopold Gmelin in *Deutsche Bauzeitung* in 1894.[46] The approach to building with its truth to materials had increasingly impressed him to the extent that he had to constantly revise his preconceptions. The term "American" is "sometimes associated with a hint of 'humbug' and 'swindle'" he notes "but from the standpoint of building this is highly unjust."[47] Natural stone and, above all, brick are the building materials of the great American cities, writes Gmelin, with a view to the huge warehouses on the banks of the Hudson River on which brick was transported to New York. Brick façades were not plastered but "demonstrate [...] consistently fine detailing – with an admirable quality of execution. The precision with which Chicago's 16 to 20-story façades are exclusively built in brick, with the possible exception of the window walls, repeatedly reawakens our respect for this technology."[48]

The lessons of Richardsonian Romanesque initially had their greatest impact in Germany as the basis for the design of national monuments. America and nationalism, stone and identity were the strands of a knot that was often difficult to disentangle. In 1890, the year of its appearance, the book *Rembrandt als Erzieher* (*Rembrandt as Educator*) by Julius Langbehn, an admirer of Nietzsche, went through 30 editions in a very short time. In a period of crisis the book very precisely struck a nerve amongst critics of civilization. The "Rembrandt-German" used his rhetorical skill to combine his critical diagnosis of the present

5.24 Primary school (now Commercial College), Wendenstrasse, Hamburg-Hammerbrook. Fritz Schumacher, 1928/29.
5.25 The Blue Hall of Stockholm City Hall by Ragnar Östberg, 1911–1923.

with a suggestion: "The Greeks had a culture of marble, the Germans should have a culture of *Granite*. Granite is a Scandinavian and Germanic stone; in the original and pure northern land, Scandinavia, it forms huge masses of rock; and it is spread across the entire lower German plain in erratic blocks."[49]

The Kaiser Wilhelm monuments by Bruno Schmitz and, above all, his Kyff-häuser Monument (1890–1896) are amongst those structures in which the transformation of mineral-based nature into architecture is enacted in a way that recalls the projects of Richardson and Olmsted. The stone tower of the

5.26 Cornice of the Chilehaus in Hamburg. Fritz Höger, 1921–1924.

Kyffhäuser Monument, with its adjacent Barbarossa courtyard, arched hall, and terrace overlooking the meadow between the Harz Mountains and the Thüringian Forest, was unveiled in 1896. The reviewer Albert Hofmann, both editor and publisher of the *Deutsche Bauzeitung*, described the development phase of the design of the monument and acclaimed the "primal energy and impact of the form" as a quality new to German architecture.[50] He praised the monument as a "work that has emerged from the natural earth."[51] According to Hofmann the inspiration for this tendency towards powerful expression came from America and could be traced back to the work of Richardson. Indeed, Schmitz had built a war memorial in Indianapolis in 1888 and, while he was in America, become acquainted with the buildings of "the American Michel-Angelo."[52] Schmitz's monument to the Battle of the Nations in Leipzig (1897–1913) took the idea of the Kyffhäuser Monument further in the spirit of the turn of the century. [Fig. 5.20] The still eclectic elements merge in Leipzig to create a more homogenous monumental impression that was still being felt in the 1930s in the work of architects such as Wilhelm Kreis. The monument to the Battle of the Nations also indicates further trajectories which point in directions other than towards the New World. The 6th-century mausoleum of Theoderic, King the

5.27 Façade detail of the Grundtvig Church in Copenhagen by Peder Vilhelm Jensen-Klint, 1913, executed 1921–1940.
5.28 Interior of the Grundtvig Church.

Ostrogoths, in Ravenna, an incunabulum of early-Germanic architecture and even buildings of the ancient Near East were also studied by representatives of the "heroic style."[53] A particularly important example of this tendency is the Main Railway Station in Stuttgart by Paul Bonatz and Friedrich Eugen Scholer (1914–1928), which was much admired when it was built and associated with both the "Cyclopean style" of Schmitz and Kreis and the monumental architecture of Babylon and Egypt.[54] [Fig. 5.21]

An important promoter of Richardsonian Romanesque in Central Europe was the office of Hans Curjel and Karl Moser, the architects of the evangelical *Lutherkirche* in Karls-ruhe (1901–1907). Moser's St. Anton's Church in Zurich Hottingen (1906–1908) exhibits such features of the style as sculpted romanizing capitals, low, compressed columns, and façades clad with ashlar masonry. [Fig. 5.22] The important new quality of this architecture is its organic integration into the architectural landscape of the city. In the architecture of

Richardson and Olmsted the granite-clad volumes combine with the rocky ground of the site. The churches of Karlsruhe or Zurich are often joined to the presbytery or communal spaces and this enables the creation of a richly graduated intermediate zone between the building volumes and the site which is made up of terraces, steps and pedestals. The Hungarian architect Aladár Árkay uses this basic disposition in his reformed church with presbytery in Budapest (Városligeti fasor, 1911–1913), where the large, block-like triumphal arch of the portal is supported on stocky columns and clad not with natural stone but with pyrogranite elements with a pattern inspired by Hungarian embroidery from the Zsolnay ceramics factory in Pécs. [Fig. 5.23] These free interpretations of the principles of Richardsonian Romanesque – the transformation of the appropriate use of material into an aesthetic of dressing – provide further proof of the elasticity of this understanding of truth.

Not only granite but also brick have been described as having educational qualities. For Fritz Schumacher brick was a material with character, quite unlike plaster. The latter permits "a shape to be effortlessly given to every callow whim and it is precisely this flawed approach that makes it a seductive material. It happily obliges every salacious instinct of inability and arrogance [...]."[55] Brick architecture is different: "Its essential acerbity enables it to rebel against these phenomena of its own accord. It is not so easy to make it comply with every arbitrary flight of fancy, its serious countenance resists prostitution, which gives it a natural barrier against the frothy excesses of stale or misunderstood entrepreneurial fantasies."[56] Today, Schumacher's buildings are principally considered against the backdrop of the reform movement of the turn of the century, as a result of which most attention tends to be paid to his earlier, decorative brick façades, despite the fact that the schools that he built in the years around 1928–1930 are excellent examples of modern masonry. Stone and brick walls were poor relations of the modern movement, too many layers of meaning which could have associated the façade with such notions as country, region, time, or work contaminated the purity of the "International Style". [Fig. 5.24]

Material and region

In Scandinavia the ideology of truth to materials was fed by not only American but also British sources. Ragnar Östberg, the architect of Stockholm City Hall (1911–1923), was inspired by Ruskin's book *The Stones of Venice* when he toured Italy in 1897/98. Like his friend and mentor Isak Gustaf Clason he railed against the "plaster devil" and historicism, for which only form mattered and material meant nothing, in the essays that he wrote around the turn of the century.[57] According to legend, the dimensions of the brick selected for the City Hall were determined by those of a brick which the architect had stolen from Gripsholm Castle in order to build it into his building.[58] The choice of brick bonding was based on studies of old Swedish buildings and hundreds of sketches. The finished object was met with enthusiasm and influenced modern brick architecture and, above all, the design of new town halls across Scandinavia for decades. In his book about brick building Konrad Werner Schulze describes the building as the "highpoint of Scandinavian dignity and refinement in architec-

5.29 The Onoma exhibition pavilion at Expo 02, Arteplage Yverdon-les-Bains. Burkhalter Sumi Architects, 2002.

ture", whose sublimeness stands "above the din of every 'direction'."[59] Schulze, who feared the "systematic removal of the soul of architecture through mechanization," hoped, like Schumacher, that the "educating factor" of brick would help to counter this trend.[60] "The architect who has never even held a brick in his hand and fingered it tenderly, who doesn't make the necessary, somewhat meditative effort to get close to the essence of this material, will never discover the secret of its formal language" wrote Schulze.[61] [Fig. 5.25]

For the Hamburg architect Fritz Höger (1877–1949) the analogy of brick and the North German people, an analogy which he himself often repeated, provided the basis for the relationship between style and material: "so much of the essence of this material is shared with us, the North German people, that we can count ourselves fortunate that this wonderful material is the one most commonly available for our buildings."[62] Monumentality is "pre-programmed" in brick architecture: "Everything is structure and nothing is texture, everything is both construction and ornament, both beauty and the fulfilling of purpose. And here, beauty is present in the thing itself; and then – the great solidity and immortality and stability convey such a powerful expression that is reminiscent of eternity!"[63] Expressionism's enthusiasm for the Gothic determined the sculptural design of the building volume of Höger's Chilehaus (1921–1924) in Hamburg. [Fig. 5.26] The reaction to the building demonstrates that his contemporaries understood the aesthetic role of brick in terms of the program of the architect quoted above. Brick was eulogized as an instrument of a heroic creative drive which was able to overcome gravity.

The work of the Danish master of brick architecture Peder Vilhelm Jensen-Klint (1853–1930) shares the spiritual roots of Höger's "old objectivity." The manner in which the enormous crystalline form of Jensen-Klint's Grundtvig's Church in Copenhagen (1913, built 1921–1940) dominates its small-scale residential surroundings demonstrates the influence of both Bruno Taut's "City

Crown" and Heinrich Tessenow's small town ideal.[64] The perfection of the church's execution is rooted in the craft ethos of the Arts and Crafts Movement but the English ideals were modified here by the Life Reform Movement and the cult of harmony of Hellerau. Jensen-Klint used no special bricks and the same yellow brick also appears in the interior as the smallest unit in the creation of the walls, vaults, and floor as well as the particularly virtuoso staircase in the tower which was executed in the form of a snail shell. [Figs. 5.27, 5.28]

In the nature of materials

The architecture of Frank Lloyd Wright, whose career began as an apprentice in the office of Dankmar Adler and Louis Sullivan in Chicago, was affected by not only the work of the *Lieber Meister* (his description of Sullivan which is German for 'Dear Master') but also many other influences. The books of Viollet-le-Duc, Ruskin, and Semper were just as familiar to Wright as the Viennese trends of around 1900 or Japanese art. In his autobiography he explains that new building materials such as steel, glass, and reinforced concrete had made it clear to him that a new material science was required in order to study the *plasticity* of architecture. But at the time there was no book about the nature of materials. In his book *An Autobiography* he wrote: "So I began to study the nature of materials, learning to *see* them. I now learned to see brick as brick, to see wood as wood, or to see concrete or glass or metal."[65] The "nature of materials" would become a central subject in Wright's thinking: "Form and function thus become one in design and execution if the nature of materials and method and purpose are all in unison."[66] He published a series of six articles in *The Architectural Record* between April and October 1928 under the title "The Meaning of Materials". These deal with the materials stone, wood, brick, ceramics (the kiln), glass, concrete, and sheet metal.[67] This was reason enough for the important and influential critic Henry-Russell Hitchcock to entitle his monograph about Wright *In the Nature of Materials*.[68]

Modern architecture adopted the doctrine of truth to materials from the architecture of the 19th century in which it had been closely associated with attempts to establish national styles. This development is made even more ironic by the fact that the modern movement saw itself as a supranational architectural tendency and – at least in its heroic period – rejected expressive materiality. Many of its representatives disagreed with the description "International Style" because they wanted to see this formal language not as a(nother) style but as a rational way of building – which explains why the topos of truth to materials was so welcome. In his important book *Bauen in Frankreich, Bauen in Eisen, Bauen in Eisenbeton* (*Building in France, Building in Iron, Building in Ferroconcrete*, 1928) the theoretician and organizer of the international modern Sigfried Giedion associated modern truth to materials with the scientifically provable "truth" of the material structure: "taking into account the molecular properties of iron, science had to study the material's specific laws, and constructors had to find a formative process that differed from the treatment of wood."[69]

The rhetoric of truth to materials is considered hollow by many of today's architects. The Swiss architect Christian Sumi formulated this with passion

5.30, 5.31 Municipal Gallery, Marktoberdorf. Bearth & Deplazes, 2000.

5.32 Façade model of the Finsbury Park residential complex in London, Sergison Bates Architects, 2015.

in the *Daidalos* double issue on the subject "Magic of Materials": Teachers at the ETH Zürich such as Bruno Reichlin, then an assistant to Aldo Rossi, have "pulled the entire prudish Modernist machinery of legitimation from the so-called moralistic swamp of so-called truth to materials."[70] As a result of this one could have "an entirely different posture regarding Modernism and constructional transposition. With respect to the question of materialization, this meant for example that we were not made unsure by a market comprising hybrid building products: concrete panels with wood fibers, wood panels with a concrete component. Instead, we could avail ourselves of it without a need for purity. The confrontation with semifabricates had broadened, unleashed, discussion and led us to reconsider architecture's sensual qualities."[71] The Onoma exhibition pavilion at Expo 02 in Yverdon-les-Bains, designed by Burkhalter Sumi Architects, addresses the outside world with a timber façade that is "pleated" (or faceted in the form of a rotating file device). The silvery glow of the white aluminum color of the surface which is inscribed with place names lends a metallic appearance to the round building within which the central projection area is separated by a glass fiber curtain. [Fig. 5.29]

The association of the idea of truth to materials with bare, massive masonry suffered a decisive defeat as a result of the first oil crisis in 1973 and the subsequent thermal insulation regulations which effectively permitted only multi-layer wall structures. Today, the use of solid masonry combined with appropriate heating systems that make use of the high heat storage capacity of such walls means that solid masonry can once again be justified. One example of this is the Municipal Gallery in Marktoberdorf, designed by Bearth & Deplazes (2000), an unplastered masonry structure built from bricks in Bavarian format. Like the donjons of the Middle Ages the large gallery spaces are surrounded by smaller spaces which nestle between the wall slabs. [Figs. 5.30, 5.31] Although the architects do not remotely intend the building to be seen as a moralistic proclamation of the theory of truth to materials, nothing here is hidden and the idea, if not the aesthetic, of truth to materials, is taken seriously. The homogeneous effect of the wall surfaces does not conform to the aesthetic ideal sought by the representatives of the aesthetic of truth to materials as a visualization of their moral principles. Here, the focus is on playing with the ambivalence of structure and texture. Similarly, Jonathan Sergison and Steven Bates make no reference to truth to materials but clearly point to Semper's theory of dressing as an inspiration for the work of their office. However, they assign the brick a specific identity, "authenticity and singularity" that they describe as *brickness*.[72] These characteristics are related not only to the simple manufacturability and prevalence of this simultaneously manual and industrial material but also to its timelessness – which results from its simplicity and geometry –, its historicity, and the multiplicity of ways in which it can be interpreted. The oscillation of the brick between an everyday object and a work of art for the gallery which distinguishes Sergison Bates' models of brick façades is a further consequence of the singularity of the material. [Fig. 5.32]

Hence, one cannot describe the search for the "essence" of the material as a relatively short-lived curiosity of architectural history. It is also a component of those regional tendencies which seek to defend the identity of a country or a region from "external" influences, globalization or mediatization. Material has a strategic function as the tough, tangible basis of resistance which cannot be swept away in media streams. We have seen how Richardsonian Romanesque, a style developed by an American architect, was able to inspire followers in 19th century Sweden, Finland, Hungary, or Switzerland who recognized it as the model of a national style which used materials in an appropriate way. Admittedly, in these countries one invoked not the American source of the style but one's own tradition – which was free of foreign influence – and, in particular, a rural culture of building which intuitively applied the rules of the appropriate use of materials. Around 1910, many architects of the reform movement were already saying that architecture had to re-establish its links with this honest, timeless tradition. However, the search for the "timeless way of building" that Christopher Alexander or Bernard Rudofsky resumed in the 1960s and 1970s generally led to the drawing up of rules that were certainly not timeless and tended to hamper rather than support creativity.[73] In a similar way, the rhetoric of the appropriate use of materials led to the canonization of certain codes that permitted specific forms to be recognized as "making appropriate use of materials." With the development of materials research and technology this theory has finally become a platitude that is no longer able to keep alive the illusion of an organic unity of place, structure, and form. The new examples mentioned above demonstrate the consequences: The architects who have recognized the compensatory function of the nostalgic search for this lost unity use materiality in a performative sense, which contradicts the simple theory of truth to materials. Semper, with his theory of *Stoffwechsel,* would have undertaken to explain the truth of these cultural performances.

Notes

1   Francesco Algarotti, *Saggio sopra l'architettura*, Venice: Graziosi a S. Apollinari, 1784. Translation by R. H. adapted from the German translation Algarotti, *Versuche über die Architectur, Mahlerey und musicalische Opera,* transl. by R[udolf] E[rich] Raspe. Kassel: Johann Friedrich Hemmerde, 1769, p. 5.

2   Ibid., p. 10.

3   Ibid., p. 11.

4   Ibid., p. 12.

5   Ibid.

6   Comp. Karsten Harries, *The Ethical Function of Architecture.* Cambridge, Mass.: The MIT Press, 1996.

7   Alberto Sartoris, *Gli elementi dell'architettura funzionale. Sintesi panoramica dell'architettura moderna.* Milan: Hoepli, 1932.

8   Joseph Rykwert, *The First Moderns. Architects of the Eighteenth Century.* Cambridge, Mass.: The MIT Press, 1980.

9   J[ean] N[icolas] L[ouis] Durand, *Précis des leçons d'architecture données à l'École Royale Polytechnique.* Brussels, Liège, 1819. Jean-Nicolas-Louis Durand, *Précis of the Lectures on Architecture,* transl. by David Britt. Los Angeles: The Getty Research Institute, 2000.

10 Ibid., p. 108.

11 Ibid., Part I, Plate 2.

12 Paul Schmitthenner, "Gedanken zu einer Einführung (1949)", in: Schmitthenner, *Gebaute Form. Variationen über ein Thema mit 60 Zeichnungen im Faksimile,* ed. Elisabeth Schmitthenner. Leinfelden-Echterdingen: Verlagsanstalt Alexander Koch, 1984, p. 8. Translation by R. H.

13 A[ugustus] Welby Pugin, *The True Principles of Pointed or Christian Architecture: Set Forth in Two Lectures Delivered at St. Marie's, Oscott.* London: John Weale, 1841.

14 A[ugustus] Welby Pugin, *Contrasts or, A Parallel between the Noble Edifices of the Middle Ages and the Corresponding Buildings of the Present Day Shewing the Present Decay of Taste.* 2nd Edition. London: Charles Dolman, 1841, p. 22.

15 Ibid.

16 Ibid.

17 The journal broke away from Cambridge University in 1845; thereafter the society was known as the Ecclesiological Society.

18 Georg Germann, *Neugotik: Geschichte ihrer Architekturtheorie.* Stuttgart: DVA, 1972, p. 93.

19 August Reichensperger, *Die christlich-germanische Baukunst und ihr Verhältniß zur Gegenwart.* 3rd edition. Trier: Verlag der Fr. Lintz'schen Buchhandlung, 1860, p. 18. Translation by R. H.

20 F.[Karl Emil Otto Fritsch], "Zu C. W. Hase's achtzigstem Geburtstage." in: *Deutsche Bauzeitung* XXXII No. 79 (1898), p. 510. Translation by R. H.

21 Propositions of the Congress of the German Evangelical Church in Barmen in 1860 in: Gerhard Langmaack (ed.), *Evangelischer Kirchenbau im 19. und 20. Jahrhundert. Geschichte, Dokumentation, Synopse.* Kassel: Johannes-Stauda-Verlag, 1971, pp. 269–271. Translation by R. H.

22 "Regulativ für den evangelischen Kirchenbau, Eisenach 1861," in: Langmaack, *Evangelischer Kirchenbau* (see note 21), pp. 272–274. Translation by R. H.

23 Wolfgang Kemp, *John Ruskin 1819–1900. Leben und Werk.* Munich: Carl Hanser, 1983, p. 461.

24 Patrick Conner, "Pugin and Ruskin", in: *Journal of the Warburg and Courtauld Institutes,* 41 (1978), pp. 344–350.

25 John Ruskin, *The Seven Lamps of Architecture,* 6th Edition. Orpington: George Allen, 1889, p. 35.

26 Ibid., p. 41.

27 Ibid., p. 56.

28 Ibid.

29 John Summerson, "William Butterfield, or, the Glory of Ugliness", in: Summerson: *Heavenly Mansions and Other Essays on Architecture* (1948). New York, London: W. W. Norton, 1963, pp. 159–176.

30 Paul Nash, "Swanage or Seaside Surrealism", in: *The Architectural Review,* April 1936, pp. 151–154.

31 Geoffrey Scott, *The Architecture of Humanism. Study in the History of Taste.* London: Constable, 1914.

32 Quoted by Sheila Kirk, *Philip Webb. Pioneer of Arts & Crafts Architecture.* Chichester: Wiley-Academy, 2005, p. 20.

33 *R.I.B.A. Journal* (VII) 1900, p. 241, quoted in Paul Thompson, *William Butterfield.* London: Routledge & Kegan Paul, 1971, p. 147.

34 George L. Hersey, *High Victorian Gothic – A Study in Associationism.* Baltimore: Johns Hopkins University Press, 1972, pp. 186–188.

35 Quoted by Eve Blau, *Ruskinian Gothic. The Architecture of Deane and Woodward 1845–1861.* Princeton: Princeton University Press, 1982, p. 58.

36 John Ruskin, *The Seven Lamps* (see note 25), p. 39.

37 Ibid.

38 Heinrich Hübsch, *In welchem Style sollen wir bauen?* Karlsruhe: Verlag der Chr. Fr. Müller'schen Hofbuchhandlung und Hofbuchdruckerey, 1828.

39 Kenneth A. Breisch, *Henry Hobson Richardson and the Small Public Library in America. A Study in Typology.* Cambridge, Mass.: The MIT Press, 1997.

40 J. H. Wolff, "Ein Prinzip und keine Parteien! Vortrag des Herrn Professor Wolff in der Architekten Versammlung zu Gotha", in: *Allgemeine Bauzeitung* XI (1846), pp. 358–367. Translation by R. H.

41 [Johann Heinrich] Wolff, review of "Sammlung architektonischer Entwürfe von Schinkel", in: *Literatur- und Anzeigeblatt für das Baufach. Beilage zur Allgemeinen Bauzeitung* 2 (1843), pp. 103–110.

42 [Ludwig] Gruner, "Der Yankee-Styl", in: *Allgemeine Bauzeitung* 39 (1874), pp. 59–62.

43 Ibid. p. 59. Translation by R. H.

44 Paul Graef (ed.), *Neubauten in Nordamerika. 100 Lichtdrucktafeln mit Grundrissen und erläuterndem Text.* Foreword by Karl Hinckeldeyn. Berlin: Julius Becker, 1897.

45 F. Rudolf Vogel, *Das amerikanische Haus,* Volume 1: *Entwicklung, Bedingungen, Anlage, Aufbau, Einrichtung, Innenraum und Umgebung.* Berlin: Wasmuth Verlag, 1910.

46 Leopold Gmelin, "Architektonisches aus Nordamerika", in: *Deutsche Bauzeitung* 28 (1894), Issue 74, pp. 453–456; 78, pp. 481–483; 79, pp. 485–487; 80, pp. 495–498; 84, pp. 520–522; 86, pp. 532–534; 92, pp. 566–570; 94, pp. 582–583, here p. 454. Translation by R. H.

47 Ibid.

48 Ibid., p. 455. Translation by R. H.

49 Julius Langbehn, *Rembrandt als Erzieher.* Leipzig: C. L. Hirschfeld, 1890. Reprint Hamburg: tredition, 2012, p. 264. Translation by R. H.

50 -H.- [Albert Hofmann], "Das Kaiser-Denkmal auf dem Kyffhäuser", in: *Deutsche Bauzeitung* XXXI (1897), p. 105f., p. 117f. Translation by R. H.

51 Fritz Schumacher, *Das Wesen des neuzeitlichen Backsteinbaues,* Munich: Verlag Georg Callwey, no year. [1920], p. 46. Translation by R. H.

52 Ibid.

53 Frank-Bertolt Raith, *Der heroische Stil. Studien zur Architektur am Ende der Weimarer Republik.* Berlin: Verlag für Bauwesen, 1997.

54 Marc Hirschfell, "Der Bahnhof von Bagdad. Orientalismen am Stuttgarter Hauptbahnhof", in: Wolfgang Voigt, Roland May (ed.), *Paul Bonatz 1877–1956.* Tübingen, Berlin: Ernst Wasmuth Verlag, pp. 62–67.

55 Schumacher, *Das Wesen des neuzeitlichen Becksteinbaues* (see note 51), p. 46. Translation by R. H.

56 Ibid.

57 Ann Kathrin Pihl Atmer, *Stockholm Town Hall and its Architect Ragnar Östberg. Dream and Reality.* Stockholm: Natur & Kultur, 2011.

58 Ibid., p. 241.

59 Konrad Werner Schulze, *Der Ziegelbau. Architektur der Gegenwart.* Volume 4. Stuttgart: Akaemischer Verlag Dr. Fritz Wedekind & Co., 1927, p. 127. Translation by R. H.

60 Ibid., p. 18, p. 21. Translation by R. H.

61 Ibid., p. 19. Translation by R. H.

62 Fritz Höger, "Backsteinbaukunst", in: Carl J. H. Westphal (ed.), *Fritz Höger. Der niederdeutsche Backstein-Baumeister.* Wolfshagen-Scharbeutz: Franz Westphal Verlag, no year [1938], pp. 16–19, here p. 18. Translation by R. H.

63 Ibid.

64 Thomas Bo Jensen, *P. V. Jensen-Klint. The Headstrong Master Builder.* Copenhagen: The Royal Danish Academy of Fine Arts, School of Architecture Publishers, 2009, pp. 288–391.

65   Frank Lloyd Wright, *An Autobiography.* 2nd revised edition. New York: Duell, Sloan and Pearce, 1943, p. 148.

66   Ibid.

67   Frank Lloyd Wright, *Collected Writings.* Volume 1: *1894–1930,* ed. Bruce Brooks Pfeiffer. New York: Rizzoli, 1992, pp. 269–309.

68   Henry-Russell Hitchcock, *In the Nature of Materials. The Buildings of Frank Lloyd Wright 1887–1941.* New York: Hawthorn Books, 1942.

69   Sigfried Giedion, *Building in France, Building in Iron, Building in Ferroconcrete,* transl. by J Duncan Berry. Los Angeles: Getty Center for the History of Art and the Humanities, 1995, p. 110.

70   Burkhalter & Sumi, "Positive Indifference", in: *Daidalos,* August 1995: *Magic of Materials II,* pp. 26–34, here p. 26.

71   Ibid., p. 26f.

72   Stephen Bates, "Wickerwork, weaving and the wall effect" and Jonathan Sergison, "Brick-ness", both in: *Sergison Bates architects, Papers 2.* Barcelona: Editorial Gustavo Gili, 2007, pp. 30–35, pp. 94–97.

73   Christopher Alexander, *The Timeless Way of Building.* New York: Oxford University Press, 1979. Bernard Rudofsky, *Architecture Without Architects. A Short Introduction to Non-Pedigreed Architecture,* New York: The Museum of Modern Art, 1964.

6.
THE LIFE OF MATTER

Development and Metamorphosis

The stability of the categories of biological, economic, and architectural theory was radically challenged in the mid-19th century by three thinkers: Charles Darwin, Karl Marx, and Gottfried Semper. Darwin's *On the Origin of Species* was published in 1859, the first volume of Semper's *Style* in 1860, and Marx's *Das Kapital* in 1867. While Semper adopted the term "*Stoffwechsel*" – metabolism –, which emanated from the natural sciences, as a design principle for the "technical and tectonic arts", Marx uses the term "metamorphosis" to describe the outcome of the process of work in which man is engaged in a constant struggle with nature. Metamorphosis raises the objects of natural history to the higher level of cultural history.[1] If the process of exchange results in the transfer of commodities from someone for whom they do not have any practical value to someone for whom they do then we can speak of the "social circulation of matter": "When once a commodity has found a resting-place where it can serve as a use value, it falls out of the sphere of exchange into that of consumption. [...] We have, therefore, now to consider exchange from a formal point of view; to investigate the change of form or metamorphosis of commodities which effectuates the social circulation of matter."[2]

According to Marx, the phases of movement of this metamorphosis of goods form a cycle consisting of "commodity-form, stripping off of this form, and return to the commodity-form."[3] Thus, for Marx, money is "a solid crystal of value, a crystal into which the commodity eagerly solidifies, and in the second, dissolves into the mere transient equivalent-form [...]."[4] Semper's approach is similar: cultural relevance emerges when an earlier material connection is represented by *Stoffwechsel*, although it, *de facto*, no longer exists. When examined from the historical perspective that considers the origin and transformations of forms, the categorical boundaries between the four elements (Semper) or between the natural and the cultural object (Marx) become blurred.

Darwin's book *On the Origin of Species* had far-reaching implications for the understanding of nature in the 19th century.[5] Semper mentions Darwin in his lecture in Zurich *Ueber Baustile* (*On Architectural Styles*, 1869), but had developed his own ideas about the laws of stylistic development long before the publication of *On the Origin of Species*. In a lecture that he delivered on 11th November 1853 in London, Semper reported on the major influence that had been exercised upon him by the collection of the founder of comparative anatomy, Georges Cuvier (1769–1832). While studying in Paris he often went to the *Jardin des Plantes*, where he "was always attracted, as it were by a magical force [...] into those Rooms, where the fossil Remains of the animal tribes of the primaeval World stand in long series ranged together with the skeletons and shells of the present creation."[6] In Cuvier's collection "we perceive the types for all the most complicated forms of the animal empire, we see progressing nature, with all its variety and immense richness, most sparing and economical in all its fundamental forms and Motives."[7] Semper also recognized the impact of this principle in architecture.

In contrast with the idea that the forms of plants and animals can be captured purely taxonomically, which was expounded by other naturalists such as Carl Linnaeus, Cuvier combined his morphology with the analysis of the functions of the organs in the overall system of the body. His basis for this was the philosophy of Aristotle: The individual organs of the body play indispensable and mutually supportive roles in preserving life. Cuvier is interested in both the functioning of the parts in the overall context and the fact that this functioning serves a higher purpose. He was convinced that the organs of an animal form a single system whose elements work together and react to each other. One cannot alter any part without altering all others accordingly. Cuvier even maintained that a scientist could reconstruct an entire animal from a single bone as long as he was acquainted with the formal laws governing the organic structure.

Cuvier's organic approach to function strongly influenced 19th-century architectural theory; Eugène E. Viollet-le-Duc has already been mentioned in this context in the chapter "The Matter of Nature". In the London lecture quoted above Semper claimed that his theory of style made use of Cuvier's methods, which may guide us "to find out the natural way of invention."[8] In this sense he was combining the analytical-historical method with the normativity of a practical aesthetic. Bemoaning the lack of books on architecture with the methodological value of Cuvier's works or Alexander von Humboldt's *Der Kosmos*, Semper set himself the task of being the first person to write such a work. He was convinced that *"every true artistic form had to be the expression of a certain law of inner necessity, just as this is certainly the case with natural forms* […]."[9]

The so-called Paris Academy dispute between Cuvier and his colleague Étienne Geoffroy Saint-Hilaire in 1830/31 was the fiercest scientific debate of its age and was followed and commented upon by both Johann Wolfgang von Goethe and Alexander von Humboldt. In contrast with Cuvier, who deduced that function was the source of similar forms in the plant and animal worlds and postulated that there was no process of formal evolution, Saint-Hilaire explained these formal correlations in terms of ancestry and kinship – a view which coincided with that of Goethe. Saint-Hilaire also found architectural support: In his entry on architecture in the *Encyclopédie Nouvelle* the architect and theorist Léonce Reynaud (1803–1880) writes that one can "in a profound sense compare human monuments to those shells formed by animals […]"[10] and was convinced that architectural organisms developed in line with the historical cultural levels of human consciousness.[11]

Semper's theory about the transformation of basic forms took a stand against Cuvier's theory (despite Semper's appreciation of the French biologist) and for the idea of development. In the lecture that he delivered in London in 1853 he explained his notion of development in architecture: "If we observe this immense variety and richness of nature notwithstanding its simplicity may we not by Analogy assume, that it will be nearly the same with the creations of our hands, with the works of industrial art? They are like those of nature, connected together by some few fundamental ideas, which have their simplest expressions in *types*. But these normal forms have given and give rise to an infinite number of varieties by development and combination according to the exigencies of their specialities, according to the gradual progress in invention and to so many other influences and circumstances which are the conditions of their embodiment."[12] As this quotation shows, it was already clear to Semper that, even though he could learn to perform Cuvier's empirical, comparative analysis, he would not adopt the rigid system of the French scholar (whom Engels described as "revolutionary in phrase and reactionary in substance").

Basic ideas, basic forms, typologies – even if such terms were never precisely defined by Semper, the question here is how certain models for the organization of a material assume concrete form. Semper's aim is to investigate the work of art as a result of a development process "with the intention of revealing the inner law" that governs the worlds of both art and nature.[13] Just as nature "in its infinite abundance is nevertheless very sparing in its motifs; it constantly repeats its basic forms, modifying them a thousand times according to the formative stage reached by living beings and the various conditions [...] Nature has its own evolutionary history, within which old motifs are discernible in every new form. In just the same way, art is based on a few standard forms and types [...]."[14] In *Style* Semper also offers examples of a force which is independent of such natural forces as the force of mass attraction and the "will power of living organisms" but which comes "into conflict with both" and which, like the "felicitous resolution" of this conflict, becomes visible in the organic form.[15] In this way, nature unfolds her "most glorious creations" such as the "elastic curve of a palm, whose majestic crown of leaves reaches vigorously upward."[16] It was on the basis of these observations that Semper defined the role of architecture: "Revealing the basic idea in the diversity of its forms and presenting a whole which is individualized and, at the same time, in harmony with the outside world, this is the great secret of architecture."[17] As he demonstrated in his conclusions about the social form of language, Semper did not explain this "basic idea" in terms of the perfection of creation. As postulated by Immanuel Kant, the only thing that one requires in order to understand the laws underlying the organic systems of nature is pure, practical reason.[18]

Mimesis and imitation

In the artistic theory of antiquity imitation is understood as mimesis (the term was related to the spectacle of mime), as the basis of literature, theater, and the fine arts and as the antithesis of artisanship. Socrates, Plato, and Aristotle speak of "imitative arts" (*mimetiké téchne)* in order to emphasize that the works produced by an artist simulate reality. However, rather than being mechanical copying, imitation is the creation of another reality and it is precisely this act of imitation which enables the artist to reveal the greater beauty behind the banality of everyday phenomena. Theorists in the relevant disciplines associate theatricality, realism, cultural reproduction, and even psychological identity with the notion of mimesis.[19]

The independence of imitation from the intention behind an image – from the idea of mimesis in literature and art – emerges at an early date. It is Vitruvius who brings the "gathering of people" around the warming fire (see p. 108) into play as the trigger of development: Architecture begins with the imitation of structures built by animals. A passage in Vitruvius' *Ten Books on Architecture* which has become a topos of architectural theory is the description of the origins of the Greek temple in the construction of the wooden roof. The individual decorative details of the stone building are explained using the structural logic of wooden building. Triglyphs, for example, originated as wooden panels which covered the sawn-off ends of the protruding roof beams.[20]

These hypotheses have been adopted by many architectural theorists. In Charles Perrault's dialogue *Parallèle des Anciens et des Modernes* (1688) the proposition of the wooden origins of the Greek temple is repeated in order to emphasize the notion of the constant development and refinement of architecture.[21] Vitruvius' treatise also played a critical role in the 19th century – the common theory of the character traits of the five orders and their proportions (which, for Perrault, was still a central question) appeared outdated as an inviolable basis of the system of architecture due to the fact that attention was steered towards material factors.

Although there is an obvious difference between the idea of mimesis of Plato and Aristotle and the use of imitation as a means of describing developments in architecture and artisanship, the meanings of the two terms overlap and they are often even used synonymously. In the mid-18th century Johann Joachim Winckelmann (1717–1768) spoke not of the "imitation of nature" but of the "imitation of ancient works of art."[22] In an important essay published in 1823 Antoine Chrysostôme Quatremère de Quincy (1755–1849), who was described as the "French Winckelmann," wrote of imitation as an act of representation rather than copying.[23] As a Platonist he endeavored to discover certain primordial forms, archetypes, and "universal models" behind the phenomenon. The "individual and dry reality" is not the true subject of the study of nature. The intellect seeks to understand the general that is expressed as an outcome of the mimetic process.[24] As someone able to recognize relationships and causalities the artist can employ imitation as a means of filtering out the higher and the ideal as a prerequisite for beauty. Understood properly, imitation is thus only possible through the appropriation of the principle of laws and has nothing to do with the copying of specific natural objects, given that these might already contain deviations from the great plan. In turn, one can only recognize these laws by observing the natural order in its entirety. Quatremère maintains that one can speak of imitation in the arts in two senses: through either the adherence to certain general rules or the consideration of individual, specific characteristics. A tree in the garden can perhaps be represented accurately by a painter but it is also possible that he doesn't need to have a concrete tree before his eyes given that he is acquainted with the formal principles of the tree. In this case his model is not an existing example, but a general image such as that of, for example, an oak tree. This is decisive for architecture: The model that is imitated in architecture is not a real, pre-existing building. This is why it is important to speak of a type rather than a model.[25] A model can be copied more-or-less exactly but a type cannot. Hence, the type is a higher entity which illustrates the essence of an object. This is where the immateriality and universality of the platonic origin of the notion of the type becomes visible as a form of reality. And this is why

Quatremère de Quincy was never able to accept the much-discussed primitive hut as a real building that was open to imitation. He understood the primitive hut as a metaphor which illustrates the essential elements of the beginning. Or, given our distinction between type and model, we could regard the primitive hut – Marc-Antoine Laugier's well-known image (see p. 61), for example – as a model that is suitable for demonstrating a type which is early, simple, and, hence, easier to study. At this point the difference between idea and image is quite clear. The idea belongs to the sphere of the spirit which finds its maximum fulfillment in its search for truth in the form of an "ideal imitation." The image, on the other hand, is a product of the senses, anchored in reality – and hence, in this case, the imitation is completely rooted in materiality. This separation of the spheres between the true and the real makes it possible to develop an artistic system based on the distance from these two poles. Architecture that imitates nothing real has a special place on this mimetic scale: It uses materials, forms, and proportions to awaken emotions and expressions of order, harmony, size, wealth, unity, permanence or eternity.[26] For architecture, type is not predetermined but, rather, derived from the definition of the program, which Semper described as "theme" or "subject".

From the standpoint of Semper's theory of *Stoffwechsel*, the most important aspect of Quatremère de Quincy's theory of imitation is his attempt to describe imitation not as copying but as a freely associating, playful activity. The most important moment of the imitation is the transformation, a process in which one has to follow existing conventions. This freedom is necessary given that executors implement models in a range of materials which influence the result. Quatremère de Quincy differentiated between three building materials in nature: earth, stone, and wood. Like most architectural theorists before him, he regarded wood as the primordial material. The process of transformational imitation turned both the original types provided by nature and the wooden primitive hut into artistic artifacts. The imitation of the wooden hut in stone denaturalized the model by using the rational system of the orders. Stone as a material was in itself incapable of providing architecture with any rules – only through the process of imitation does architecture become an *art raisonné*. If wooden buildings had only ever imitated other wooden buildings then the classical column would never have emerged. It was the fact that the architect always had to interpret wood architecture as soon as he built with stone that led to the vast formal wealth of stone and brick architecture. The imitation of a wooden building in stone is an idealizing, interpretative process that generates both identity and difference – a distance between the original and the work of art like that between a person and their portrait.

According to Quatremère de Quincy the pleasure of imitation can be traced back to working with a different material: It is the "prétention de voir une image produite par une *matière* étrangère à son modèle. Voilà le principe du jeu de l'illusion" (the demand to see an image in a material unlike that of his model. That is the principle of the game of illusion).[27] A change of material emphasizes the difference between reality as factual truth and ideality as a higher, more intellectual truth. This also explains Quatremère's opposition to the picturesque English garden, which he viewed as a soulless reproduction of nature. The true imitation of nature is not to be found in arrangements that appear natural but in geometrical gardens that imitate the lawfulness and not the randomness of nature. Hence, in the eyes of Quatremère de Quincy, imitation links the real with the ideal and employs similarity to bridge distance. For Quatremère de Quincy Greek temples are honest deceivers because they are open about their mimetic character, about their failure to be identical with the imitated model.[28] These thoughts inspired Semper but he clearly rejected Quatremère's "fruitless brooding" about the imitation of concrete models such as the wooden hut, the cave or the tent.[29]

Imitation and the laws governing form

In the 19th and 20th centuries imitation was discussed by many philosophers as a general artistic principle. In a text published in 1795 Goethe had already written that the great feats of architecture demand a reflective consideration which is able to recognize and acknowledge appearance *per se*: "Architecture is not an art of imitation, but rather an autonomous art; yet at the highest level it cannot do without imitation. It carries over the qualities and appearance of one material into another: every order of columns, for example, imitates buildings in wood; it carries over the characteristics of one building into another: for example by the union of columns and pilasters with walls; and it does this for variety and richness. And just as it is difficult for the artist to know whether he is doing the right thing here, so it is difficult for the connoisseur to know whether the right thing has been done."[30] Goethe's ideas on imitation and the evolution of form are inspired by his observation of nature and, in particular, his theory about the metamorphosis of plants.

In his *Philosophie der Kunst* (*Philosophy of Art*, 1802/03) Friedrich Wilhelm Joseph Schelling differentiated between organic and inorganic art forms as a prelude to a demand that architecture as art should imitate its own forms: "*In order to be beautiful, architecture must be the power or imitation of itself as the art of necessity. The proof of this is that it ultimately remains subordinate to the relationship with purpose due to the fact that the inorganic as such can only have an indirect relationship with reason and, hence, never a symbolic significance. Thus, in order to both obey necessity and rise above it, to transform subjective utility into objective utility, it has to become an object itself, imitate itself.*"[31] Schelling adds the comment that: "It is self-evident that this imitation should only go so far as to truly grant utility to the *object* itself."[32]

Schelling points to the Vitruvian genealogy of the Doric temple as proof of the fact that architecture "creates the ideal," throwing off its original "crude forms" as it rises above mere necessity.[33] In this sense, the "axed tree trunk," the origin of the Doric order, discards its natural archetype in order to become a "portent of something higher."[34] Schelling's thesis that architecture as art has to "throw off" immediate need anticipated one of Semper's central ideas. The marble imitation of a wooden building is a means of releasing architecture from being a mere act of building rooted in needs and materials and enabling it to become true architecture or "frozen music."[35] For both Schelling and Semper, architecture is an act of building which provides a permanent image of both the purpose of the whole and the functions of the parts.

With their "reconstructions" of the structural principles of the temples of antiquity and their interpretations of details such as capitals and triglyphs, the architects and theorists of the 19th century who sought to justify the paradigmatic character of Greek antiquity also performed important groundwork for Semper's theories of *Stoffwechsel* and dressing. In his major work *Die Baukunst nach den Grundsätzen der Alten* (*Architecture According to the Principles of the Ancients*, 1809) the archaeologist Aloys Hirt (1759–1837), a teacher of Karl Friedrich Schinkel and Leo von Klenze at Berlin's *Bauakademie*, asserts that architecture is not an art that imitates nature in the same sense as sculpture or painting: "Its essence is based upon the laws of true mechanics of which nature has provided no model for imitation. It is the work of the experience and invention of many individuals, ages, and peoples."[36] The resulting laws "progressively granted structures the broadening, stability, and simplicity that raised them to a level of perfection equivalent to that of a natural body. Only then, when art had arrived at this point, was it possible for a form of general model to emerge that was largely based on the skill of the carpenter."[37] The illustrations in Hirt's work sought to demonstrate the development of wooden architecture out of the "roof-shaped hut." [Fig. 6.1] Goethe had already sarcastically rejected Laugier's model of the primitive hut: "Two stakes at each end, crossed at their apex, with another as ridgepole are, as you may daily see in the huts of field and vineyard, a far more basic invention, from which you could not even extract a principle for your pig-sty."[38] Hirt's drawing appears to correspond precisely with this description of the simplest hut. According to him, stone building was based on wooden building: "Here, the stonemason took the work of the carpenter as his model. This was a fundamental law for all ancient art."[39] For Hirt, this process of "refining and perfecting" embodied the exemplary nature, "the essence or the ideal," of Greek architecture.[40] It is character that can transform even an austere structure into a work of architecture. [Fig. 6.2] Hirt compiled a collection of the typological development of the plan forms of simple genetic configurations, based on comparative tables. [Fig. 6.3]

The imitation of forms was a central theme in the publications about the architecture of antiquity by the French architect and archaeologist Charles Chipiez. Chipiez was a professor at the École spéciale d'Architecture, a private architecture school in Paris. *Histoire de l'art dans l'antiquité* (1882–1889), which he published in eight volumes together with Georges Perrot, contained opulent, highly detailed drawings which were, however, largely ignored by the architects of the 19th century. In 1876 Chipiez published an essay *Histoire critique des origines et de formation des ordres grecs* (*A critical history of the origins and development of the Greek orders*) in which he presented his drawn reconstructions of primordial wooden forms.[41] [Fig. 6.4] In France, graphic arguments made a major contribution to the dissemination of the notion that the Doric order is an imitation of the system of wooden architecture. In his book *Une maison – un palais* (1928) even Le Corbusier reproduces the "ancestrales demeures des paysans de la Mésopotamie" (traditional houses of Mesopotamian peasants) from Chipiez's book.[42] [Fig. 6.5] The much admired, powerful axonometric drawings with which the French architect and architectural theorist Auguste Choisy illustrated his work *Historie de l'architecture* (1899) vividly demonstrate the "petrification" of wooden architecture in the architecture of antiquity.[43] [Fig. 6.6] Choisy also reports the critical words of Heinrich Hübsch who, in his book *Ueber griechische Architektur* (*On Greek Architecture*, 1822), had saved his fiercest criticism for Hirt as he sought to prove that the perfection of the temple

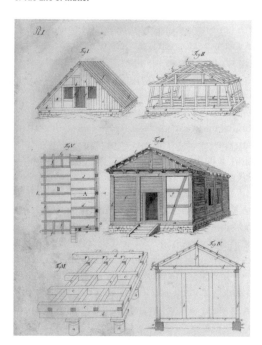

6.1 The roof-shaped hut (Fig. I), the hut in the form of an articulated roof (Fig. II), and the wooden house with section and plan (Figs. III–VI). Plate in A[loys] Hirt, *Die Baukunst nach den Grundsätzen der Alten*, Berlin, 1809.
6.2 Plan and view of the Tuscan temple after Vitruvius (Figs. 1–2), plan and view of a Doric temple (Figs. 3–4). Plate in A[loys] Hirt, *Die Baukunst nach den Grund-sätzen der Alten*, Berlin, 1809.

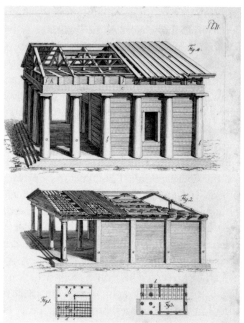

of antiquity resulted from detailed knowledge of the rules of stone building and of the characteristics of materials and that talk of the imitation of primitive wooden building was thus, completely misplaced.[44] Choisy accepted Hübsch's objection regarding the correspondence of the fluting of the columns with stone architecture but maintained that the two hypotheses were reconcilable –

6.3 Central building types from Aloys Hirt, *Die Geschichte der Baukunst bei den Alten*, Berlin, 1821.

Greek roof structures were, after all, *maçonneries de bois,* wooden masonry. If one accepted Hübsch's theory then the relationship between stone construction and form should be closest in the earliest structures. It was here, however, that Choisy found the greatest disparity.[45]

Stoffwechsel and evolution

The task of archaeological anthropology is to reconstruct chains of development from the fragments of the past – a process that is known as "seriation." One assumption of the process is that formal similarities point to typological relationships. Modifications in form indicate the improvement or adaptation of an everyday object. The recording of this process leads to diagrams that also indicate bifurcations in these chains of development such as those that correspond with local adaptations of a type. Imitation, as an instinctive repetitive pattern in the development of forms, has been addressed from the very beginnings of architectural theory. The ethnographic exhibits in the Crystal Palace necessitated the creation of systems of classification. The British Lieutenant-General Augustus Lane-Fox Pitt Rivers expressly compiled a large collection and produced diagrams which recorded the (hypothetical) evolu-

6.4 Wooden hut in Asia Minor as a model for the Doric order, in Charles Chipiez, *Histoire critique des origines et de formation des ordres grecs*, Paris, 1876.
6.5 Le Corbusier's drawing of the Mesopotamian farmhouse and its development in his book *Une maison – un palais*, Paris, 1928.

tionary stages of such individual implements as the weapons of the Australian aborigines. In order to demonstrate the divergence of evolutionary trajectories in terms of time and geographical unit (in this case, the various regions of Australia), clubs, boomerangs, shields, and lances are arranged in the form of a star around a wooden stick which represents the basic form.[46] As Philip Steadman argues, it was not a case of evolution ensuring that a form always better fulfilled a certain purpose – the function itself developed together with the form.[47] [Fig. 6.7] Pitt Rivers' system was developed in London at around the same time as Semper's proposal for an ideal museum and many of the ethnographic objects that he investigated were precisely those that were also studied by Owen Jones and Semper.[48]

The curator of the ethnographic collection of Oxford University, Henry Balfour – who wrote the introduction to Pitt Rivers' *The Evolution of Culture* – and the anthropologist and zoologist Alfred C. Haddon each investigated a large number of the objects in their collections. They discovered that craftsmen in tribal societies were not prepared to find new forms for new materials and new uses: "To many minds new designs are unvalued; they awaken no sympathy, they are devoid of associations; like alien plants, they pine away and die," writes Haddon in his book *Evolution in Art* (1895).[49] Instead of discovering something new, craftsmen adopted old forms with certain alterations. The fact that imitation is the motor of the evolutionary process is also confirmed by Balfour in *The Evolution of Decorative Art*: "Imitation is the mother of art, and it is the outcome of this desire to possess some object or to reproduce some effect which is

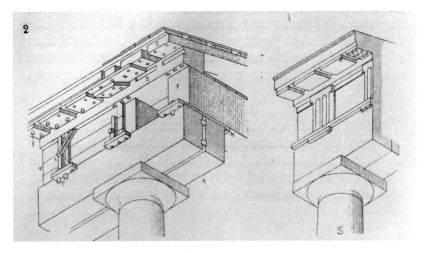

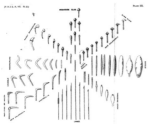

6.6 The material transformation of the wooden temple in Auguste Choisy, *Histoire de l'architecture*, Volume 1, Paris 1899.
6.7 The evolution of weapons in A[ugustus] Lane-Fox Pitt Rivers, *The Evolution of Culture and Other Essays*, ed. J. L. Myres, Oxford, 1906.

admired; it is inherent in our nature, and is perhaps the principal stimulus in the early development of the fine arts."[50]

In *Evolution in Art* Haddon offers some even more graphic examples of this process. He shows, for example, how stone blades were slotted into timber handles and fixed in place by a diagonal binding made of fibers. Later, as the knife or dagger was manufactured in a single piece or the blade was attached to the handle with bolts, this binding had become superfluous and yet its form remained as painted or carved ornament. Haddon introduced new terms for the various forms in order to label the ways in which ornament could represent natural or constructional models. These models could be vegetable (*phyllomorphs)* or animal (*zoomorphs)* or represent another object or activity (*physicomorphs)*. Haddon paid particular attention to the forms that he called "skeuomorphic" (*skeuomorphs*). [Figs. 6.8 a, b] Skeuomorphic forms imitate an earlier constructional form such as the above-mentioned example of the binding. He identified the phenomenon more often amongst clay pots which were bound with fibers before being baked in order to stop them falling apart in the oven. Later, when people worked with firmer clay, these bindings were no longer necessary but their form survived as ornament. Haddon presented monumental Lycian tombs as the most powerful evidence for the phenomenon of skeuomorphism in architecture, supporting his argument by quoting the description by H. Colley March. These tombs (one of which, the so-called "Tomb of Payava" is still to be found in the British Museum) were also discussed by Semper (see p. 193).[51]

Haddon's system became even more complex when he described hybrids of types of *Stoffwechsel* – *heteromorphs of skeuomorphs, heteromorphs of biomorphs* and even *heteromorphs of skeuo-biomorphs*.[52] The term "skeuomorph" has since been revived: In her book *How We Became Posthuman* (1999), N. Katherine Hayles suggests that forms from analog culture that continue to exist in the digital age (e. g. the hand, lever or pedal as symbols on a screen) should be described as skeuomorphic.[53] This would confirm the "principle of laziness" in the history of the development of everyday objects: until forms have been found that are more appropriate to an age and its technology skeuomorphs can act as placeholders.

The work of Leopold Eidlitz (1823–1908) in the United States was influenced by the British architectural theory inspired by evolutionism, American transcendentalism, and German idealism as well as by the psycho-physiological research which was one of the novelties of his age. Eidlitz, who had been born in Prague and studied at the Polytechnic Institute in Vienna, moved to the USA in 1843. In 1881 he published his book *The Nature and Function of Art, More Especially of Architecture,* in which he postulated a complex theory of imitation. He writes that all natural organisms possess the mechanical ability to exercise certain functions. But rather than merely fulfilling these functions they also express these, "they tell the story of their being."[54] By imitating this natural condition of the material the architect models his forms in such a way that these also reveal their functions – the mechanical conditions of force or rest. This 'narration' becomes possible if the expressive power of the simple constructional forms which follow the laws of nature is enhanced through decoration. Eidlitz warns, however, that carved and polychrome decoration must be governed by the laws of mechanics. If this is not the case then disharmony between the building volume and the decoration will result.[55] Although Eidlitz was himself active as an architect his eclectic aesthetic is best expressed in the work of Frank Furness (1839–1912). Alongside his contemporary Henry Hobson Richardson Furness was one of the most original North American architects of the 19th century and his influences, in addition to Eidlitz, included Eugène E. Viollet-le-Duc and John Ruskin. His Pennsylvania Academy of the Fine Arts in Philadelphia (1871–1876) and the library of the University of Pennsylvania (1888–1891) are hybrid structures which combine historic architectural forms with exposed iron structures and biomorphic details. [Figs. 6.9, 6.10]

Semper, Darwin and the organic work of art

Darwin replaces the admiration of creation in the works of nature with a new understanding of nature that is not without tragedy. We must not forget, writes the naturalist, "that each at some period of its life, during some season of the year, during each generation or at intervals, has to struggle for life, and to suffer great destruction. When we reflect on this struggle, we may console ourselves with the full belief, that the war of nature is not incessant, that no fear is felt, that death is generally prompt, and that the vigorous, the healthy, and the happy survive and multiply."[56]

6.8 a, b Illustrations from Alfred C. Haddon, *Evolution in Art as Illustrated by the Life-Histories of Designs*, London, 1895. Skeuomorphs of basketry and of timbering.

Semper strikes a similarly tragic tone in the foreword to *Style*: "A never-ending struggle – a frightful law of the stronger according to which one eats another only to be eaten in turn – pervades nature, but it manifests its full cruelty and harshness in the animal world, which is closest to us. It forms the content of our earthly existence and that of history."[57] In his lecture "On Architectural Styles," which he delivered on 4th March 1869 in Zurich City Hall, Semper spoke critically about those architects who saw the return to Gothic principles as offering an opportunity for the creation of national formal languages. Alongside these "practical solutions to the question of style" there is another notion "according to which architectural styles cannot be invented at all, but evolve in different ways in conformance with the laws of natural selection, heredity, and adaptation from a few primitive types *(Urtypen)*, rather similar to the way the species are presumed to evolve in the realm of organic creation."[58]

The reference to Darwin is clear. Semper, however, makes it equally clear that he regards the insights gained from the observation of nature as not necessarily transferable to architecture: "This application of the famous axiom, 'nature makes no leaps' and of Darwin's theory on the origin of species to the special world of the small re-creator – man – seems somewhat questionable to us, in view of what the study of monuments shows. Very often they present the monumental symbols of national cultures continuing alongside or following behind one another in a consciously retained opposition."[59] For Semper there is a clear difference between the forms of nature and the forms of human technology. Hence, his explanation of the origin of forms differs radically from those of such contemporaries as Alois Riegl, who explained the emergence of the work of art in terms of the "artistic will *(Kunstwollen)*" of the epoch or the subject of the artist. The "divining sense" may well play a defining role in Semper's theory but, in his view, this is associated with the ability of the artist to internalize those factors which determine the work of art from without. The influence of material on form is thus neither direct nor mechanical but conveyed by the subject of the formative artist. Semper clearly expressed this conviction in his Zurich lecture (which also reminds us of Reynaud's comment, see p. 164): "We can quite rightly describe the old monuments as fossilized receptacles of extinct social organizations, but these did not grow on the backs of society like shells on the backs of snails, nor did they spring forth from blind natural processes, like coral reefs. They are the free creations of man, on which he employed his understanding, observation of nature, genius, will, knowledge, and power."[60] The most important factor concerning the origin of styles is "the free will of the creative human spirit […] although, of course, man's creative power is confined by certain higher laws of tradition, demand, and necessity. Yet man appropriated these laws and made them subservient, as it were, to his free, objective interpretation and exploitation (*Verwertung*)."[61]

Semper's category of the organic work of art had nothing to do with biomorphism, the imitation of nature. He demands a form "in which free human work appears as a necessity of nature and becomes the generally understood and perceived formal expression of an idea."[62] This was the spirit in which he also interpreted the leaden projectiles of the slingshots of the Greeks, carrying out his own calculations to confirm their optimal ballistic form. He assumes that the ancient Greeks not only observed but truly researched the laws of nature. In other words, rather than copying natural forms they created "their own forms, free of all imitation […] that only coincided with those of nature in the commonality of the law."[63] [Fig. 6.11] The same applies to architecture's role of shaping an organic unity which is structured by laws yet has nothing to do with the direct imitation of natural forms.

A Darwinian view of the development of style

In 1890 the Cologne architect Georg Heuser began the publication of a series of essays entitled *Darwinistisches über Kunst und Technik* (*Darwinian Remarks on Art and Technology*) in Ludwig Förster's *Allgemeine Bauzeitung* – in the same issues that carried reports on the new Forth Bridge in Scotland.[64] Heuser quoted Darwin with regard to natural selection in nature and technology and refers to the work of the geographer, philosopher, and teacher Ernst Kapp, whose book *Grundlinien einer Philosophie der Technik* (*Principles of a Philosophy of Technology*, 1877) had outlined an evolutionary theory which saw tools as projections of human organs (*Organprojektionen*).[65] Heuser sums up this theory by equating a hammer with an arm and a fist and a saw with a set of teeth while also pointing to further parallels between the animal and human organism and tools and machines. His ideal, a modern and expressive iron architecture, is the result of the evolution of building technology "in the Darwinian sense": The development of the cross-sectional form of columns progresses from solid timber and stone profiles towards lighter structural members which are a consequence of, for example, the removal of material during the construction of vaults.[66] [Fig. 6.12] This evolution of the column leads to the emergence of the latticework style, an architecture of iron and glass which uses less material. "Here it is the same as everywhere; more appropriate nutrition, improved raw materials lead to the enhancement of the organs and their projections."[67]

Adolf Göller, professor at the Stuttgart Polytechnic School, reevaluated Semper's view and interpretation of material in the light of the latest find-

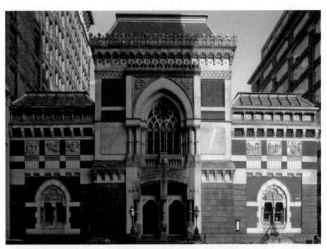

6.9, 6.10 Pennsylvania Academy of the Fine Arts, Philadelphia. Frank Furness, 1871–1876.

ings of cognitive psychology in his book *Die Entstehung der architektonischen Stilformen. Eine Geschichte der Baukunst aus dem Werden und Wandern der Formgedanken (The Origin of Architectural Style-Forms. A History of Architecture Based on the Emergence and Migration of Notions of Form*, 1888).[68] Göller differentiates between the two sources of forms in architecture and the applied arts as, on the one hand, "creation based on geometrical *formal rules* which are identified in nature and the things of working life and recognized as a source of pleasure" and, on the other hand, "the *imitation* of nature and other external forms as a means of perpetuating the evocative and gratifying affinity with earlier forms and works."[69] Göller notes that new design in architecture principally occurs *"through the remodeling of existing architecture"* and, like Semper, compares the development of the language of architectural forms with *"the languages of peoples."*[70] He meticulously distinguishes between three basic principles in the development of forms: transmission, remodeling, and connection or combination. In the spirit of Semper's theory of *Stoffwechsel* he writes that transmission includes the *"transmission of an architectural form onto another material"* but also the *"representation of a non-existent structural feat"* or the *"transmission of a decorative form developed in a certain technique onto another technique"* (e.g. Gothic tracery onto a turret roof).[71] According to Göller, the category of remodeling includes the replacement of *"individual features of a form,"* the *"moderate adjustment of the proportions,"* the alteration of the elements of a form *"while retaining their method of composition,"* the simplification or omission of certain elements, and the *"intensification of the attractiveness of a form or remodeling through the reinforcement of certain characteristics."*[72]

Göller concludes his book with a model of development based on psychological saturation, aesthetic *Stoffwechsel* and the erosion of forms through social exposure: "Just as the flame can only keep burning by consuming itself and organic life can only keep going through the slow *consumption* and metamorphosis of the materials out of which it is formed, just as aesthetic sensibility is nourished by the slow *consumption* of the beauty and the grandeur of the things upon which it is focused, the beauty of *architecture* also exists only as a continuously changing feeling that has to continuously recreate itself in new forms or *extinguish* itself while its works are an ever evolving reflection with which the ever evolving human spirit projects itself in space as if through its own inner light."[73] This conclusion enables Göller, like Riegl, to create a new psychological basis for the theory of the transformation of form without, however, contradicting that of Semper. His conclusion is pessimistic because it is based on the organic model of growth and decay: *"mature* civilizations" which are past their prime can no longer create "either architectural style or language; they can only develop both of these to a higher state of perfection, which they achieve either internally or through assimilation from other peoples and ages, and which they eventually consume through endless remodeling."[74]

Evolutionist models for explaining the development of style retained their place in the theories of architecture and the applied arts for many years without ever rediscovering the conceptual complexity of Göller. The Hungarian architect Ödön Lechner (1845–1914) explained his use of forms borrowed from both historical styles and vernacular art as "experiments in crossbreeding" aimed at steering stylistic development in a direction that was both modern-urban and

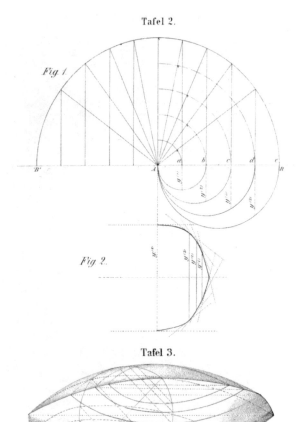

Tafel 2.

Fig. 1.

Fig. 2.

Tafel 3.

6.11 The form of an ancient Greek lead slingshot projectile with the calculation of minimum resistance, Gottfried Semper, *Ueber die blei-ernen Schleudergeschosse der Alten und über zweckmässige Gestaltung der Wurfkörper im Allgemeinen,* Frankfurt am Main, 1959.

nationalistic; referring in the process to the analogy of language and architecture (see Fig. 8.31).[75]

In his lecture *Das Formproblem im Ingenieurbau* (*The Problem of Form in Engineering Structures*), which was reproduced in the 1913 Yearbook of the German *Werkbund*, Hermann Muthesius reiterated Haddon's principle of laziness in the development of appropriate technical forms: "The history of human technology demonstrates at every turn that, although the invention of new machines is relatively rapid and, apparently, effortless, man has constantly found it difficult to discover the final form of these new creations. Confusion is common. And one regularly turns to the familiar forms of similar earlier objects. The first railway carriages were created by placing stagecoaches on the tracks, the first steamships were sailing ships with a built-in steam engine, the first outlets of gas lamps imitated the wax candle."[76] Even the columns of the Doric temple are then subordinate to the change of material in that, cast in iron, they become the "supporting members" in machines. The idea of evolution was natural to the Werkbund Movement while progressive education and the establishment of craft-based schools in Europe and the United States developed in a process of close cooperation. In an article in the *Kunstgewerbeblatt* which

6.12 The evolution of constructional types, G[eorg] Heuser, "Darwinistisches über Kunst und Technik", in *Allgemeine Bauzeitung*, 1890.

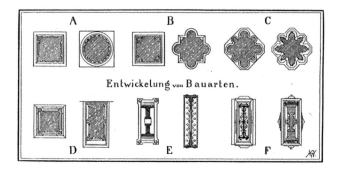

he wrote after visiting the Educational Exhibition in St. Louis in 1904, Alwin Pabst, Head of the School of Arts and Crafts in Leipzig, compared German and American axes, attributing perfect utility and beauty to the latter due to the fact that it was two to three times more efficient than its German counterpart. The evolution of tools is a process of anthropomorphization, the progressive adaptation to the human body in line with Ernst Kapp's teachings on organ projection, coupled with an ever more efficient use of energy. Referring to Goethe and Emerson, Pabst emphasizes the need for practical manual experience which can never be replaced by purely theoretical study.[77] [Figs. 6.13]

Like Muthesius, Adolf Loos and Le Corbusier also speak about the evolution of everyday objects. The trajectory of this development is towards forms which are free of all historical associations: The electric lamps of Peter Behrens replaced the candle-filled chandelier and the latest Citroën model the horse-drawn carriage. At the same time, an approach to design which was true to materials and constructional principles signified a growing freedom from the past while ornament, the residue of now meaningless structural forms, was removed.[78] [Fig. 6.14]

Mimesis in the artistic theory of the 20th century

Mimesis plays a central role in both Georg Lukács' concept of realism and Theodor W. Adorno's aesthetic theory. In his book *Aesthetic Theory* Adorno describes mimesis as the shadow of the enlightenment in the sense of the modern glorification of reason and as another, more ancient path to knowledge: "Art is a refuge for mimetic comportment."[79] A work of art originates from a mimetic impulse, albeit one which is regulated by rationality: "Art is rationality that criticizes this rationality without withdrawing from it [...]."[80] The mimetic moment explains the critical capacity of the work of art. Although imitation is often rejected in modern society as an irrational principle that is rooted in magic, art is one of those few areas in which it is not only tolerated but expected. With its mimetic quality, art has an important role as a counterbalance, particularly in a society in which everything is judged from a rational perspective. This role is subversive because art cannot create any sort of counter-world

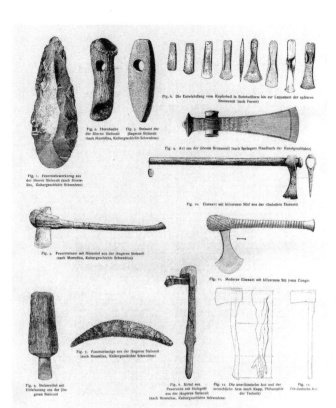

6.13 Alwin Pabst, illustration to the article "Technische Arbeit als Erziehungsmittel", in *Kunstgewerbeblatt*, 19 (1908).

without, at the same time, imitating reality as a means of adding a toxic agent to the imitated reality with the aim of both denying it and highlighting its problems: "The opposition of artworks to domination is mimesis of domination. They must assimilate themselves to the comportment of domination in order to produce something qualitatively distinct from the world of domination."[81]

Both Lukács and Adorno associate imitation with the origins of art, with daily reality and its imitation in magic. More recent authors also examine this relationship. In his book *The Transfiguration of the Commonplace* Arthur C. Danto examines the question of how such banal objects as a urinal (in the work of Marcel Duchamp) or cans of soup and boxes of washing powder (Andy Warhol) can be regarded as works of art.[82] He answers from the postmodern perspective: The issue is always the transformation of something banal which society then recognizes as art. The mysterious nature of this process is highlighted by the adoption of the theological term "transfiguration" which had already been used by Semper.

All these examples further broaden the spectrum of meaning of *Stoffwechsel*. We can refer to *Stoffwechsel* in describing the mimetic process that begins with the sketching of the first ideas about a building but, rather than ending with its completion, continues through the phases of alteration, expansion, interpretation and, eventually, restoration and reconstruction. The fate of Ludwig Mies van Rohe's Barcelona Pavilion (1929) is a well-known example: Fritz Neumeyer compares Mies' reduction to the essential with Laugier's illustration

6.14 The search for a type. The evolution of the automobile in Le Corbusier's *Vers une architecture*, 2nd edition, Paris, 1929.

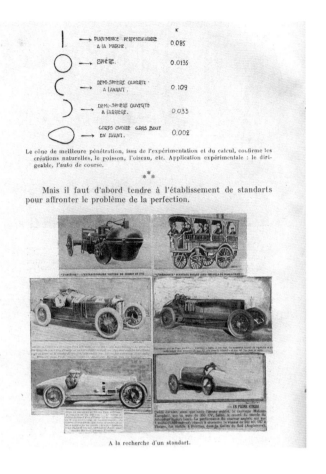

of the Vitruvian primitive hut while Rem Koolhaas presents the pavilion as "Casa Palestra" in his exhibition at the 17th Triennale in Milan (1986). There were a number of suggestions of how the pavilion which had been demolished at the end of the exhibition could be reconstructed (including a reconstruction in black and white as in the photographs). Today, the rebuilt pavilion is interpreted by artists, photographers, and architectural historians. Mimesis and *Stoffwechsel* are at work here, from conception via interpretation and transformation to destruction and possibly, as in the case of the Barcelona Pavilion, to the building of a copy. Koolhaas maintains that he has always regarded working with the existing fabric as a central task and now, in the age of "starchitecture," the conservation of historic monuments and the preservation and remodeling of the built fabric have become a place of refuge from iconic architecture.[83] [Fig. 6.15] If "originality" is increasingly becoming a category of an ever more uninhibited economy of spectacle and the architectural icons of the star architects are being increasingly used and misused by policy makers as symbols of political consensus, then the significance and urgency of the metamorphosis of the existing can only increase.

6.15 Window in the "Golden Tower" of the Fondazione Prada. The remodeling of an industrial complex in Milan, OMA / Rem Koolhaas, 2015.

Notes

1   Karl Marx, *Capital. A Critique of Political Economy,* transl. by Samuel Moore and Edward Aveling. New York: The Modern Library, 1906.

2   Ibid., p. 117.

3   Ibid., p. 125.

4   Ibid.

5   Charles Darwin, *On the Origin of Species by Means of Natural Selection, or the Preservation of Favoured Races in the Struggle for Life.* London: John Murray, 1859.

6   Gottfried Semper, "London Lecture of November 11, 1853", ed. with a commentary by Harry Francis Mallgrave, foreword by Joseph Rykwert, in *Res 6* (Autumn, 1983) pp. 5–22, here p. 8.

7   Ibid.

8   Ibid., p. 9.

9   Gottfried Semper, *Ueber die bleiernen Schleudergeschosse der Alten und über zweckmässige Gestaltung der Wurfkörper im Allgemeinen. Ein Versuch die dynamische Entstehung gewisser Formen in der Natur und in der Kunst nachzuweisen.* Frankfurt am Main: Verlag für Kunst und Wissenschaft, 1859, p. 1f. Translation by R. H.

10   Léonce Reynaud, "Architecture", in: *Encyclopédie nouvelle* (1834–1841). Volume 1, p. 773, quoted in: David Van Zanten, *Designing Paris. The Architecture of Duban, Labrouste, Duc, and Vaudoyer.* Cambridge, Mass.: The MIT Press, 1987, p. 57.

11   Léonce Reynaud, *Traité d'architecture.* 2 Volumes with Atlas. Paris: Carlian-Goeury & Dalmont, Volume 1: 1850, Volume 2: 1858.

12   Semper, "London Lecture of November 11, 1853" (see note 6), p. 8.

13   Gottfried Semper, *Style in the Technical and Tectonic Arts; or, Practical Aesthetics,* transl. by Harry Francis Mallgrave and Michael Robinson. Los Angeles: Getty Research Institute, 2004, p. 72.

14   Ibid.

15   Ibid., p. 90.

16   Ibid.

17   Gottfried Semper, "Vergleichende Baulehre. Vorwort", in: Wolfgang Herrmann, Gottfried Semper, *Theoretischer Nachlass an der ETH Zürich. Katalog und Kommentare.* Basel, Boston, Stuttgart: Birkhäuser Verlag, 1981, pp. 180–184, here p. 184. Translation by R. H.

18   Immanuel Kant, "Critique of Practical Reason (1788)" in Kant, *Practical Philosophy,* transl. and ed. by Mary J. Gregor. Cambridge: Cambridge University Press, 1996, pp. 133–272. Comp. Mari Hvattum, *Gottfried Semper and the Problem of Historicism.* Cambridge: Cambridge University Press, 2004.

19   Matthew Potolsky, *Mimesis.* New York, London: Routledge, 2006.

20   Vitruvius, *Ten Books on Architecture,* transl. by Morris Hicky Morgan. Cambridge, Mass.: Harvard University Press, 1914, p. 107.

21   Charles Perrault, *Parallèle des Anciens et des Modernes,* Volume 1 (1688), reproduced in: Françoise Fichet, *La théorie architecturale à l'âge classique. Essai d'anthologie critique.* Brussels: Pierre Mardaga, 1979, p. 186.

22   Johann Joachim Winckelmann, *Gedanken über die Nachahmung der griechischen Werke in der Malerei und Bildhauerkunst.* 2nd Edition 1756. Stuttgart: Philipp Reclam jun., 1969. Translation by R. H.

23   Antoine Chrisostôme Quatremère de Quincy, *Essai sur la nature, le but et les modes de l'imitation dans les Beaux Arts.* Paris: Treuttel et Würtz, 1823. Reprint Brussels: Archives d'Architecture Moderne, 1980, p. 3.

24   Ibid., p. 180.

25   [Antoine Chrisostôme] Quatremère de Quincy, "Type", in Quatremère de Quincy, *Dictionnaire historique d'architecture comprenant dans son plan les notions historiques, descriptives, archælogiques, biographiques, théoriques, didactiques et pratiques de cet art.* Vol. II. Paris: Librairie d'Adrien le Clere et Cie, 1832, pp. 629–630.

26   Quatremère de Quincy, *Essai* (see note 23), p. 147.

27   Ibid., p. 125.

28   Quatremère de Quincy, *Dictionnaire d'architecture.* Volume 3, partly by Charles-Joseph Panckoucke (ed.), *Encyclopédie méthodique par ordre des matières* (Paris 1788–1825), Volume 1, p. 115. Quoted from Sylvia Lavin, *Quatremère de Quincy and the Invention of a Modern Language of Architecture.* Cambridge, Mass.: The MIT Press, 1992, p. 253.

29   Semper, *Style* (see note 13), p. 103.

30   Johann Wolfgang von Goethe, "On German Architecture (1772)", transl. by John Gage in Gage (ed.) *Goethe on Art* Berkeley/Los Angeles: University of California Press, 1980, p. 197.

31   Friedrich Wilhelm Joseph von Schelling, "Philosophie der Kunst", reproduced in: von Schelling, *Schriften,* Volume 2, Frankfurt am Main: Suhrkamp, 1985, p. 409. Translation by R. H.

32   Ibid.

33   Ibid., p. 420.

34   Ibid.

35   Ibid., p. 421.

36   A[loys] Hirt, *Die Baukunst nach den Grundsätzen der Alten.* Berlin: Realschulbuchhandlung, 1809, p. 27. Translation by R. H.

37   Ibid.

38   Johann Wolfgang von Goethe, "Architecture (1795)", transl. by John Gage in Gage (ed.) *Goethe on Art* (see note 30), p. 106.

39   Hirt, *Die Baukunst* (see note 36), p. 38.

40   Ibid.

41   Charles Chipiez, *Histoire critique des origines et de formation des ordres grecs.* Paris: A. Morel, 1876.

42   Le Corbusier, *Une maison – un palais. "A la recherche d'une unité architecturale."* Paris: G. Crès et Cie, 1928.

43   Auguste Choisy, *Histoire de l'architecture.* Volume 1. Paris: Gauthier-Villars, 1899, p. 300.

44   Heinrich Hübsch, *Über griechische Architektur.* Heidelberg: J. C. B. Mohr, 1822.

45   Choisy, *Histoire de l'architecture* (see note 43), p. 302.

46   A[ugustus] Lane-Fox Pitt-Rivers, *The Evolution of Culture and Other Essays*, ed. J. L. Myres. Oxford: Clarendon Press, 1906.

47   Philip Steadman, *The Evolution of Designs. Biological Analogy in Architecture and the Applied Arts.* Cambridge, London: Cambridge University Press, 1979, p. 90.

48   Ibid., p. 96.

49   Alfred C. Haddon, *Evolution in Art as Illustrated by the Life-Histories of Designs.* London: Walter Scott, 1895, p. 116.

50   Henry Balfour, *The Evolution of Decorative Art. An Essay Upon its Origin and Development as Illustrated by the Art of Modern Races of Mankind.* New York: Macmillan, 1893, p. 22.

51   Ibid., p. 114f.

52   Ibid., p. 192f.

53   N. Katherine Hayles, *How We Became Posthuman. Virtual Bodies in Cybernetics, Literature, and Informatics.* Chicago, London: The University of Chicago Press, 1999.

54   Leopold Eidlitz, *The Nature and Function of Art, More Especially of Architecture.* New York: A. C. Armstrong & Son, 1881. Reprint New York: Da Capo Press, 1977, p. 223.

55   Ibid., p. 251.

56   Darwin, *On the Origin of Species by Means of Natural Selection, or the Preservation of Favoured Races in the Struggle for Life* (see note 5), p. 79.

57   Semper, *Style* (see note 13), p. 82.

58   Gottfried Semper, "On Architectural Styles. A Lecture Delivered at the Rathaus in Zurich (1869)", in: Semper, *The Four Elements of Architecture and Other Writings,* transl. by Harry Francis Mallgrave and Wolfgang Herrmann, Cambridge: Cambridge University Press, 1989, pp. 264–284, here p. 268.

59   Ibid.

60   Ibid.

61   Ibid.

62   Semper, *Style* (see note 13), p. 75.

63   Semper, *Ueber die bleiernen Schleudergeschosse* (see note 9), p. 6.

64   G[eorg] Heuser, "Darwinistisches über Kunst und Technik", in: *Allgemeine Bauzeitung,* Vol. 55 (1890), pp. 17–19, pp. 25–27.

65   Ernst Kapp, *Grundlinien einer Philosophie der Technik. Zur Entstehungsgeschichte der Cultur aus neuen Gesichtspunkten.* Braunschweig: George Westermann, 1877.

66   Heuser, "Darwinistisches über Kunst und Technik" (see note 64), p. 19.

67   Ibid., p. 26.

68   Adolf Göller, *Die Entstehung der architektonischen Stilformen. Eine Geschichte der Baukunst aus dem Werden und Wandern der Formgedanken.* Stuttgart: Verlag von Konrad Wittwer, 1888.

69   Ibid., p. 20.

70   Ibid., p. 27f.

71   Ibid., p. 29f.

72   Ibid., p. 31f.

73   Ibid., p. 453.

74   Ibid., p. 447.

75   Edmund [sic!] Lechner, "Mein Lebens- und Werdegang", in: *Bildende Künstler. Monatsschrift für Künstler und Kunstfreunde,* Issue 11, 1911, pp. 558–576.

76   Hermann Muthesius, "Das Formproblem im Ingenieurbau", in: *Die Kunst in Industrie und Handel. Jahrbuch des Deutschen Werkbundes 1913.* Jena: Eugen Diederichs, 1913, p. 24.

77   [Alwin] Pabst, "Technische Arbeit als Erziehungsmittel", in: *Kunstgewerbeblatt,* 19 (1908), pp. 81–90. Comp. Ákos Moravánszky, "Educated Evolution. Darwinism, Design Education and American Influence in Central Europe, 1898–1918," in: Martha Pollak (ed.), *The Education of the Architect: Historiography, Urbanism, and the Growth of Architectural Knowledge.* Cambridge, Mass.: The MIT Press, 1997, pp. 113–117.

78   Le Corbusier, *Vers une architecture. Nouvelle édition revue et augmentée.* Paris: G. Crès et Cie, 1924, p. 116.

79   Theodor W. Adorno, *Aesthetic Theory,* transl. by Robert Hullot-Kentor. London: Bloomsbury Academic, 2013, p. 73.

80   Ibid., p. 74.

81   Ibid., p. 385.

82   Arthur C. Danto, *The Transfiguration of the Commonplace. A Philosophy of Art.* Cambridge, Mass.: Harvard University Press, 1981.

83   Rem Koolhaas, *Preservation is Overtaking Us.* New York: GSAPP Books, 2014.

7.
THE THEORY AND PRACTICE OF METAMORPHISM

Gottfried Semper prefaced his study *Vorläufige Bemerkungen über bemalte Architektur und Plastik bei den Alten* (*Preliminary Remarks on Polychrome Architecture and Sculpture in Antiquity*, 1834) with a quotation from *Faust*: "Gray, dear friend, is all theory / And green the golden tree of life."[1] Inspired in part by Johann Wolfgang von Goethe's ideas about the metamorphosis of forms in nature, Semper's own theory of *Stoffwechsel* has lost none of its fascination to this day. Supported by shrewd observations or ingenious ideas about subjects ranging from the pierced lower lips of the "Botocudo Indians" to the "wooden clumsiness" of American rubber shoes, his texts demonstrate that theory can be highly colorful.

The principle of *Stoffwechsel* combines the most important elements of Semper's theory with wider religious and materialistic ideas: Concepts that emerged in the fields of alchemy, biology, biochemistry, linguistics, political economy, ecology, art, and architecture. Above all it is a theory that combines artistic production not with a rejection of that which came before but with reflective, creative continuity.

Stoffwechsel as transubstantiation – in the liturgy the church celebrates the essential transformation of bread and wine into the body and blood of Christ in the symbolic reenactment of the Last Supper. By "substance" we understand the sensorially imperceptible essence of an object. It is unlikely that the doctrine of the Eucharist provided Semper with direct inspiration. Yet, without this dogmatic background, the idea of metamorphosis between body-related tectonics and an immaterial signifier (e.g. polychromy) is barely conceivable.[2] Semper describes the assumption of "monumental form" by the "essentially material, structural, and technical notion" of the dwelling as "true architecture" and the "mystery of transfiguration."[3]

It is clear that Semper was more interested in the scientific history than the theological background of the notion of *Stoffwechsel*. The concept and term were introduced to the fields of physiology, biology, and biochemistry at the beginning of the 19th century. The physician and natural philosopher Johann Bernhard Wilbrand summed up the principle clearly in *Physiologie des Menschen* (*Human Physiology*, 1815): "Given that one and the same unlimited stream of life flows through the vibrant unity of all of nature in all of its manifestations there is a constant interaction between the individual elements. As a result of this constant interaction external influences are absorbed by each organic individual and, conversely, it is as if this same stream of life flows out from the individual into the surrounding nature."[4] The anatomist and physiologist Friedrich Tiedemann subsequently used the term *Stoffwechsel* in 1830 in his book *Physiologie des Menschen* (*The Physiology of Man*): "*Die Schnelligkeit des das*

Situla. Hydria.

7.1 Situla and hydria from Semper, *Style*, Volume II.

Leben der Thiere begleitenden Stoffwechsels in den festen Theilen läuft parallel mit dem Grade der Combination ihres Baues und der damit in Verbindung stehenden Mannigfaltigkeit ihrer Lebens-Aeusserungen (The rapidity of the *Stoffwechsel* in solid parts, which accompanies the life of animals, is in a direct ratio to the degree of complication of their structure, and the variety of their vital manifestations, itself dependent on the former circumstance)."[5]

The German chemist Justus von Liebig, who investigated the phenomenon of metabolism in plants and animals in a series of experiments in the 1830s, was no materialist. He regarded the investigation of nature as a means of recognizing the "omnipotence, the perfection," and the "inscrutable wisdom of an infinitely higher being" without the awareness of which "the immortal spirit of man cannot attain to a consciousness of its own dignity."[6] Liebig's observations of nature, which were published from 1844 onwards as his *Chemische Briefe* (*Familiar Letters on Chemistry*) contributed significantly to the dissemination of the idea of *Stoffwechsel*. The reader can understand the book as a rehabilitation of alchemy as the science of the changeable and the changing. Liebig compared chemistry with the philosopher's stone "which changes the ingredients of the crust of the earth into useful products, to be further transformed, by commerce, into gold."[7]

Semper's fellow professor at the ETH Zürich, the Dutch-born physician and physiologist Jakob Moleschott was, in contrast to Liebig, a materialist, who replaced God with the "creative omnipotence" of *Stoffwechsel*. He published his best-known book *Der Kreislauf des Lebens* (*The Circulation of Life*) in 1852 as a criticism of his colleague, which explains his subtitle *Physiologische Antworten auf Liebig's Chemische Briefe* (*Psychological Responses to Liebig's Letters on Chemistry*). The book was an attempt to demonstrate the superiority of matter over consciousness.[8] "The expression 'history of creation' will disappear from the natural sciences because it is contrary to nature,"[9] maintains Moleschott, before repeating the incriminating phrase: "There is no thought without phosphorus, without grease, without water."[10] It is no surprise that the Protestant priest at Semper's funeral in Rome in 1879 was so outraged by Moleschott's eulogy that the architect's son had to intervene in order to avoid a scandal.[11]

The idea of understanding history as a chain of transformations which had already been formulated in antiquity was investigated in the epoch of historicism with a positivistic inclination to precision and documented with many examples. Semper was well aware of Franz Bopp's *Vergleichende Grammatik* (*Comparative Grammar*, 1833). The classification of languages by the science of linguistics also developed in the direction of more dynamic models. In his book *Prinzipien der Sprachgeschichte* (*Principles of the History of Language*, 1880) Hermann Paul observes that the role played by purpose in the development of "language" is the same as that "assigned to it by Darwin in the development of organic nature."[12] He classifies the evolution of linguistic usage by examining changes in pronunciation and meaning. Although it is not clear whether Paul had read Semper's theory of style, the methodological similarity is clear. He also recognizes the importance of "analogies which might be drawn from organic nature."[13]

Semper's theory of *Stoffwechsel*

In the chapter "The Life of Matter" we saw that the phenomenon of the transfer of form to another material described by various architectural critics and theorists as atavism was evaluated as a reversion to earlier stages of development. Semper, on the other hand, recognized *Stoffwechsel* as a principle that granted objects both the ability to remember and a cultural significance that considerably outstripped the value of their everyday usefulness.

The best example of Semper's concept of *Stoffwechsel*, which illustrates the key aspects of his theory, is his comparison between two antique ceramic vessels: the situla, described as the "sacred Nile pail" of the Egyptians, and the hydria, an urn-shaped water jug used by the Greeks. For Semper, such ceramic vessels were cult objects and symbols of belief, the fired clay the "least perishable of materials." Even precious metals are inferior to fired clay in terms of durability because they "incite the human urge to steal and the associated urge to destroy."[14] [Fig. 7.1]

Semper clearly differentiates between purpose and function in that he first analyses each vessel in terms of its purpose: "both [vessels] have the same original purpose of collecting water," but each works differently and this determines the functioning of their parts.[15] The Egyptians used the situla to scoop water from the Nile, which is why the form is "characteristic of Egypt [...] which has no water sources trickling from rocks. Two such pails were carried on a yoke by Egyptian water bearers, one in front and the other behind. The heaviest part of the vessel is lowest, and it tapers toward the top to prevent spilling. It is shaped like a water drop and both its overall look and its ornamentation recall the original leather tube that was customarily used for drawing water in the earliest period of Egyptian civilization [...]."[16] The transition from leather tube to ceramic vessel has made the object easier to hold while the form has remained because it corresponds with the hydraulic laws of nature which had shaped the elastic leather tube.

In contrast, the Greek hydria bears the traits of another landscape, a humanistic culture. Its purpose was "not to draw water but to catch it as it flows from the fountain. This is the reason for the funnel-shaped neck and the kettlelike belly, which places the center of gravity as close to the mouth as possible. Etruscan and Greek women carried the hydria on their heads – Carrying the hydria upright when full, horizontal when empty [...]."[17] It is easier to balance a stick on the tip of the fingers when the heavy end is uppermost: This explains the form of the hydria, "which when complete has two horizontal handles at the center of gravity to lift the vessel when full and a third vertical one for carrying and suspending the empty vessel. The third handle was perhaps also a grip with which a second person helping the women carrying the water could lift the full vessel onto the other's head."[18] A figurative scene applied to the belly of the hydria – to a structurally neutral position ("the resting point of the structure") – demonstrates the destiny, the purpose of the object, i.e. the ritual act. In contrast, Semper identifies function as the supporting or basic role of one element of an overall structure – of, for example, the handle, the neck or the foot – in conjunction with the other elements and with the vessel as a whole.[19]

Semper describes the transformation of an everyday object into a cultural object which can speak of the landscape and the culture of the people that have shaped it: "How significantly the soaring, spiritual, and lucid essence of the spring-worshiping Hellenes emerges symbolically from this subordinated artistic form, in contrast to the situla, which expresses the physical law of gravity and balance in a way quite opposite but no less appropriate to the spirit of the Egyptian people!"[20] He uses this poetic example to clearly and memorably explain the emergence of the monumental form. The ceramic imitation of the form of a leather tube visualizes time: It leaves its traces on the surface of the clay situla. According to Semper, this process offers a sensorially perceptible expression to topographical features, social behavior, and cultural gestures. Here, the shaping factors of Semper's formula $U = C x, y, z, t, v, w$ lead to another style – to a "result" which is different to that produced by the factors which shape the Hydria (see p. 53).

"And there is more!" Semper finally declares with enthusiasm. "The basic features of Egyptian architecture seem to be contained in embryo in the Nile pail, and the formal relation of the hydria to certain types of the Doric style is no less striking! Both forms are precursors of what architecture invented as it struggled to give monumental expression to the respective natures of these two peoples."[21] He states that there is a correspondence between a form and a culture (as expressed in the cultivation of land and the way of life) in that this culture becomes concrete and visible in the form of the vessel. It is *Stoffwechsel*, the transformation of the original form into a durable material and the associated continuity, which renders the vessel monumental because monumentality correlates with memory (*monere* = warn, admonish). Semper was convinced that the principles of architecture and the fine arts were first developed in the technical arts, in artisanship. This position is diametrically opposed to the dominant academic opinion which saw the products of "domesticity" as a mere inferior derivative of high culture.

Metamorphism and monumentality

Semper writes that the starting point of *Stoffwechsel* is a creative process which makes an appropriate use of materials. Every material dictates a certain form of representation due to "the properties that distinguish it from other materials, and each demands its own treatment or technique."[22] Thus, primary technical forms emerge that become artistic motifs upon being transferred to another material. "When an artistic motive undergoes any kind of material treatment, its original type will be modified; it will receive, so to speak, a specific coloring. The type is no longer in its primary stage of development but has undergone a more or less pronounced metamorphosis."[23] Semper even speaks of multiple transformations, of the stages of material development.[24] As an example he mentions statuary art, the technique of making statues in antiquity, which developed in a number of stages from a core wrapped in a polychrome crust to marble sculptures. The material metamorphoses of wood, clay, wax, sheet metal, and marble play an active and productive role in the history of style.

The early architectural examples most commonly discussed by Semper are those victory or funerary monuments in which the "commemorative immortalization" of an event, its anchoring in the collective memory of a society, is

7.2 Ara Pacis, Rome, 13–9 B.C. Detail of the dividing wall as a metamorphosis of the wooden fence enclosing the sacrificial altar.

marked by the transfer of the forms of a provisional structure into enduring materials. The triumphal arches of antiquity can be interpreted with the help of the theory of *Stoffwechsel*: Built to mark the entrance of victorious armies into their cities these gateways were initially improvised wooden scaffolds adorned with captured weapons, trophies, sacrificial offerings, and garlands of flowers. Even Caesar Augustus' Ara Pacis altar of peace in Rome (13–9 B.C.) was much more than a place for sacrificial rites due to the fact that it was also designed to ensure that the reason for its construction remained in the collective memory. Hence, the decoration of the marble wall between the altar and the temple imitated the wooden planks, decorated with garlands of flowers, which screened off the sacred space. [Fig. 7.2] Semper writes that the provisional timber scaffold "which was made of boards but richly decorated and dressed" was then rebuilt with enduring materials in order to pass the memory of the victory on to the coming generations.[25] His notion of the monument remains faithful to the original etymological meaning of the word "monument": The monumental work reminds society of an event. Semper sees the "improvised scaffold" which was required for the dramatic performances as the starting point for "monumental

7.3 Detail of the entrance gate
to the All-Russian Agricultural,
Handicraft and Industrial
Exhibition in Moscow in 1923 by
Ivan Zholtovsky. From S[elim]
O[mirovitsch] Chan-Magomedow,
Ivan Scholtowski, Moscow, 2010.
7.4 Design for a wall in the
aula of the Eidgenössisches
Polytechnikum in Zurich,
Gottfried Semper, 1865, gta Archiv,
Zurich.

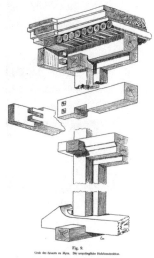

Fig. 9.
Grab des Amacts es Myra. Die ursprüngliche Holzkonstruktion.

7.5 Viollet-le-Duc's representation of a Lycian funerary monument in his work *Entretiens sur l'architecture*, Paris, 1864.
7.6 Constantin Uhde's reconstruction of the timber origins of the Lycian funerary monument in Uhde, *Der Holzbau*, Berlin, 1903.

undertakings." If there is a wish to "commemorate and immortalize some religious or solemn act, an event in world history, or an act of state," then a "festival apparatus – the improvised scaffold with all its splendor and frills that specifically marks the occasion for celebrating, enhances, decorates, and adorns the glorification of the feast, and is hung with tapestries, dressed with festoons and garlands, and decorated with fluttering bands and trophies [captured weapons, Á. M.] – is the motive for the permanent monument, which is intended to proclaim to future generations the solemn act or event celebrated. Thus Egyptian temples arose from the motive of the improvised pilgrim's market, which even in later times was often knocked together from poles and tent coverings […]."[26] This image of the dressed, decorated "festival apparatus" would go on to occupy Otto Wagner and his students for many years (see p. 230).

The stone replica immortalizes the historic moment. This act of monumentalization is the role of architecture as the art of building: It illustrates the relationship between fast-flowing time and the peaceful haven of permanence. The urban role of the stone triumphal arch is different to that of a wooden structure: Rather than framing a triumphal procession it assumes a central position. Such 19th-century triumphal arches as the Arc de Triomphe de l'Étoile in Paris (1806–1836) are no longer gateways. They shift to the center of the city and structure its social life. The temporary triumphal arch built from wooden poles appears as a motif in Russian architecture after 1917 as exemplified by the entrance gate designed by Ivan Zholtovsky for the 1923 All-Russian Agricultural, Handicraft, and Industrial Exhibition in Moscow. [Fig. 7.3] The final link in the chain of metamorphoses of the triumphal arch is its dematerialization as exemplified by the version painted by Semper in the auditorium of the Polytechnikum (now the ETH) in Zurich. [Fig. 7.4]

Semper described the Lycian funerary monument, which was carved from stone in the form of a wooden scaffold, as a "funeral pyre monumentally received." He was able to study an example of such structures – which have also found their way into other handbooks on architectural history as documents of material transformation – in the British Museum. E. Viollet-le-Duc also included a representation of a "Lycian tomb" [27] amongst the illustrations in his work *Entretiens sur l'architecture*. [Fig. 7.5] The Braunschweig architect and university professor Constantin Uhde, who attended Viollet-le-Duc's lectures in Paris, went on to analyze these tombs in his handbook about wooden building (1903) as a means of depicting the different principles of wooden and stone construction. [Fig. 7.6] The peculiarity of wooden construction is that the "clear constructional arrangement" already suffices to produce an aesthetic effect. In stone building, the constructional elements often merge into each other "without clear boundaries" as a result of which it is left to the secondary "artistic form" to emphasize these elements and articulate the construction.[28] It is on the basis of such observations that Uhde develops his theory of the parallel development and reciprocal influence of stone and wooden building: "One progressed from the tent to the stone-filled frame and then to exclusively stone building, which explains why stone building initially adopted the forms of wooden building. Later, the decorative forms of stone building developed over centuries had a shaping influence on the ornamentation of the wooden buildings that were being realized at the same time. The forms of the stone buildings even retroactively altered the forms and constructional expression of the materials to which they themselves often owed their origin."[29]

Semper is the big absentee in Uhde's book, which contains numerous examples of *Stoffwechsel* between wood and stone. *Style* is not mentioned in the bibliography despite the fact that Uhde even presents drawn reconstructions of textile or wooden models for stone buildings. Semper, however, who also critically addressed the Vitruvian notion of the wood-built primeval temple, would have regarded such hypothetical illustrations as being far too concrete. For him, the wooden hut was the "mystical-poetic and artistic motive for the temple [...]" rather than a concrete model that was to be imitated directly.[30]

In *Style*, Semper discusses numerous examples of *Stoffwechsel* in connection with the four basic techniques of textiles, ceramics, tectonics, and stereotomy (see Chapter 4). In the volume on textiles he presents reels of strings of pearls that become ornamentation on vessels and architectural members, carpet-like mosaic floors, and Chinese lattices which resemble tracery. Semper describes Phrygian tombs such as that of Midas, which was first illustrated in Charles Texier's *Description de l'Asie Mineure*, as "colossal tapestry walls hewn in rock," which were once "stuccoed and richly adorned with paint and gilding."[31] [Figs. 7.7, 7.8] Semper principally finds "metamorphosed" ceramic forms in metallurgy and the design of capitals. He discovers the "frameworks" of tec-

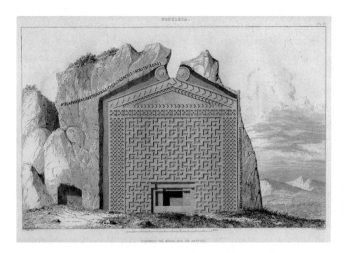

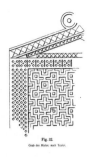

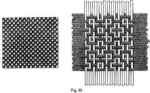

7.7 The tomb of Midas in Charles Texier, *Description de l'Asie Mineure*, Volume 1, Paris, 1839.
7.8 Constantin Uhde's reconstruction of the textile origins of the tomb of Midas in Uhde, *Der Holzbau*, Berlin, 1903.

tonics in the metal supporting structures of candelabras. In addition to this he notes the "malleability" of iron as a result of which he cannot simply insert this material into his system. "Metal, like glass, is used as a material in three states: first as a hard, very strong, homogeneous and dense body that can be given a desired shape by removing parts; second as a molten mass poured onto molds and fixed to them as it cools; and third as a tough, extremely ductile substance that can be given a suitable form for various purposes by hammering, pressing, and other procedures."[32]

The destruction of material

The form of a leather tube was determined by the laws of nature but, in the case of the situla, this compelling contingency no longer exists. This leads us to Semper's central statement which he put in a long footnote in *Style*. The impression of a coercive, involuntary relationship between material and form must be "destroyed": "I think that *dressing* and the *mask* are as old as human civilization and that the joy in both is identical to the joy in those things that led men to be sculptors, architects, poets, musicians, dramatists – in short, artists. Every artistic creation, every artistic pleasure, presumes a certain carnival spirit, or to express it in a modern way, the haze of carnival candles is the true atmosphere of art. The destruction of reality, of the material, is necessary if form is to emerge as a meaningful symbol, as an autonomous human creation. Let us not forget the means that must be used to achieve a desired artistic effect, and not burst them out and thus woefully forget ourselves."[33]

The destruction or masking of reality signifies for Semper not the escape from but the potentialization of reality: The universal is accentuated and rendered timeless. The tangible, empirical reality of material is destroyed, whereby 'material' is not necessarily physical matter but can also be, for example, a subject such as a historical event. For Semper, potentialization signifies that a stage play, a monument or a building symbolically represents transitory, time-dependent reality and, hence, a connection with the particular event that gave rise to the work. To return to the example of the situla: The original leather tube was, indeed, "destroyed" and yet its form lives on "monumentally" in the ceramic vessel. This monumentality is related not only to the permanence of the object but also to the ability of its form to recall its origins and create historical continuity.

The idea of the destruction of material was formulated by Friedrich Schiller in the final years of the 18th century in his letters about the aesthetic education of man: "However vast and sublime it may be, the substance always exercises a restrictive action on the mind, and true aesthetic liberty can only be expected from the form. Consequently the true search of the master consists in destroying matter by the form."[34] "Aesthetic appearance" must be treated as something autonomous that is to be clearly differentiated from reality. For Schiller, this dialectic interplay between reality and appearance is one of those opportunities to blossom which the "aesthetic state" of the future will offer to its citizens.[35]

Semper used this notion that masking is a destruction of reality as a way of synthesizing ideality and reality, aesthetic form and construction in art. The carnival atmosphere has something to do with the interplay of familiar and new, of similar and strange. The significance of "material" as subject, as raw material for the drama, was important to him as a way of emphasizing the necessity of artistic adaptation. He points out that the narrative material *"the material to be treated"* should itself be reworked, enhanced, and monumentalized in the form of the fate of an individual in order to move us as an expression of general human beauty and greatness: "The spirit of the mask breathes in Shakespeare's dramas. We meet the humor of masks and the haze of candles, the carnival spirit (which, in truth, is not always joyous), in Mozart's *Don Giovanni*. For even music needs a means to destroy reality. Hecuba means nothing to the musician, either, or should mean nothing."[36] The interest in material, in subject, is a dependent, unconditional interest which occurs outside the artistic realm. Given that we have no feelings for the Trojan Queen Hecuba, whom we have never met, we can only be shaken by her tragic fate after her *"Stoffwechsel"* into a dramatic figure.[37] The word "person" is derived from the Latin *persona* which was the name given to an actor's mask.

Possibly the most serious of all misinterpretations of Semper is the interpretation of his enthusiasm for the spirit of the mask and the atmosphere of the carnival, which fit perfectly into the clichéd image of historicism as a masked ball, as a call for the free use of set pieces from the depository of history. While Alois Riegl or Peter Behrens criticize Semper as a materialist, the architectural evolutionists ridicule him as a dreamer. "*Semper's* so highly valued candlelit carnival service [sic!], which was particularly appreciated by a Cologne architect who worked for a winter in Rome, may have the same influence on the creation of fantasy forms as the atmosphere of churchly incense or the fragrance of perfume in a lady's boudoir," writes Georg Heuser, the author of Darwinist architectural studies (see p. 176) in 1884, not without sarcasm.[38] The works of the artist "belong to a general process of evolution, [...] General laws apply to architecture similar to those which Charles *Darwin* established for nature."[38] Failing to share Semper's insistence on the freedom of the artist who had internalized the limits to this freedom, Heuser wanted to see architecture determined by the laws of evolution: "It is natural selection that determines the viability of mature new forms."[39]

There is a certain irony in reviewing Semper's – and Schiller's – arguments in the light of the early, neo-Kantian *Heidelberger* Ästhetik (1916–1918) of the later Marxist and theorist of realism Georg Lukács: "[…] it is precisely the specific role of aesthetic form to be the form of a specific material, to comprise a material in such a way that it transforms its materiality into form so that it is 'destroyed' as material."[40]

Stoffwechsel in 20th-century architecture

The tracks which Semper laid with his theory of *Stoffwechsel* may have remained redundant for some time in other parts of the world but Friedrich Achleitner's conclusion that they were heavily used (see p. 26) is unquestionably true for Viennese 20th-century architecture. Otto Wagner's work is particularly interesting in this respect, not least because he appeared to take a radically Darwinist position in *Die Baukunst unserer Zeit* (Modern Architecture, 1914). He criticizes Semper: "Like Darwin […] he lacked the courage to complete his theories from above and below and had to make do with a symbolism of construction, instead of naming construction itself as the primitive cell of architecture."[41] The criticism of Semper in Rudolf Redtenbacher's handbooks on tectonics struck a similar tone. In the introduction to *Architektonik der modernen Baukunst* (*The Architectonics of Modern Architecture*, 1883), Redtenbacher admitted that, although the principle of dressing had dominated "the beginnings of architecture" this didn't mean that "making construction the starting point of building design would be an inartistic idea. Architecture begins with construction and ends when there is nothing left to construct. Hence we are taking the different path of seeking architectural motifs in construction."[42]

Despite the similar tone of their pronouncements there is a fundamental difference between the positions of Redtenbacher and Wagner. While Redtenbacher's criticism prepares the ground for an investigation, supported by the latest psycho-physiological research ideas, of structural forms that express weight, equilibrium or dynamic force, Wagner's work avoided such simple mechanical thinking. In his publication *Architektonische Zeitfragen* (*Contemporary Architectural Questions*, 1898) the Munich architectural historian Richard Streiter rightly questions how Wagner would be able to adhere "to a 'symbolism of construction' when it is precisely this symbolism that allows the art-form to develop out of constructional form […]. It would not be wrong to assume that Wagner's objection to Semper results only from a theoretical misunderstanding, since even in his own practice Wagner cannot do away with the symbolism of construction."[43] It is a false assumption, writes Streiter, that "construction and technology are in themselves crucial to the making of form, to style."[44] Wagner himself criticizes the thinking of engineers who fail to consider "art-form" in their designs – in the very chapter of his book in which he criticizes

Semper's lack of courage: "*The engineer who does not consider the nascent art-form but only the structural calculation and the expense will therefore speak a language unsympathetic to man, while on the other hand, the architect's mode of expression will remain unintelligible if in the creation of the art-form he does not start from construction.* Both are great errors."[45] This means in turn that the transformation of the work-form of the engineer into the art-form of the architect clearly requires a symbolism of construction which extends beyond mere structural purpose.

Wagner emphasized the artistic potential of forms like riveted or screwed connections which result from such modern industrial methods as material processing and assembly in order to understand them as aesthetic motifs. The combination of the profit motive with the quest to reduce the consumption of time and materials led to the emergence of a new aesthetic. In his *Modern Architecture* Wagner rejected "Art-forms in which the time of production is not consistent with the effect or with the material or mode of production" – these "always had something false or vexing about them."[46] He condemned "Consoles and keystones that carry nothing" and "plaster buildings that display a full stone pattern," but "when construction attempts to combine a shorter time of production with the same or greater solidity and with an artistic form of equal value, then it correctly understands the task."[47]

Otto Wagner's building for the Postal Savings Bank in Vienna (1903–1906, extension 1910–1912) is defined by the idea of saving. [Fig. 7.9] The institution of the Postal Savings Bank was introduced in Austria by Georg Coch with the support of the Christian Social Party as the bank of the "ordinary people." The Vienna headquarters should express reliability and the security of the money. The façade was structured in line with the principle of the four elements: the base, as the stereotomic element, is dressed with 10-cm-thick slabs of granite as a transformation of the rusticated stories of Renaissance palaces (see Fig. 8.20). A powerful cornice emphasizes the presence of the roof (tectonics), whose form can be seen as a technical, machine-like metamorphosis of the woodwork of the temples of antiquity. The façade to the upper stories is covered with 2-cm-thin slabs of Sterzing marble which are "nailed" to the load-bearing masonry with iron bolts whose heads are fitted with aluminum caps. The slabs of marble are, however, laid in a mortar bed. According to Wagner the bolts were intended to support the stone until the mortar set. The extent to which this solution is orchestrated by material transformation is much greater than Wagner would like to admit. The sought-after effect, the establishment of a rhythm on the façade, is achieved through the technical form of the bolted fixings which are otherwise used in the erection of iron loadbearing structures. Wagner invokes a higher "constructional truth": The modern achievement of saving time and money by using thin stone slabs rather than heavy stone blocks is only visualized by the bolt heads on the façade. [Fig. 7.10]

In order to exemplify this position Wagner refers to Semper's *Burgtheater* (*Court Theater*) in Vienna as a "mistaken building method" in contrast with his own architecture of dressing that he describes as a "modern way of building." The theater was "constructed in courses of stone and the material was procured with a great expenditure of time and money."[48] In order to build the main cornice "immense stone blocks, reminiscent of the Roman method of construction, were employed. [...] The preparation and procurement of these

7.9, 7.10 Main façade and cornice detail of the Postal Savings Bank in Vienna. Otto Wagner, 1903–1906.

blocks required great temporal and pecuniary sacrifice."[49] In accordance with the modern way of building the façade of the Postal Savings Bank is dressed with slabs which are thinner than the dressing of the façade of the *Burgtheater* but which are made from a nobler material. As a result of this the thickness of the slabs of stone falls to 1/10 to 1/50 of that required by the old method, "the monumental effect will be enhanced by the nobler material; the money spent will decrease enormously, and the production time will be reduced to the normal and desired amount."[50] The architect can employ this method to develop a new aesthetic: *"In this way a number of new artistic motifs will emerge* [...] whose development the artist will not only find very desirable, but also [...] which he must seize with alacrity and enthusiasm so as to make genuine progress in art."[51]

Wagner's architectural work is an encyclopedia of the possibilities of metamorphism. His buildings convincingly demonstrate that, far from the theory of *Stoffwechsel* becoming obsolete with the fall of historicism, the opposite was the case. Its aesthetic possibilities could be significantly broadened through the integration of modern materials. And it was through the conscious application of the theory of *Stoffwechsel* that employees and pupils of Wagner including Max Fabiani, Jože Plečnik, and István Medgyaszay realized radical innovations.

Wagner's Slovenian pupil Plečnik reinterpreted these subjects in his buildings in Vienna, Prague, and Ljubljana and placed the idea of metamorphism at the heart of his approach to architecture. In this context, however, 'reinterpreted' means that he combined his knowledge of archaic forms of building with his virtuoso ability to create works in which distortion, disassociation, the given, and the completely invented counterbalance each other. In such early buildings as the Church of the Holy Spirit in Vienna (1910–1913) Plečnik was already experimenting with the transmission of tectonic forms in reinforced concrete. [Fig. 7.11] The façade of his Church of the Most Sacred Heart of Our Lord in Prague (1928–1931) is very clearly divided into a brick-clad lower zone and a white-rendered upper zone. Blocks of granite burst from the dark clinker brick cladding; heavy, stereometric and light, textile forms interacting with one another. [Fig. 7.12]

The design of Žale Cemetery in Ljubljana and the two pavilions of the castle in Begunje (1939) offered Plečnik welcome opportunities to present such primordial architectural forms as the tumulus and the primitive hut and their historicist metamorphoses together with hybrid combinations of these forms in a narrative spirit enlivened with a touch of both humor and the grotesque. The façade of the workshop building of Žale Cemetery (1939/40) is held between a powerful base with natural stone cladding and a wide overhanging roof. The stone base supports the pillars which are clad with terrazzo between the ground-floor windows and topped not by capitals but by figurative representations of Saints. [Fig. 7.13] Plečnik created the main columns of the Church of St Michael on the Marshes in Ljubljana (1937/38, interior 1940) from sanded and ornamentally painted concrete drainage pipes which directly support a ring of wooden beams. [Fig. 7.14] Thin wooden posts give additional support to these beams between the concrete pipes. This creates a nesting effect common to Plečnik in which slender structural elements are protectively surrounded by stronger and more enduring ones. His projects and those of his pupils demonstrate the almost limitless possibilities for transforming, combining, and vary-

7.11 Crypt of the Church of the Holy Spirit in Vienna-Ottakring. Jože Plečnik, 1910–1913.
7.12 Church of the Most Sacred Heart of Our Lord, Prague. Jože Plečnik, 1928–1931.
7.13 Workshop building in Žale Cemetery in Ljubljana. Jože Plečnik, 1939/40.

ing historical forms up to the very limits of deformability.[52] Despite later interpretations in terms of postmodernism *avant la lettre* these projects are never "quotations" or attempts to fall back on concrete examples from architectural history. Rather, they are based on an intimate knowledge of the handling of "material" – as both building material and subject – and of the way in which it is produced.

The term metabolism was interpreted by the Japanese architecture of the 1960s in a way which was quite independent of Semper's theory of *Stoffwechsel*. The then 26-year-old architect Kisho Kurokawa appeared in public together with his colleagues Fumihiko Maki, Masato Otaka, and Kiyonori Kikutake, and the critic Noboru Kawazoe at the World Design Conference in Tokyo in 1960 with their manifesto *Metabolism* (the English word for *Stoffwechsel*). Their starting point was the analogy between city, building, and nature. Highrise buildings in the form of conglomerations of cells and DNA helices, whose modules were envisaged as being interchangeable, stood as symbols of urban

7.14 Interior of the Church of St Michael on the Marshes (na Barje)
with the use of painted concrete drainage pipes, Ljubljana. Jože Plečnik,
1937/38, decoration 1940.

vitality. Kurokawa and the Metabolists had more than constructional flexibility in mind: They understood Metabolism as a metaphor for building for the
information society, as a process of metamorphosis that creates order out of
chaos. It is because of this "occupation" of the term *metabolism* in architectural
history that Semper's theory of *Stoffwechsel* is translated into English in the
specialist literature as the "theory of material change" or the "theory of material
metamorphosis."

Postmodern transformations

Although the aesthetic affinity between the works of Wagner's pupils and those
of the American office of Robert Venturi and Denise Scott Brown is obvious, the Venturi solutions, whose two-dimensionality was inspired by commercial *billboards,* come across as somewhat paper-thin in comparison with
those of Plečnik or Fabiani. Venturi's proposal for the renovation of the Ponte
dell'Accademia in Venice (1985) envisaged the transformation of the existing
provisional bridge of wood and iron into a collage-like form built from fiber-
glass panels with stylized renaissance ornamentation which appeared two-

7.15 The floor of the vestibule of Aarhus City Hall. Arne Jacobsen and Erik Møller, 1938–1941.
7.16 Façade of the office center for Basler Versicherung, Vienna. Boris Podrecca with Suter + Suter, 1990–1993.

dimensional as it spanned the Canal Grande.[53] Encouraged by the success of Venturi's postmodernism a younger generation of Central European architects also turned with newly aroused interest to the architecture of Wagner and his school in the 1970s. Alongside Semper's aesthetic, his theories of dressing and *Stoffwechsel*, the cultural oscillation between myth and rationality mentioned in the previous chapter and the theme of transformation which was ubiquitous in the Habsburg Monarchy also played a role. For the exhibition *Die Türken vor Wien* (*The Turks at the Gates of Vienna*, 1983) Hans Hollein disguised the Künstlerhaus on Vienna's Karlsplatz as a huge tent whose aesthetic affinity with Wagner's nearby Stadtbahn stations is no coincidence.

7.17 Institute du Monde Arabe, Paris. Jean Nouvel, 1981–1987.

Boris Podrecca is one of those Vienna architects who consciously refer to Semper's theory and to its earlier interpretations in the architecture of Wagner and his pupils and employees. In his office center for Basler Versicherung in Vienna-Brigittenau (designed together with Suter + Suter, 1990–1993) he reflects the location on the Danube Canal in a similar way to Wagner in his Schützenhaus (1904–1908). The scale-like cladding of the canal façade floats above a hard plinth. Ashlar masonry with a recessed face would be a "stylistic nonsense" writes Semper, given that it should express "resistance" and that "this expression intensifies […] as the projection is increased."[54] If, on the other hand, one creates ashlar from metal "then a recessed filling would make stylistic sense."[55] The blue painted metal base with its recessed horizontal fields follows this recommendation. [Fig. 7.16]

Postmodernism's search for a historically reflected approach to ornamentation also leads indirectly to Semper's theory on the subject of metamorphoses. Jean Nouvel's *Institut du Monde Arabe* in Paris (1981–1987) translates the ornamental richness of repetitive Islamic wall texture to a high-tech curtain wall. The metal structure consists of cassettes with smaller and larger openings which are designed to work like the iris diaphragms of cameras: Under strong sunlight the blades reduce the openings through which the light can pass. [Fig. 7.17]

Monoblue: art – architecture transformations

In February 1961 the French artist Yves Klein undertook a pilgrimage to the small Umbrian town of Cascia near Perugia in order to present a votive offering to Saint Rita di Cascia, the patron saint of his family. The offering took the form of an opening clear plastic box of around 30 × 40 cm which was divided into an upper and a lower part. The three upper compartments contained ultramarine and pink colored pigments and gold leaf and the lower one three tiny gold bars on a layer of ultramarine pigment. A folded piece of paper with a text in which Klein prayed for success, beauty, and eternal life was placed in the slot in-between. Klein had previously participated in the exhibition *Vision in Motion* in Antwerp and demanded pure gold as payment for his work "Zones of Immaterial Pictorial Sensibility."[56] If a buyer wanted to acquire the immaterial value of a zone he had to ceremoniously burn the invoice for the purchased immaterial zone, which indicated the weight of the corresponding gold. Thereupon Klein threw half of the gold into the sea or a river in the presence of art experts as witnesses. He placed the other half in the votive casket.

7.18 Façade detail of the Barcelona Fórum. Herzog & de Meuron, 2001–2004.

Many elements in the myth of the artist, of his talent and his readiness to make sacrifices, find an almost formal expression in Klein's votive offering. An important idea here is transubstantiation, the transmutability of immateriality and materiality. The depth that one can never buy with money but only with gold is the blue depth of the sea. Herzog and de Meuron chose the Yves Klein blue as the color of the huge triangle of the Barcelona Fórum (2001–2004) which stands at the point where Avenida Diagonal – the avenue that slices across the square grid of the city – meets the Mediterranean shoreline. The earthen haptic and weight of the surface combine in such a way that the blue sprayed concrete volume with its glazed cracks floats surreally over the golden and silver reflections and highlights of its hollowed-out base. [Fig. 7.18] Inside the exhibition space one feels as if one is in a deep-sea aquarium, a world recalling Captain Nemo's submarine *Nautilus* in Jules Verne's novel *Twenty Thousand Leagues Under the Sea*. Thus, Klein's "blue revolution" continues to colorize and colonize new shores long after his death – even if money has meanwhile become an accepted form of payment for spatial sensibility.[57]

The role of metamorphism in art also pertains to technical processes such as the casting of bronze statues. The manufacture of the mold begins with the creation of a wax positive which is then melted in a *cire perdue* process before the liquid alloy of copper and tin is poured into the mold. The modeling of a spatial form in wax – the additive method – leads to results that differ from those of the converse, subtractive method which involves the sculptural removal of material. This also explains the creative difference between statues originally conceived in bronze and bronze copies of marble statues. [Fig. 7.19]

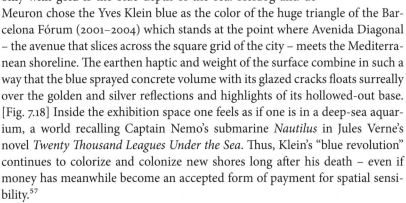

7.19 Mold for an equestrian statue using a *cire perdue* process, engraving by Bernard Durand.

The presentation of everyday life through the transposition of the private into the public is amongst the subjects addressed by artists such as Gordon Matta Clark, Dan Graham or Rachel Whiteread. For Whiteread, metamorphism is also the result of the pouring out of a form. The surfaces of the artifacts reveal the traces of the mold as evidence of the contact that envelops the object in an aura. Her Holocaust Memorial in Vienna (2000) is a rectangular concrete prism whose surfaces are modeled like bookshelves, lined with countless copies of one and the same book. Yet they face the viewer not with their spines but with their fore edges. [Fig. 7.20] The use of concrete castings is increasing amongst architects. Diener & Diener, for example, employed them in the reconstruction of the Museum of Natural History in Berlin (1995–2010) which had suffered heavy damage during the Second World War. Polyurethane templates of the surviving parts of the brick façade were created which then served as molds for the casting of the concrete elements. [Fig. 7.21]

Joseph Beuys combined biological metabolism with cycles of social energy influenced by Rudolf Steiner's anthroposophy. Material substances contain certain primary qualities which remain even after metamorphosis. Beuys' installation Honey Pump functions like the human and, at the same time, the social organism that connects and regulates the different functional areas of the body

7.20 Holocaust Memorial in Vienna. Rachel Whiteread, 2000.

and social life. *7000 Oaks – City Forestation Instead of City Administration,* which Beuys presented at documenta 7 (1982), is particularly important in this context. He oversaw the building of a triangle of 7,000 basalt columns in front of the Fridericianum in Kassel. Each person who donated 500 deutschmarks received a stone and was permitted to plant an oak tree somewhere in the city next to which the stone was set into the ground. Beuys regarded the work as finished as soon as its materiality had completely evaporated away due to the fact that all the stones had been removed and become part of a "natural" cycle. This should have taken five years.

The Japanese artist Noriyuki Haraguchi employed metamorphism as a critical strategy when he recreated an American Skyhawk fighter jet in wood. A machine of war which had been deployed against Japan during the Second World War loses its threatening power when it is made of fragile wood. Haraguchi's replica of a Japanese house – an image idealized by European modernism – appears beautiful from a distance or as an illustration in the exhibition catalog. In reality, however, the copy was made of painted plywood and the dark, shimmering pool of water was filled with black, foul-smelling waste oil. The German artist Thomas Demand also recreates places of memory from paper – the photographs of the full-size models reflect the ambivalent

7.21 Remodeling and restoration of the Museum of Natural History,
Berlin. Diener & Diener, 1995–2010.

relationship between fragility and monumentality. In contrast to Semper, both Haraguchi and Demand employ metamorphism as a strategy of ephemeralization.

Stoffwechsel and ultra-materials

The wealth of newly developed materials and the search for principles that can explain or even justify their use lends Semper's theory of *Stoffwechsel* a new relevance. Andrea Deplazes summarizes the implications of the evolution of timber building when he speaks of the reconstituted wood which is created from combining ground cellular material and chemical additives as a synthetic material: "The growing interest in new timber building technologies endorses the theory that we are witnessing a general development from solid building towards timber building, which belongs to the category of filigree building (tectonics), for the first time in the history of architecture. Take the example of Gottfried Semper's so-called 'theory of *Stoffwechsel*', which is less concerned with building technology itself than with its effect on the expression of architectural forms at the moment of transition from tectonics to stereotomy, a form of transfer of timber building onto solid building (a conflict that I describe as 'technological immanence versus cultural permanence') or the first reinforced concrete structures of Hennebique which, with their hierarchically structured uprights, primary beams, and secondary joists, are still fully indebted to the tectonic structure of timber buildings."[58]

The Meuli House in Fläsch in Graubünden by Bearth & Deplazes (1997–2001) is a five-sided building volume on the edge of the village. Due to the gray-white color of its 50-cm-thick walls of cast insulating concrete the house seems like a material transformation of the wood-paneled Willimann-Lötscher House in Sevgein (1997–1998), which was also designed by Bearth & Deplazes. Expanded clay was used in the production of the insulating concrete, removing the need for a further layer of insulation and creating a homogenous masonry volume which was cast in one piece. The impression of the timber formwork on the concrete surface – a controversial issue in a modernist aesthetic that was dominated by the theory of truth to materials – is explained by the architects with the help of the theory of *Stoffwechsel*: "A Semperian metamorphosis is perhaps detectable in the way the traces of the wooden formwork have been retained, thereby integrating the monolith more with the nearby farm buildings."[59] [Figs. 7.22, 7.23]

The term *Stoffwechsel* makes something in art and architecture visible that is otherwise difficult to explain: the alchemistic transition between materiality and immateriality ("techniques are the very basis of poetry", as Le Corbusier put it).[60] The preoccupation of Semper's ideas with continuity in change makes it possible to knit them into the fabric of the computer age. The Austrian architect Adolf Krischanitz sees "analog-digital transformation via the computer" as an emancipation of form from the purely material and, hence, *Stoffwechsel* as described by Semper. Krischanitz extrapolates Semper's definition of *Stoffwechsel* as a means of detecting permeability between the categories city, type, structure, and ornament or writing. He speaks, for example, about the use of

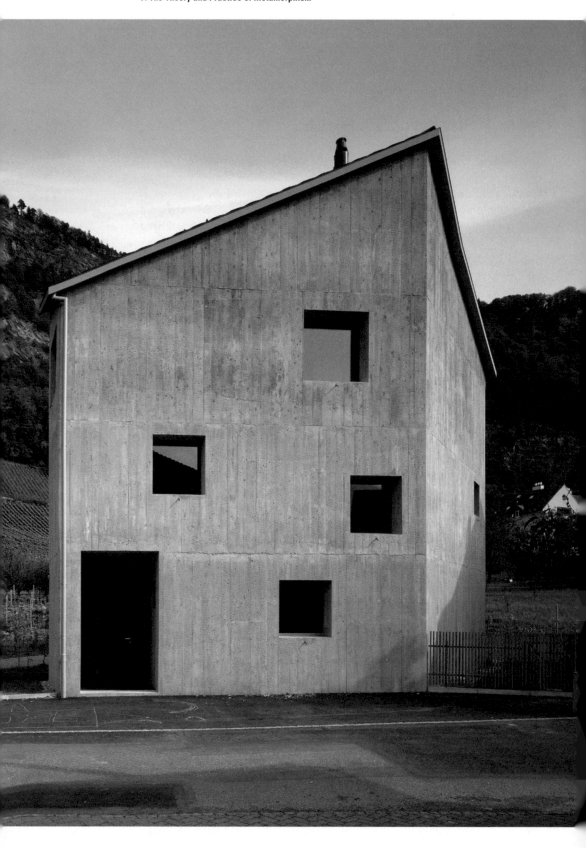

7.22 Meuli House in Fläsch. Bearth & Deplazes, 1997–2001.
7.23 Willimann-Lötscher House in Sevgein. Bearth & Deplazes, 1998/99.

terms which facilitate "*dynamische 'Stoffwechselvorgänge*" (dynamic 'metabolism processes')[61] or about "*stadtstrukturelle Stoffwechselapparate*" (urban structural metabolic apparatus), which can support a range of use scenarios.[62] [Fig. 7.24]

Contemporary theorists in the field of digital design such as Bernard Cache refer readily to Semper's theory of *Stoffwechsel*.[63] The French architect expands Semper's matrix of the four primordial techniques to the world of information technology. He devised a number of tables for his lecture "Digital Semper" at the *Anymore* conference in Paris (1999) as a means of depicting the transformational potential of the "historic and traditional materials." He then expanded

211

7.24 Remodeling and extension
of the Museum Rietberg, Zurich.
Adolf Krischanitz with Alfred
Grazioli, 2002–2007.

Semper's system of the four elements by adding a fifth category – the metals –
and then went further with concrete, glass, biology, and information. He maintains that Semper's categories of textiles, ceramics, and tectonics correspond in
information technology with - respectively - modulation, work with rotations
and radial coordinates, and the Cartesian coordinate system. And Cache associates stereotomy – as the art of tiling and paving – with work with Boolean
algorithms.[64]

The transformation of mineral urban walls into green façades or of recycled
waste and by-products into building materials is regarded as a sign of environ-
mentally-friendly design but this alone is not enough to signify an ecological or
social transition. A much more promising approach would be to reflect upon
what Karl Marx described as "metamorphosis between man and nature," and
to reconsider the interaction between technology and nature in the light of
current social conditions. The term "*Stoffwechsel*" is thus still able to render
something visible in science, culture, art, and architecture that is otherwise
difficult to grasp. "Form persists and comes to preside over a built work in a

world where functions continually become modified; and in a form, material is modified. The material of a bell is modified into a cannon ball; the form of an amphitheater into that of a city; the form of a city into a palace," writes Aldo Rossi, explaining his concept of analogy in his *Scientific Autobiography*.[65] The issue here is change and continuity, the constant renewal of form which reflects the story of its own creation. This freedom is not unlimited, the new materials and objects are integrated in a pre-structured system which is adequately elastic and which promotes rather than restricts reinvention. In this sense, *Stoffwechsel* is an old hypothesis but one which signifies constant renewal.

Notes

1   Gottfried Semper, "Preliminary Remarks on Polychrome Architecture and Sculpture in Antiquity" (1834), in Semper, *The Four Elements of Architecture and Other Writings*, transl. by Harry Francis Mallgrave and Wolfgang Herrmann. Cambridge: Cambridge University Press, 1989, pp. 45–73, here p. 45.

2   Michael Gnehm proposes this interpretation in his essay about Semper's theory of *Stoffwechsel*: "Just as the material body of Christ is merely the epiphany of a higher being into which it transforms itself, Semper understands architectural *Stoffwechsel* as the transformation of (dead) material into (living) spirituality", in: Gnehm, "Stoffwechseltheorie", in: *ARCH+* 221, Winter 2015, p. 155.

3   Gottfried Semper, *Style in the Technical and Tectonic Arts; or, Practical Aesthetics,* transl. by Harry Francis Mallgrave and Michael Robinson. Los Angeles: Getty Research Institute, 2004, p. 248.

4   Johann Bernhard Wilbrand, *Physiologie des Menschen*. Gießen: Georg Friedrich Tasché, 1815, p. 322. Translation by R. H.

5   Friedrich Tiedemann, *A Systematic Treatise on Comparative Physiology, Introductory to the Physiology of Man,* Volume 1, transl. by James Manby Gully and J. Hunter Lake. London: John Churchill, 1834, p. 180.

6   Justus von Liebig, *Familiar Letters on Chemistry in its Relations to Physiology, Dietetics, Agriculture, Commerce, and Political Economy*. London: Taylor, Walter, & Maberly, 1851, p. 40f.

7   Ibid., p. 46.

8   Jac[ob] Moleschott, *Der Kreislauf des Lebens. Physiologische Antworten auf Liebig's Chemische Briefe.* 4th Edition. Mainz: Verlag von Victor von Zabern, 1863, p. 333f. Translation by R. H.

9   Jacob Moleschott, *Der Kreislauf des Lebens*, 5th Edition. Gießen: Emil Roth, 1887, p. 593. Translation by R. H.

10 Ibid., p. 599. English translation quoted in Hans Schwarz, *Theology in a Global Context. The Last Two Hundred Years*. Grand Rapids, Michigan, Cambridge: William B. Eerdman, 2005. p. 191.

11 Harry Francis Mallgrave, *Gottfried Semper. Architect of the Nineteenth Century*. New Haven, London: Yale University Press, 1996.

12 Hermann Paul, *Principles of the History of Language (revised edition, 1890),* transl. by H. A. Strong. London: Longmans, Green, and Co., 1891, p. 13.

13 Ibid., p. 20.

14 Semper, *Style* (see note 3), p. 468.

15 Ibid., p.469.

16 Ibid.

17 Ibid.

18 Ibid.

19 Comp. Ute Poerschke, *Funktionen und Formen. Architekturtheorie der Moderne*. Bielefeld: transcript Verlag, 2014, p. 83.

20 Semper, *Style* (see note 3), p. 469.

21 Ibid., p. 470.

22 Ibid., p. 250.

23   Ibid.

24   Ibid.

25   Ibid. Semper's interpretation has not been confirmed by archaeology. Comp. Heinz Kähler, "Triumphbogen (Ehrenbogen)", in: *Paulys Real-Enzyklopädie der classischen Altertumswissenschaft,* Volume 7, A1. Stuttgart: Metzler, 1939, pp. 373–493.

26   Semper, *Style* (see note 3), p. 249.

27   Ibid.

28   Constantin Uhde, *Die Konstruktionen und die Kunstformen der Architektur. Ihre Entstehung und geschichtliche Entwickelung bei den verschiedenen Völkern.* Volume 2: *Der Holzbau: Seine künstlerische und geschichtlich geographische Entwickelung, sowie sein Einfluss auf die Steinarchitektur.* Berlin: Ernst Wasmuth, 1903, p. 20. Translation by R. H.

29   Ibid., p. 2.

30   Semper, *Style* (see note 3), p. 665.

31   Semper, *Style* (see note 3), p. 369f. The image of the "Tomb of Midas" first appeared in: Charles Texier, *Description de l'Asie Mineure,* Volume 1. Paris: Firmin Didot Frères, 1839.

32   Semper, *Style* (see note 3), p. 824.

33   Ibid., p. 438f.

34   Friedrich Schiller, "Letters upon the Aesthetic Education of Man", in The Harvard Classics, *Literary and Philosophical Essays.* New York: P.F Collier & Son, 1910, pp. 221–322, here p. 286.

35   Ibid., p. 311ff.

36   Semper, *Style* (see note 3), p. 439.

37   The quotation "What's Hecuba to him" is found in William Shakespeare's *Hamlet*, and came to be used as an expression for one's indifference to the fate of another.

38   G[eorg] Heuser, "Die Stabilrahmen, Strukturformen der Metall-Tektonik und ihre Nachbildung in anderem Rohstoffe," in: *Allgemeine Bauzeitung,* Vol. 49 (1884), pp. 97–103, here p. 98. Translation by R. H.

38   Ibid., p. 102.

39   Ibid.

40   Georg Lukács, *Heidelberger Ästhetik (1916–1918),* ed. György Márkus, Frank Benseler. Darmstadt, Neuwied: Hermann Luchterhand Verlag, 1974, p. 144f. Translation by R. H.

41   Otto Wagner, *Modern Architecture,* transl. by Harry Francis Mallgrave. Santa Monica, CA: The Getty Center for the History of Art and the Humanities, 1988, p. 93.

42   Rudolph [Rudolf] Redtenbacher, *Die Architektonik der modernen Baukunst. Ein Hülfsbuch bei der Bearbeitung architektonischer Aufgaben.* Berlin: Verlag von Ernst & Korn, 1883, p. 1. Translation by R. H.

43   Richard Streiter, "Architektonische Zeitfragen" (1898), in: Streiter, *Ausgewählte Schriften zur Aesthetik und Kunst-Geschichte,* ed. Franz von Reber, Emil Sulger-Gebing. Munich: Delphin-Verlag, 1913, translation after Ákos Moravánszky, "The Aesthetics of the Mask. The Critical Reception of Wagner's *Moderne Architektur* and Architectural Theory in Central Europe", transl. by Harry Francis Mallgrave, in: Mallgrave, ed., *Otto Wagner. Reflections on the Raiment of Modernity.* Santa Monica: The Getty Center for the History of Art and the Humanities, 1993, pp. 198–239, here p. 209f.

44   Ibid., p. 210.

45   Wagner, *Modern Architecture* (see note 41), p. 94.

46   Ibid., p. 95.

47   Ibid., p. 95f.

48   Ibid., p. 96.

49   Ibid.

50   Ibid.

51   Ibid.

52   France Stelè, Anton Trstenjak (eds.), *Jože Plečnik. Architectura Perennis.* Ljubljana: Mestna Občina Ljubljanska, 1941. Reprint Ljubljana: DESSA, 1993. France Stelè, *Esej o arhitekturi. Napori. Josip Plečnik, Dela.* Ljubljana: Slovenska Akademija Znanosti in Umetnosti, 1955. Reprint Ljubljana: DESSA, 1993.

53   Stanislaus von Moos, *Venturi, Rauch & Scott Brown, Buildings and Projects.* New York: Rizzoli, 1987, pp. 141–143.

54   Semper, *Style* (see note 3), p. 731.

55   Ibid., p. 749, note 8.

56   Pierre Restany, *Yves Klein e la mistica di Santa Rita da Cascia.* Milan: Domus, 1981.

57   Comp. Sandra Stich, *Yves Klein.* Stuttgart: Cantz, 1994, pp. 131–156.

58   Andrea Deplazes, "Indifferent, synthetisch, abstract – Kunststoff. Präfabrikationstechnol-
      ogie im Holzbau: aktuelle Situation und Prognose", in: *Werk, Bauen+Wohnen* 1–2/2001,
      pp. 10–17. Translation by R. H.

59   Heinz Wirz (ed.), *Bearth & Deplazes. Konstrukte/Constructs*. Lucerne: Quart Verlag, 2005,
      p. 75.

60   "Les techniques sont l'assiette même du lyrisme", in Le Corbusier, *Précisions sur un état
      présent de l'architecture et de l'urbanisme*, Paris: Éditions Vincent, Fréal & Cie, 1960. Quo-
      tation in English from Le Corbusier, *Precisions on the Present State of Architecture and City
      Planning*, transl. by Edith Schreiber-Aujame. Cambridge, Mass.: MIT Press, 1991, p. 37.

61   Adolf Krischanitz, *Architektur ist der Unterschied zwischen Architektur*. Ostfildern: Hatje
      Cantz, 2010, pp. 116/117.

62   Ibid., pp. 70/71.

63   Bernard Cache, "Digital Semper", in: Cynthia Davidson (ed.), *Anymore*. Cambridge, Mass.,
      London: The MIT Press, 2000, pp. 190–197.

64   Ibid., p. 195.

65   Aldo Rossi, *A Scientific Autobiography,* transl. by Lawrence Venuti. Cambridge, Mass., Lon-
      don: The MIT Press, 1981, p. 1.

8.
THE PRINCIPLE
OF DRESSING[1]

Semper and Polychromy

The image of a colored marble temple in the Greek landscape was a challenge to the imagination in the 19th century – and remains so to this day. Nonetheless, some aesthetes of the period were enthused by the notion that "dead antiquity" could be brought to life by color. Josef Bayer, Professor of Aesthetics at the Technical University in Vienna, wrote in 1890 that the "dogmatic idea of 'classicism' and 'noble simplicity'" that, for them, was synonymous with "noble tedium" had finally become unbearable.[2]

In his *Vorläufigen Bemerkungen über bemalte Architectur und Plastik bei den Alten* (*Preliminary Remarks on Polychrome Architecture and Sculpture in Antiquity*, 1834) Gottfried Semper paid tribute to the British architects James Stuart and Nicholas Revett, who had surveyed the ruins of the Parthenon in Athens in 1757.[3] In the three folio volumes of their much-vaunted publication *The Antiquities of Athens* (1762–1794) they mentioned that traces of the architectural color scheme had been preserved.[4] Stuart and Revett's discovery was, however, barely noticed by their contemporaries and would certainly have been difficult to reconcile with their own notion of antiquity. Like Georges Cuvier's theoretical reconstruction of the plumage of the extinct pterodactyl, the colored surfaces of a marble temple must have appeared monstrous and a colorful statue well-nigh barbaric. But at the beginning of the 19th century, polychromy was grabbing the attention of many French and German architects, who started to study precisely this aspect of Stuart and Revett's work.

The first important contribution to the discussion on polychromy in the context of the theory of imitation came from Antoine Chrisostôme Quatremère de Quincy, professor and *Secrétaire perpétuel* (Secretary-for-life) at the Académie des Beaux-Arts, in the form of his monumental publication *Le Jupiter Olympien* (1814).[5] In this folio volume he published his colored reconstruction of Phidias' huge gold and ivory statue of Zeus which had stood in the cella of the temple in Olympia. In terms of architecture, however, Quatremère de Quincy felt bound to Johann Joachim Winckelmann's classical ideal of beauty and the notion of colored temple architecture must have appalled him. And yet two architects in Paris with German origins, Jakob Ignaz Hittorff (1792–1867) and Franz Christian Gau (1790–1854), who had studied at Quatremère de Quincy's École des Beaux-Arts, not only carried out research which contributed to the polychromy debate but also delivered their own built examples of a new colored architecture. Gau exhibited his illustrations of vividly colored Egyptian façades and tomb interiors at the Paris Salon of 1822 and Hittorff published chromolithographs entitled *Architecture antique de la Sicile* in 1827,[6] in collaboration with Karl Ludwig Wilhelm Zanth, the architect of the Moorish Villa Wilhelma in Cannstatt near Stuttgart (1837–1851).

Semper made two visits of several months to Paris between 1826 and 1830 in order to study at Gau's school of architecture. In 1830 he travelled on with his friend Jules Goury to Italy and then to Greece in order to investigate the traces of color on ancient buildings. In Greece they met the young Owen Jones, who would go on to compile the highly influential sourcebook *The Grammar of Ornament* (1856) and was also commissioned with the color design of the Crystal Palace in London.[7] In 1833 Semper travelled to Berlin to personally present his drawings showing colored reconstructions of the Acropolis to Karl Friedrich Schinkel who, over the course of the next few years, produced a grandiose polychrome design for the Orianda Palace on the Crimean Peninsula (1838). [Fig. 8.1]

Textile walls assume an important role in Semper's description: He states that, alongside painting, "the metal ornaments, gilding, tapestrylike draperies, baldachins, curtains, and movable implements must not be forgotten. From the beginning the monuments were designed with all these things in mind, even for the surroundings – the crowds of people, priests, and the processions. The monuments were the scaffolding intended to bring together these elements on a common stage."[8] This text includes statements that he would later develop into his theory of dressing. He demanded that each material should speak for itself and appear unveiled, brick as brick, wood as wood, "each according to its own statistical laws."[9] In the next sentence, however, he clarifies that he is not a spokesman for the theory of truth to materials: "true simplicity" alone is not enough and we should "let our fondness for the harmless embroidery of decoration run free. Wood, iron, and every metal need a coating to protect them against the corroding effect of the air. This need can be fulfilled quite naturally, in a way that contributes at the same time to their embellishment. Instead of a dull coat of paint we could select a pleasant diversity of color. Polychromy thus becomes natural and necessary."[10] In this text he already describes the decoration of the temple of Selinunt as "color dressing" (Farbenbekleidung).[11] These words are guided by a vision not of a white marble temple juxtaposed with nature but of a building and its natural surroundings which have become a single colorful entity: "In a bright, consuming southern light and strongly tinted environment, the effect of refraction on well-ordered tones of color placed next to one another is so mild that the colors do not offend the eye but soothe it."[12] It is clear that archaeological discoveries alone cannot explain the newly ignited interest in polychromy – the aesthetic vision was, at the very least, equally important.

Bötticher's tectonics

The German architect and archaeologist Karl Bötticher (1806–1889), a pupil of Schinkel, took upon himself the role of drawing up a consistent theory which corresponded with the built works and the remaining fragments of the architectural teachings of his master. Bötticher's important work *Die Tektonik der Hellenen* (*The Tectonics of the Greeks*, 1844–1852) broke with traditional

8.1 Colored view of the entablature of the Parthenon, Athens. Gottfried Semper, 1836. gta Archiv, Zurich.

treatises on the architecture of Ancient Greece by proposing a set of underlying rules for this architecture that was distilled from a detailed analysis of its forms. His aim in doing so was not only to interpret the historical material but also to provide a design theory for his own time. Bötticher believed that the principle of form in antiquity worked in a similar way to "creating nature." On the basis of this he drew up a "law of form" that stands "far above individual arbitrariness." He described tectonics as "the activity of building or of making objects of use, as soon as this activity is *ethically suffused*, and can rise to the charges placed upon it by intellectual or physical life. At that point, this activity not only seeks to satisfy mere needs by *forming a volume* in accordance with material necessity but instead may elevate that volume to a *Kunstform* (art-form)."[13] [Fig. 8.2]

Bötticher describes the Greek temple as an ideal organism, "one that is *skillfully articulated* in order to produce a *spatial* entity. This space-producing organism is thoroughly considered, from the whole to the smallest of its parts – membra. It belongs to the imagination of the human soul and has no precedent in its natural surroundings from which it could have been created."[14] The form

8.2, 8.3 Ornamentation of column bases, vessels and umbelliferous plant. Karl Bötticher, *Die Tektonik der Hellenen,* 1844–1852.

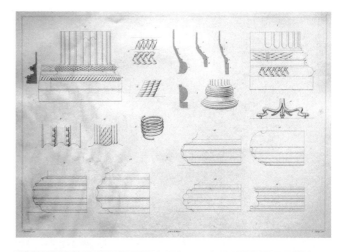

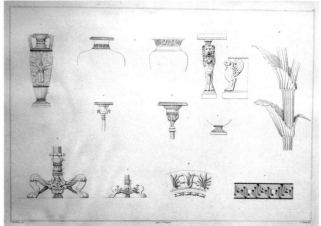

of a constructional element is lent to the building material and "inasmuch as *all* these members are related within a self-sufficient construct, then the vital force that inhabits a building material but *lies latent* as long as the material is formless, will be actualized in a dynamic expression and forced to assume a *static* function. By this means, the self-same material is lent a higher existence, because it now functions as a member of an *ideal* organism."[15] In his analysis Bötticher considers every constructional element as consisting of two components: "core form" (Kernform) and "art form" (Kunstform). He defines these components as follows: "The core form of every element is the *mechanically necessary,* the *structurally* functioning scheme; the art form, on the other hand, is merely the *characteristic that explains* this function."[16] The core form is an abstraction, the immaterial, diagrammatic image of the constructional component. The art form, on the other hand, is not pure decoration but, rather, the visually perceptible appearance of this component which not only fulfills but also has to symbolically represent the structural function. A special role in Bötticher's theory is played by "juncture", the point of connection between elements, which takes the form of a capital, abacus, cyma or plinth, etc. These are shaped in line with models from nature as a way of expressing their precise function in the structural system. [Fig. 8.3]

The idea of coherence, the correlation of the visible and the concealed, can be largely traced back to Karl Otfried Müller's *Handbuch der Archäologie der Kunst* (*A Manual of the Archaeology of Art*, 1830) which proved to be useful reading matter for both Bötticher and Semper.[17] Despite Bötticher's characterization of the core form as a "scheme", some of his formulations and terms can be read in another way – namely, that the core form could be thought of as a concrete constructional element stripped of its covering skin – a cylindrical column, perhaps, without a base or capital – an interpretation which would be taken up later by modernism.

Bötticher's theory had a great impact upon being published. Semper first read *Die Tektonik der Hellenen* during his stay in London in December 1852. He immediately recognized the relevance of the book for his own research although this didn't prevent him from reacting with biting criticism. Nonetheless, his reading spurred him on to refine his own theory on the emergence of artistic forms – which was then less developed than that of Bötticher – and to highlight the differences between his ideas and *Die Tektonik der Hellenen*.

Semper's principle of dressing

Semper used the term "*Stoffwechsel*" in his book *Style* in order to justify the principle of dressing.[18] Textile art was, for Semper, the original art, given that all other technical arts "borrowed their types and symbols" from textiles.[19] For him, there was no doubt that "*the beginning of building coincides with the beginning of textiles.*"[20] The basic motif of textiles is the rhythmic sequencing of the knot, which itself is "perhaps the oldest technical symbol and […] the expression for the earliest cosmogonic ideas that sprang up among nations."[21] The knot is primarily a "means of connection" and the arrangement of knots creates netting, mesh, felt, and fabric – materials for dressing both human bodies and buildings. [Fig. 8.4] Textiles are strictly structured in line with the rules of artisanship, but the limitations of technique permit a wide range of variations of patterns and colors, a fact which undoubtedly contributed to Semper's enthusiasm. He even suspected that the words, "Naht (stitch)", "Knoten (knot)", and "Not (distress)" were etymologically interrelated; and he used a reference to the Gordian knot to speculate about the "association of ideas […] between *Naht* and *Knoten* […] between the tied-up Ἀνάγκη (necessity) and the inextricable entwinement through which again only *Noth* can cut […]."[22] In this sense, the adage "*aus der Noth eine Tugend zu machen* (make a virtue out of necessity)" is a reference to the contribution of the knot to the creation of a coherent fabric out of individual elements.[23] Hence we can summarize: The necessity of connection is solved by the technical gesture of the knot whose labyrinthine spatial calligraphy is registered in the image of the knot. The decorative fabric, in the form of both dress and spatial boundary, is a product of the rhythmic repetition of knots: Textile substance creates space where there was once void. Order and ornamentation (the terms share the same linguistic root) coincide

8.4 Drawing of a knot in Gottfried Semper, *Style*, Volume I.

in the act and the motif of the knot. This same knot, portrayed as a spatial figure, went on to play a similarly universal role in the modern constructional teaching of Konrad Wachsmann, which is rooted in mechanization and standardization.[24] [Fig. 8.5]

"In all Germanic languages the word *Wand,* (wall), which has the same root and basic meaning as *Gewand* (garment) directly alludes to the ancient origins and type of the visible spatial enclosure", writes Semper, continuing his etymology.[25] Terms such as "*Decke* (cover, ceiling)", "*Bekleidung* (clothing, dressing)", "*Schranke* (barrier, gate)" or "*Zaun* (hedge, fence)" – which, according to Semper, has the same meaning as *Saum* (hem, fillet) – are "clear indications of the textile origin of these building elements."[26] The first house – which was made of wickerwork – illustrates not only the need to escape the weather but also a certain pleasure in ornamentation:

"The dressing of the wall was thus the origin and, in terms of its spatial and architectural significance, the essence; the wall itself was secondary."[27] These are the linguistically founded premises of Semper's theory of dressing which addresses the architectural object not, like Bötticher, by starting with its construction but by emphasizing its anthropological-historical evolution and the role of dressing.

In his manuscript *Vergleichenden Baulehre* (*Comparative Theory of Building*) Semper traces the development of architecture back to the texture and colors of the textiles of the Assyrians. He writes that the dressing of walls only became significant "when these walls were made not of carpet but of alternative materials such as stucco or wooden, alabaster, or metal panels for reasons which included durability, economy, cleanliness, and a fondness for grandeur."[28] These new forms of dressing – painted wood, stucco, stone, ceramics or metal – are imitations of the colorful embroidery of the carpet walls. The overwhelming importance of textile art for Semper can be seen in the fact that he dedicated the whole of the first volume of *Style* to this technique while the other three primeval techniques had to be satisfied with their place alongside metallurgy in the second volume. It was in conjunction with textile art that Semper developed the most important theories about the "Principle of Dressing in Architecture" and the "Masking of Reality in the Arts." In the second part of the first volume he then presented, subordinate to the principle of dressing, his depiction of the forms which emerged from the textile arts in a number of European and non-European cultures.

Architecture begins with dressing: This central thesis of Semper was incompatible with Bötticher's concept of tectonics. However, given that the heyday of classicism-inspired theories had already come to an end by the second half of the 19th century the new aesthetic appeared to be an attractive alternative. "The 'Hellenic renaissance' is over," scoffed Richard Streiter in 1896: "The 'last disciples of tectonics' regard the 'arbitrariness and degeneration' of today's architecture with resentment."[29] The precedence of decoration over construction also meant that the question of space, of its enclosure and structure, became more central than in the architectural theory of the early 19th century. "The need for protection, cover, and spatial enclosure" are emphasized by Semper

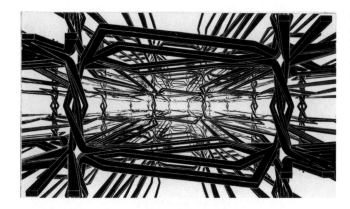

8.5 Perspective of a structure using a standard structural element, by Konrad Wachsmann. Academy of Arts, Berlin, Konrad Wachsmann Archive.

as he begins his observations on the *Decke* (cover). "The cover's purpose is the opposite to that of binding. Everything closed, protected, enclosed, enveloped, and covered presents itself as *unified*, as a collective; whereas everything bound reveals itself as articulated, as a plurality."[30] Hence, he displays much more interest in the *Decke* as a horizontal enclosure (ceiling) than in the *Decke* as structure (slab).

Semper, however, was not alone in the mid-19th century in regarding architecture as a form of spatial dressing: Hermann Weiß, a professor at the Akademie der Künste in Berlin, published his *Kostümkunde* (*The Lore of Dressing*), whose first double volume was subtitled *Handbuch der Geschichte der Tracht, des Baues und des Geräthes der Völker des Alterthums* (*A Handbook of the History of the Traditional Costumes, Buildings and Tools of the Peoples of Antiquity*), in 1860. Semper refers to this publication in *Style*.[31] The French architects and archaeologists Georges Perrot and Charles Chipiez, who were less well-known in architectural circles, published an eight-volume history of the art of antiquity between 1882 and 1903. This is opulently illustrated with drawings showing large-scale reconstructions of Egyptian, Assyrian, Phoenician, and Roman art.[32] Perrot and Chipiez refer to Semper's *Style* and also find confirmation for his theory in the ornamental decoration of Egyptian tombs.[33] These drawings, which underline the textile character of ancient façades, subsequently found their way into many handbooks of architectural history. [Figs. 8.6, 8.7]

It is not easy to be more precise about the similarities and differences between the theories of dressing of Bötticher and Semper, especially given the breadth of interpretations of the positions of the authors by their contemporaries. They were generally presented as rivals: Bötticher as the protagonist of a clear system which was determined by frameworks and subservient to the classicist idea of beauty and Semper as the advocate of the decorative surface effect of the colorful dressing of the façade and of its ability to determine space. These are different approaches but these differences should not be overestimated. For example, their positions regarding the interaction between envelope and core appear to be essentially similar. Bötticher tends more towards the interplay between core form and art form, which guarantees the coherence of the "total form," while Semper emphasizes: "But masking does not help when the thing *behind* the mask is not right or when the mask is no good."[34] Clearly this doesn't

8.6 Detail of the ceiling of the hypostyle hall of Xerxes in Persepolis. Georges Perrot and Charles Chipiez, *Historie de l'art dans l'antiquité*, Volume V, Paris, 1890, Plate VI.

explain everything: When is "the thing not right," when is the mask "no good"? There is nothing easier than understanding Semper's principle of dressing in terms of the decadent Habsburg obsession with pompousness, of the ceremonial processions devised by Hans Makart, but also by Otto Wagner.

The architect Rudolf Redtenbacher, son of the founder of the theoretical study of machines, Ferdinand Redtenbacher, responded brutally to Semper's theory of dressing in his book *Tektonik* (*Tectonics*): "To name the principle of dressing rather than construction, material, and purpose as the highest principle of tectonics, as *Semper* has done, is to deny the products of nature their right to be regarded as beautiful, and to suggest that a rose or a melon would only be beautiful if it had been coated in oil paints; and it would also mean sliding backwards and falling into barbarism [...]. Tectonics retains everything of value that the past has produced as long as it is still of use and everything else is cast into the waste bin of history".[35] This is the birth of the modernist rhetoric of unveiling.[36]

8.7 Isometric view of the ceiling and upper wall surface in the tomb of Ptah-Hotep. Georges Perrot and Charles Chipiez, *Historie de l'art dans l'antiquité*, Volume I, Paris, 1882, Plate XIII.

It was Josef Bayer, the art historian mentioned at the start of this chapter, who took upon himself to interpret Semper's principle of dressing as the theoretical groundwork for the establishment of a new style. In 1879, the year of Semper's death, he published the first in-depth analysis of the theory and the built oeuvre of the architect in the *Zeitschrift für bildende Kunst*.[37] He emphasized Semper's definition of necessity as the only one master of art[38] as a means of demonstrating that this program was motivated by the "desire for freedom of the age": A "dominated people" is not aware of its own need. Bayer states that the "built organism" is a "symbolic representation of the social organism": The driving forces within modern society differ significantly from those that caused the great buildings of the past to soar skywards.[39] In his short article "Stilkrisen der Zeit" ("Stylistic Crises of the Present", 1886) he went further, quite in the spirit of Semper's theory of dressing: "Our repository of available forms is richer because much more building history lies behind us; a much *greater variety* of articles of dress is at our disposal for use in our buildings. But at the same time the new building-organism requires an alteration in the cut of the adapted raiment of forms; there are times when even stylistic dressing bursts at the seams and one must somehow seek help."[40] This figurative formulation finds its architectural counterpart a decade later in the exhibition building for the Vienna Secession (1897/98) by Joseph Maria Olbrich: a cube, whose outer façade layers, profiled like fragments of a "classical" building, peel away from the core under the vegetable pressure of a gold-incrusted layer of floral ornamentation. What could better visualize the impossibility of representing bursting stylistic dressing as this solution (which Adolf Loos would then immediately toss into the waste bin of superfluous artistic ornament)? [Fig. 8.8]

The potential for an almost unlimited metaphorical extension of the terms "fabric" and "textile" into other areas of culture and human life is already mythologically expressed in, for example, the figures of the three Fates (Moirai or Parcae), who weave and cut the threads of the life of man. But the idea also lives on in modern literary theory and philosophy. "The text is a tissue [fabric] of quotations drawn from innumerable centers of culture", writes Roland Barthes.[41] Viktor Shklovsky, the literary critic of Russian formalism, also speaks of the web-like nature of texts, of their generative behavior or, in short, of texture.[42] The French philosopher Maurice Merleau-Ponty describes the phenomenological materiality of the world as a network of the seeing and the visible.[43] From this perspective, Semper's Caribbean hut appears not only as a house with wickerwork walls but as an element of the global spatial network.

The aesthetic of dressing in Semper's work

"Proud Genoa is glowing most unexpectedly in sober Zurich," was Josef Bayer's comment about Semper's building for the Zurich Polytechnikum (with Johann Caspar Wolff, 1859–1863), which is now the main building of the ETH Zürich.[44] The north façade demonstrates how Semper implemented the theory of dressing in his own work.[45] The building stands on a broad terrace which enjoys views of the city on the Limmat, Lake Zurich, and the mountains. The terrace, with its dressing of huge blocks of stone, detaches the building somewhat from

8.8 Vienna Secession exhibition building, detail of the portal. Joseph Maria Olbrich, 1897/98.

its surroundings while increasing its monumentality in the cityscape. Bayer speaks of the "bold earthiness of the bossage" which is comparable with the fortified gateways built by Michele Sanmicheli in the Late Renaissance.[46] The ground-floor façade has a rusticated dressing similar to that of the Florentine Renaissance palace. In contrast with the west façade, which is dominated by an *avant-corps* with powerful pilasters, the two upper stories of the north façade are covered with extremely rich sgraffito decoration. [Figs. 8.9, 8.10]

The visitor climbing from the city center to the Polytechnikum between 1864 and 1872 would also have been able to see the Treichler, the laundry ship which was also designed by Semper, lying at anchor on the Limmat before he saw the north façade of the Polytechnikum. The ship served as a laundry for the housewives of Zurich due to the fact that the city had no running water before 1869. Semper designed it with a light superstructure of iron profiles dressed on the inside with wooden planking and on the outside with metal panels inspired by Pompeian wall paintings. Semper may have been unable to give Zurich the imperial forum that he built in Vienna but he still managed to string a narrative thread through the streets of the city on the Limmat up to the Confederate Observatory (1860–1864) above the Polytechnikum. [Fig. 8.11]

8.9 West façade of the Eidgenössisches Polytechnikum in Zurich.
Gottfried Semper, around 1859, gta Archiv, Zurich.
8.10 North façade of the Eidgenössisches Polytechnikum in Zurich.
Gottfried Semper, 1859–1868.

Otto Wagner and his school

Semper's theory was interpreted in Vienna by Otto Wagner and Wagner's employees and pupils in the form of a modern aesthetic of dressing. The effect of the theory of dressing is ever-present in Wagner's architecture. Such early buildings as the Orthodox Synagogue in Budapest (1868–1873) already displayed richly textured surfaces: in this case a façade carpeted with glazed blue ceramic tiles and stone-like areas of plaster which suggest the influence of the

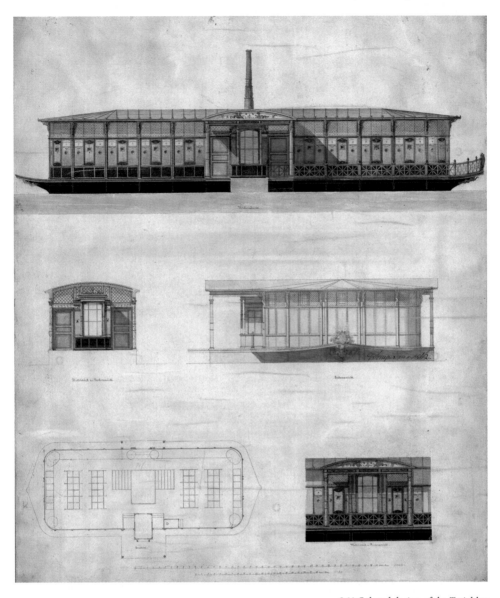

8.11 Colored design of the Treichler laundry ship in Zurich. Gottfried Semper, 1862, gta Archiv, Zurich.

Dresden Synagogue where Semper had employed similarly orientalized detailing (1838) and the study of (principally British) pattern books on Moorish ornamentation. [Fig. 8.12] The second half of the 19th century saw the appearance of such important pattern books as Owen Jones' *Grammar of Ornament* (1856) and Edmund W. Smith's *Portfolio of Indian Architectural Drawings* (1897), which also included oriental examples.[47] [Fig. 8.13] Simplifying somewhat, one could suggest that the transition from Bötticher's tectonics to Semper's theory of dressing also represented a shift from ancient and Christian models in the

8.12 Orthodox synagogue in Budapest. Otto Wagner, 1868–1873.

direction of a form of orientalism, a phenomenon which was also reflected in various fields of culture ranging from philosophy to literature.

Wagner's early designs include such festive decorations as the marquee for the silver wedding of Kaiser Franz Josef I and Elisabeth (1879) and the baldachin for the arrival of the Belgian Princess Stephanie in Vienna (1881), where the architect even suggested incorporating "electric flames" and girls clad in white below the pergola of the Elisabethbrücke.[48] [Fig. 8.14] The bridges for the Stadtbahn (City Railway) that Wagner designed during the last decade of the 19th century were "engineering-like" riveted iron structures wrapped in a layer of floral details combined with the trophies of the imperial capital. The dressing-like nature of these elements emphasizes metal fixings which imitate textile forms such as ribbons or ropes. The stations of the Stadtbahn on Karlsplatz or the imperial pavilion of the Stadtbahn in Vienna are metamorphoses of provisional tents in the sense of Semper's theory of *Stoffwechsel* and display a wide range of forms with textile origins. The dualism of a framework with an ornamental cover is articulated with great clarity in every detail of the columns, railings, and candelabras. [Figs. 8.15, 8.16]

8.13 Detail of the tomb of Salim Chishti, Fatehpur Sikri. Edmund W. Smith, *Portfolio of Indian Architectural Drawings*, London 1897, Plate XXXIX.

8.14 Festive decorations for the arrival of the Belgian Princess Stephanie in Vienna. Otto Wagner, 1881. Joseph August Lux, *Otto Wagner. Eine Monographie*, Munich, 1914.

8.15 The Court Pavilion of the Stadtbahn, Vienna. Otto Wagner, 1898/99.
8.16 Central hall of the Court Pavilion.
8.17 Apartment building on the Linke Wienzeile (Majolikahaus) in Vienna. Otto Wagner, 1898/99.
8.18 Detail of the façade of the Majolikahaus.
8.19 Cornice detail of the Majolikahaus.

Wagner's aesthetic of dressing is most richly developed in the apartment building on Linke Wienzeile known as the Majolikahaus (1898/99), the Church of St. Leopold, which is known as the *Kirche am Steinhof* (1904–1907), and the Postal Savings Bank (1904–1906), all of which are in Vienna. In the description of the façade of the Majolikahaus that he wrote in 1907 the art historian Josef Strzygowski commented that Wagner "is attempting to awaken the impression that a colorfully painted curtain has been fixed in front of it", and compares this solution with the façade of a mosque in the Turkish city of Konya.[49] Crowned with a widely projecting Florentine cornice, the façade of the Majolikahaus

is separated from its neighbors by deeply recessed bays with balconies which further emphasize the autonomy of the building and the layered nature of the façade. This is finished with shimmering tiles which are arranged in such a way that the floral decoration is densest below the cornice. Below this point, the number of undecorated tiles increases and the ornamentation is concentrated on the façade's central axis. Cut into the façade without regard to the ornamentation, the window openings convey the impression of a hanging carpet. This only serves to increase the emphasis on the lions' heads below the cornice which Strzygowski interprets as hooks for the symbolic hanging of

8.20 Granite dressing to the base of the Postal Savings Bank in Vienna. Otto Wagner, 1903–1906.
8.21 Stucco dressing to the base of the apartment building at Döblergasse 4, Vienna. Otto Wagner, 1911/12.

the dressing. Wagner mentions that "the installation of elevators" will make "the rental values of the individual floors […] almost identical," as a result of which the hierarchy of values between the *bel étage* and the attic level will be a thing of the past. Architectural treatments "that seek their motives in the architecture of palaces are completely inappropriate to such cellular conglomerates, simply because they contradict the interior structure of the building."[50] Like his contemporary Ödön Lechner in Budapest, Wagner uses the smoke and soot in the city air to justify his choice of ceramic as a dressing: "they can be [countered] only by employing the simplest possible forms and smooth surfaces; by using materials such as porcelain and majolica, stone and mosaic pictures; and by systematically cleaning the artworks."[51] [Figs. 8.17–8.19]

The development of Wagner's architecture from the orientalizing synagogue in Budapest via the major Vienna palaces in the "free Renaissance" style to the objectively ornament-free apartment buildings can certainly be interpreted in the sense of a tabula rasa. At the same time, however, even those buildings that he most radically "cleansed" of ornament are articulated in line with Semper's theory. As the stereotomic element of the building their bases are always reinforced – albeit through the use of ever simpler techniques: from plastered rusticated blocks or bands in the early works (building in Universitätsstraße, 1888) to irregular sandstone masonry (Church of St. Leopold, 1904–1907), granite slabs (Postal Savings Bank, 1904–1906) or horizontal-grooved plasterwork (apartment building on Döblergasse, 1911/12) in the later ones. [Figs. 8.20, 8.21]

The façade of the Church of St. Leopold am Steinhof (1904–1097) is also developed in line with Semper's theory of the four elements which, following the abandonment of the classicist concept of tectonics, came to serve as the basis for a clear structure. The *opus incertum* of the base underlines the origin of this component in the geological matter of the earth. The dressing of the upper part of the façade with alternating layers of 2-mm-thick marble panels and 4-mm-thick marble strips which are held in place by fixing bolts with visible heads establishes a clear contrast with the weight of the base. The portico is a baldachin which is spanned between thin iron beams and pierced by four columns supporting angels sculpted by Othmar Schimkowitz. The idea of the tent also determines the interior. The ceiling consists of a light lattice construction made from T-shaped iron profiles suspended from the load-bearing iron framework of the high dome. The undersides of the iron profiles are gilded and panels of plastered wire mesh span between them. The floating effect of this light shell is principally explained by the stained glass windows which slice through the walls in places which would not

8.22 Church of St. Leopold am Steinhof, Vienna. Otto Wagner, 1904–1907.
8.23 Plasterboard ceiling suspended from the dome structure of the Church of St. Leopold am Steinhof.
8.24 Ceiling of the banking hall of the Postal Savings Bank, Vienna.

have been permitted by a load-bearing dome structure. [Fig. 8.22, 8.23] Wagner finds another, no less effective solution for the banking hall of his Postal Savings Bank. Here, the columns slice through the glass skin of the ceiling which is similarly suspended from an iron roof structure, remaining visible through the translucent glass panels. [Fig. 8.24]

The wall surface also retained its textile character in Wagner's later works. The fact that this consists of surface texture rather than load-bearing elements in-filled with panels is demonstrated by such elements as the visible heads to the fixing bolts on the façade of the Postal Savings Bank or the fine gridlines on the façade of the apartment building in Neustiftgasse (1910) where the only ornamentation is provided by a thin frame of glazed blue tiles. The presence of roofs is principally emphasized by cornices supported by consoles modeled in line with the machine aesthetic.

The proliferation of narrative decoration which went so far as to transform entire façades into engraved panels in the designs of Wagner's pupils around 1900 is clear evidence of the crisis of ornament in conjunction with the principle of dressing. The flocks of migratory birds, beech forests, and flower meadows appear interchangeable, as if they could be simply wiped away. [Fig. 8.25] One of the most radical examples is the Portois & Fix apartment and commercial building in Vienna (1899/1900) which was the work of Max Fabiani, the Karst-born pupil of Wagner who was active in both Vienna and Trieste. [Figs. 8.26, 8.28] Clad in green and brown Zsolnay ceramic tiles the façade has the appearance of a geometric-abstract Majolikahaus. It traces its texture back to their shared prototype, the façade of the Doge's Palace in Venice, which was admired by many architects of the Wagner school for the way in which it appeared to be floating on the lagoon. In his book *The Stones of Venice* John Ruskin described such façades as 'wall veils' (see p. 139).[52] Fabiani continued this approach to façade design in his Slovenian National Hall in Trieste (1904/05). And in Vienna, where Venice and Byzantium were never lost from view – a fact to which Gustav Klimt is the main witness –, many variations on the theme were built. Josef Hoffmann (1870–1956), a pupil of Wagner between 1902 and 1905, dressed the façade of the Palais Stoclet in Brussels (1905–1911) with white marble panels from Norway. Floating above a base, these areas of façade are edged with embossed, ornamented, and gilded metal profiles which appear like jets of water cascading downwards from the tower-like structure which rises from the building. These framing profiles break down the façade to such an extent that it appears like a house of cards whose smooth surfaces have been fully relieved of any load-bearing function. [Fig. 8.29, 8.30]

The relationship between the dressed façade and such other elements as the roof and the canopy was a specific conceptual challenge for Wagner's circle that demanded considerable amounts of both empathy and fantasy. Given that non-tectonic façade dressing can carry no loads, canopies require their own load-bearing structures which mostly consist of thin metal bars that support the glass or copper baldachins. A particularly interesting detail is the junction between the ceramic-clad façade and roof cornice of the Portois & Fix apartment and commercial building, which optically relieves the façade. The roof structure resembles a form of airship which has landed on the building while the dynamic, snaking ornament of the cornice strongly recalls the framing metal bordures of Hoffmann's Palais Stoclet. [Fig. 8.27] For Wagner, this clear

8.25 Façade design for an apartment building. Hans Schlechta, 1900. *Aus der Wagner-Schule MCM,* Vienna 1901.

HANS SCHLECHTA. MIETHAUS. FAÇADENDETAIL.
SCHULPROJECT. I. JAHRGANG.

upper edge to the façade with its "Florentine" cornice is important because it reinforces the perspective effect of the street, the "major gesture" of the modern city. Those amongst his pupils such as Hoffmann who were happy to experiment with non-tectonic, decorative effects often omitted the cornice altogether. The upper windows of the Palais Stoclet rise above the marble-clad area of the façade while the bordure meanders to continue around their lintels. Further inventions resulting from Hoffmann's creative freedom and the suspension of the structural legibility of the volume are the fluting of entire surfaces of façade or the equal treatment of load-bearing and in-filling elements.

The question of the materiality of the façade was intensely addressed in the Viennese architecture of the late 19th century. The buildings of the Ringstraße convincingly illustrated the potential and scale of the attainable polychrome effects. In other cities, particularly in the Hungarian half of the Danube

8.26 Portois & Fix apartment and commercial building in Vienna. Max Fabiani, 1899/1900.

Monarchy, the colored city became a theme for architects such as Ödön Lechner (1845–1914),[53] a theme which was taken up again in the 1970s by his compatriot the Op Art artist Victor Vasarely from his home in France.[54] Lechner wanted Budapest to differentiate itself as a national capital from the other, gray major cities of the time through its colorful, shimmering ceramic façades, which were particularly resistant against pollution. He worked with Vilmos Zsolnay, the owner of the Zsolnay ceramics factory in Pécs and inventor of pyrogranite, a ceramic material that, burnt to a higher temperature, was not only hard but also frost-resistant.[55] [Fig. 8.31] Pyrogranite products such as decorative objects, ovens, and constructional ceramics were marketed around the globe and used by Vienna architects including Wagner and Fabiani in the dressing of the façades of their buildings.

COURS D'ARCHITECTURE

PL. XXIX

DU PALAIS DES DOGES (VENISE)

8.27 Cornice detail of the Portois & Fix building.
8.28 The Palazzo Ducale in Venice, from E. E. Viollet-le-Duc, *Entretiens sur l'architecture. Atlas*, Paris, 1864.

Jože Plečnik's Zacherlhaus in Vienna (1903–1905) continues the dressing aesthetic of Wagner and Fabiani. [Figs. 8.32, 8.33] A special feature of the dressing of the façade is the way in which the polished granite slabs are held in place. In contrast with the fixing bolts with visible heads used by Wagner, Plečnik anchored the slabs invisibly with the help of nickel-plated iron castings which were fixed into the masonry with wedge-shaped wooden dowels. The vertical joints are covered by round granite strips which lend a rhythm to the façade. In contrast to the "Nordic" granite façades discussed in the chapter "The Nature of Matter", Plečnik takes his motif directly from textiles. By positioning copper tassels over the mezzanine windows he interprets the granite-clad surface of the façade as a "curtain wall."[56] Ornaments, which still played an important role in his competition entry, were very sparingly used on the façade.

8.29 Palais Stoclet in Brussels, Josef Hoffmann, 1905–1911, from *Moderne Bauformen,* Vol. XIII (1914).
8.30 Detail of the framing metal profiles on the façade of the Palais Stoclet.

The principle of dressing continued to inform the work of Wagner's former pupils during the interwar period and beyond. The façade of Plečnik's University Library in Ljubljana (1936–1941) appears to be crafted from a fabric woven from stone and brick which is perhaps intended to symbolize Slovenia's dual relationship with the building traditions of both Central Europe and the Mediterranean. [Fig. 8.34] Plečnik's pupils in Ljubljana and, in particular, Edvard Ravnikar (1907–1993), whose buildings of the 1960s and 1970s shaped the image of the city, pursued the aesthetic of dressing of their master in the direction of an expressive concrete and brick architecture.

Iron and the covering of façades in France

Between 1825 and 1830, the years of Semper's studies in Paris and travels in Italy, a small group of architects was forming at the French Academy in Rome. On the basis of their studies of ancient monuments in Pompeii and Paestum this group was developing the idea of structural rationalism which held that the dissociation between the load-bearing framework and the space-defining surfaces should be clearly apparent. An important early work in this direction is Henri

8.31 Detail of the main façade of the Museum of Applied Arts in Budapest. Ödön Lechner, 1893–1896.
8.32, 8.33. Zacherlhaus in Vienna. Jože Plečnik, 1903–1905.

8.34 Façade of the Slovenian National and University Library, Ljubljana.
Jože Plečnik, 1936–1941.

Labrouste's Bibliothèque Sainte-Geneviève in Paris (1843–1851). [Fig. 8.35, 8.36]
The duality of the prefabricated iron frame and external masonry skin is modulated here by a broad range of materials including cast iron, forged iron profiles, sheet iron, bronze, ceramic, porcelain, and plaster that ensures finely graded light and color effects in the interior. The arcade of the façade is inspired by Leon Battista Alberti's Malatesta Temple in Rimini (see p. 42) and the parapets below the windows are inscribed with the names of great authors. Together with the Pantheon the library thus forms a sort of sacred precinct dedicated to the outstanding minds of the world and, above all, the nation. Labrouste's reading room in the Bibliothèque Nationale in Paris (1854–1875) is a space divided into a square 3 x 3 grid; the light domes formed of panels of terracotta are supported by thin cast iron columns. The glazed surface of the skin of the domes created the reflections and color effects which added intensity to the vision of antiquity described by Gau, Hittorff, and Semper. [Fig. 8.37]

Semper took a critical view of slender iron structures; he regarded the Bibliothèque Sainte-Geneviève as a failure because the reading room "lacked the comfortable seclusion required for serious study."[57] In *Style* he writes derisively that it is not possible to speak of a monumental iron or cast-iron style because "their ideal is *invisible architecture!* For the thinner the metal tissue, the more perfect it is."[58] This explains why the architecture of the Crystal Palace – in comparison with the Caribbean hut that is exhibited within it – is ignored by Semper in the book, despite the fact that Paxton's building should not be so far removed from his way of thinking. However, according to Wolfgang Herrmann, Semper was thoroughly complimentary about the Crystal Palace in his unpublished manuscripts.[59] Paxton described the basic idea of his building – the relationship between the load-bearing framework and the envelope of iron

8.35, 8.36 Bibliothèque Sainte-Geneviève in Paris. Henri Labrouste, 1843–1851. Façade and reading room.

243

8.37 Bibliothèque Nationale in Paris. Henri Labrouste, 1854–1875.

and glass – with the image of a table and a tablecloth, which led Adolf Max Vogt to comment that the Crystal Palace was itself an enlarged Caribbean hut, "the embryonic or original form or, in short, the egg of the Crystal Palace within which it itself was exhibited."[60] Semper could have been inspired by more than the idea of the glass façade as a textile wall. Owen Jones' color scheme for the structural elements of the hall in the primary colors of red, yellow, and blue which served to increase the transparency and the levels of light reflected his own preference for polychrome architecture. And he used cast iron columns himself in a "utilitarian structure," the scene dock of the opera house in Vienna (1874–1877).

Labrouste had visited the Crystal Palace in London and met Owen Jones and his libraries attest to these influences. The clear differentiation between load-bearing structure and dressing, which evidently also corresponds with the

8.38 Residential building and studio of the Agence Perret in Rue Franklin, Paris. Auguste Perret, 1903/04.

position represented by Viollet-le-Duc, is rediscovered in the architecture of Auguste Perret who constructed his building in Rue Franklin in Paris (1903/04) using a reinforced concrete frame in-filled with brick. He dressed both the load-bearing structure and the masonry infill, first with tiles decorated with a sunflower pattern and then with sculpted ceramic foliage and small discs embedded in cement mortar. [Fig. 8.38]

Brick pattern books from the 19th century such as Bernhard Liebold's *Ziegelrohbau* (1879), Pierre Chabat's two-volume *La Brique et la Terre* (1881, 1888) or Jean Lacroux's *Constructions en briques* (1878) demonstrate the diversity of decorative possibilities that arise from the use of colored, and often also glazed, bricks. [Fig. 8.39] Such façades are fruits of the same artistic period as pointillism in French painting: Georges Seurat painted his famous work *A Sunday Afternoon on the Island of La Grand Jatte* between 1884 and 1886. Around the

8.39 Terracotta dressing of the Ministry of Public Works in Paris. Fernand de Dartein, 1878, from Pierre Chabat, *La brique et la terre cuite*, Paris, 1881.

MINISTERE DES TRAVAUX PUBLICS

turn of the century many companies were offering a broad selection of such ceramic dressing elements as tiles, profiles, and a vast range of sculptural forms – or would produce these in line with an architect's specific wishes. The experiments of the architect Henri Sauvage with tile cladding on the façades of dwelling houses which step back at every story in order to allow more sunlight and fresh air to reach street level are particularly important in this context. In January 1912 Sauvage patented his system for the construction of terraced apartment blocks (*système de construction en gradins*). He justified the terracing with reference to the hygienic improvement of living conditions in the large city. His system was first used in his apartment building in Rue Vavin, a terraced block with a projecting central part (1912/13). Constructed as a reinforced concrete frame in-filled with brick, the façade was dressed – also in the spirit of hygiene – with blue and white glazed tiles known for their use in Paris' metro

8.40 Apartment building in Rue Vavin, Paris. Henri Sauvage, 1912/13.

8.41 Wainwright Building in St. Louis. Louis H. Sullivan, 1890/91.
8.42 Cornice detail of the Wainwright Building.

stations. This reflective material had previously only been used as a façade dressing within lightwells.[61] [Fig. 8.40]

Woven façades in America

Semper's theory was well-known in the large architectural offices of Chicago, not least due to the fact that many architects were, like Louis Sullivan's partner Dankmar Adler, migrants from Germany. John Wellborn Root translated the text of Semper's final lecture in Zurich, "Ueber Baustile" (On Architectural Styles, 1869), for the Chicago-based architectural magazine *The Inland Architect and News Record* in 1889 while Bernard Maybeck, who was principally active in San Francisco, began his translation of *Style* the following year. It was never completed.[62]

Sullivan's Wainwright Building in St. Louis (1890/91) and Guaranty Building in Buffalo (1894–1896) are early examples of high-rise buildings whose

8.43 Guaranty Building, Buffalo. Louis H. Sullivan, 1894–1896.
8.44 National Farmers' Bank, Owatonna, Minnesota. Louis H. Sullivan, 1906–1908.

8.45 The "textile block" façade of the Storer Residence in Hollywood Hills, Los Angeles. Frank Lloyd Wright, 1923.

construction is closely related to the evolution of Sullivan's important essay "The Tall Office Building Aesthetically Considered" (1896). The Wainwright Building is a nine-story, steel-framed building whose base, which contains the ground-floor and mezzanine, is clad with granite and sandstone. The steel posts of the façade are hidden between the windows in each second column. The bases and capitals to these columns, the window parapets, the fascia, and the panel-like cornice have a richly ornamental terracotta dressing. The building volume is clearly structured in line with the tripartite model (classical columns with the ground floor and mezzanine as base, the office floors as shaft, and the fascia and cornice as capital). [Figs. 8.41, 8.42] At the Guaranty Building the fascia and cornice merge organically and the entire building is overlaid with a ceramic skin whose ornamentation follows its own rules and is only ever skin-deep. [Fig. 8.43]

The brick façades of the smaller bank buildings which Sullivan built in the rural centers of the American Midwest, in Minnesota, Iowa, and Ohio, were conceived as valuable "jewel boxes". The cubic red-brick façade panels of the National Farmers' Bank in Owatonna, Minnesota (1906–1908) are framed by shiny strips of glazed green terracotta. The decorative details were designed by George Elmslie who, as a partner of William Gray Purcell, was to become the most important architect of the Prairie School alongside Frank Lloyd Wright. [Fig. 8.44] Sullivan consciously sought the effect of textile surfaces, "a texture with a nap-like effect, suggesting somewhat an Anatolian rug; a texture giving innumerable highlights and shadows, and a mosslike appearance. Thus the

8.46 Design for the hall of the commodities exchange in Amsterdam. Hendrik P. Berlage, 1897, from Jan Gratama, *Dr. H. P. Berlage Bouwmeester*. Rotterdam 1925.

rough brick became really a fine brick and brought with it new suggestions of use and beauty."[63]

Claude Bragdon, architect, graphic artist, and author of texts on architectural theory and esoteric subjects, explained the return of color in architecture as a reflection of the return of the enjoyment of democratic life. In his book *Architecture and Democracy* (1918), which was inspired by the architecture of Sullivan, he writes that one only needs to compare the ashen-colored brown or grey walls of metropolises such as Paris, London or Chicago with the colors of Rome, Siena or Venice in order to recognize the loss resulting from the elimination of color.[64] In his chapter "Color and Ceramics" Bragdon differentiates between "inherent" and "incrusted" architecture. The former regards construction and architecture as identical, the latter as separate. Modern architecture resulting from the steel frame is incrusted and requires the dressing of the "bony framework of steel" with a sumptuous coat for which ceramic is an ideal choice of material as a result of its color, texture, hardness, and durability: "Ours is a period of Incrusted architecture – one which demands the encasement, rather than the exposure of structure and therefore logically admits of the enrichment of surfaces by means of 'veneers' of materials more precious and beautiful than those employed in the structure, which becomes, as it were, the canvas of the picture, and not the picture itself."[65]

Wright, who regarded himself as Sullivan's heir, used the so-called textile block system in his Californian buildings. Here, masonry is constructed from prefabricated light concrete blocks into which reinforcing bars are inserted *in*

8.47 AEG Turbine Factory, Berlin-Moabit. Peter Behrens, 1908/09.

situ. The appropriate choice of casting molds created an ornamental, fabric-like effect although the material soon started to crumble, even in the Californian climate. Wright described himself as "the Weaver" – in contrast with the sculptor-architect –, as a means of characterizing the façades of such Californian buildings as La Miniatura in Pasadena or the Storer Residence in Hollywood Hills (1923).[66] [Fig. 8.45] In such early works as the Unity Temple (Oak Park near Chicago, 1905–1908) Wright was already accompanying the opening up of the closed building volume, which he described as "the destruction of the box," with the weaving together of the horizontal and vertical surfaces of the interior spaces through the use of the ornamental lines with which he would go on to weave together every aspect of later projects ranging from gardens to light fittings.[67]

Berlage and the architecture of impressionism

The Dutch architect Hendrik Petrus Berlage (1856–1934) studied at the Poly-technikum in Zurich between 1875 and 1878, shortly after Semper's departure from the school (1871).[68] In the texts in which he searched for the aesthetic bases of a modern architectural style he referred to Semper and Viollet-le-Duc as the "two great practical aestheticians."[69] His aim was to bridge the gap be-tween the two positions. The main ideas that he adopted from the theory of Viollet-le-Duc were an appreciation of the architecture of the Middle Ages (e.g. the asymmetrical form of the building volume) and an interest in the use of iron structures for spanning large distances. At the same time, he criticized Semper for his "fatal sympathy for the Italian High Renaissance" and his lack of understanding of the Gothic architecture which Berlage regarded as the one true constructional architecture.[70] The starting point for his stylistic theory was Semper's theory of dressing but this underwent significant revisions inspired by Viollet-le-Duc. The architect must start by studying the skeleton because, as with "every natural object," the dressing is an exact reflection of the inner struc-ture. The dressing should never appear like a "loose covering entirely negating the construction" but "totally rooted in the inner building" and as "decorated construction."[71]

Berlage emphasized the social relevance of this idea. It is the responsibility of architects to create spaces for a just society and this means that the material enclosures of these spaces are to be designed as if they were the clothing of this society. In the lectures that he delivered in the Kunstgewerbemuseum in Zurich and published in 1908 under the title *Grundlagen und Entwicklung der Architektur* (*The Foundations and Development of Architecture*) he compared the struggle against style-based architecture with the labor movement: The ob-jective of the latter is "material evolution" as a means of striving for universal equality whereas architecture is the showplace of a "spiritual evolution."[72] For Berlage, the truth of architecture signified the elimination of all "architecture of a parasitic nature," of all decorative additions which only served to express social positions and differences. Berlage praised Semper in the most exalted tones, declaring that his words "should be hung as a motto on the walls in every artist's studio" but then makes the decisive move of simplifying his theory of dressing because he wants to study "the dry construction in all its robustness" in order "to arrive once again at the full body" without the "confusion of cloth-ing. Even the last covering, the fig leaf, must go, for the truth that we desire is utterly naked."[73] The metaphor of dressing leads inevitably to the counter-metaphor of undressing: as a search for truth in the sense of *nuda veritas* but also driven by the desire to strip away "brutally" the "fig-leaf" of the covering from the body.

It was on the basis of these considerations that Berlage saw the role of masonry as being upgraded to that of a "full body". In his essay "Architecture and Impressionism" he demanded that decorative details be reduced in number or absorbed into the body of the building: "Away with all these time-consuming details, which cannot be executed the way one wants anyway; away with all those things that do not matter within the overall impression! Let us look only for some characteristic large planes and edges. The architect of today should become an impressionist!"[74] The brick façade of his Amsterdam Stock Exchange (1896–1903) demonstrates the use of this principle, which leads to the intensification of the impact of the mass and the use of filigree iron structures to cover large spans. [Fig. 8.46] With regard to the design of "naked truth": Berlage dedicated most of his book *Grundlagen & Entwicklung der Architektur* to speculation about triangles and squares, about the system of Egyptian triangles and other "secrets" of the ancient builders with the help of which plans and façades could be organized and coordinated. Berlage quotes Semper: "*nothing in this is arbitrary*" – while watering down Semper's theory by merging it with the counter model of Viollet-le-Duc.

Structure and façade covering

The rhetorical references to dressing and undressing and the human body were augmented around 1900 by the even deeper metaphoric of skin, flesh, and skeleton. The "fleshless" impression of the slender cross-section of iron structures was a much-debated issue at the start of the 20th century, as exemplified by *Eisenbauten* (*Iron Buildings*, 1907)[75] by Alfred Gotthold Meyer or *Ingenieur-Aesthetik* (*Engineer Aesthetic*, 1910) by Joseph August Lux, the critic, editor, and biographer of Otto Wagner.[76] "It is simply not true that the objective content, the bare skeleton, is the last word in beauty," writes Lux. "A railway bridge, an Eiffel Tower, and similar works of engineering are mere skeletons. They can satisfy my understanding but never my heart. And the artistic eye sees with the heart and not the understanding. Allow me to choose a comparison: The human skeleton is the most perfect work of engineering. But for my beauty-seeking eye it is the blooming flesh that decides."[77]

Peter Behrens, who repeated Alois Riegl's criticism of Semper almost verbatim in his writings, represented a position that appears quite compatible with Semper's principle of dressing: Monumental effects of mass can be created in an age of slender iron structures by suitably designed dressing which hides the "wiriness" that he so hated. In his lecture "Art and Technology" (1909) he quoted the engineer Alois Riedler: "Where a simple, calm look cannot be achieved by the structure alone, cladding should be consciously used in order to achieve the simplest formal effects."[78] Solutions such as the hollow volumes which appear like massive pilasters supporting the gable ends of the AEG Turbine Factory in Berlin-Moabit (1908/09) demonstrate his interpretation of his stated objective of the "form-based calming of the machine by cladding."[79] [Fig. 8.47]

8.48 Wall cladding in the Villa Karma in Clarens near Montreux. Adolf Loos, 1903–1906.

Adolf Loos and the principle of cladding

At first glance it may appear surprising that Adolf Loos, the sharp-tongued critic of the superfluous in architecture, appropriated Semper's theory of dressing. In his essay "The Principle of Cladding" he adopted Semper's theory almost word-for-word.[80] The human being seeks protection from the weather, which explains why the covering is "the oldest architectural detail" which was originally made out of "animal skins or textile products." The textile walls require a "structural frame to hold them in their correct place. To invent this frame is the architect's second task."[81] He finds the confirmation for the correctness of this principle in nature: "The principle of cladding, which was first

8.49 Main signal box, Basel. Herzog & de Meuron, 1994–1999.

articulated by Semper, extends to nature as well. Man is covered with skin, the tree with bark."[82]

Loos maintained that every material develops its own formal language and no material should claim the forms of another material for itself: "For forms have been constituted out of the applicability and the methods of production of materials. They have come into being with and through materials. No material permits an encroachment into its own circle of forms. Whoever dares to make such an encroachment notwithstanding this is branded by the world a counterfeiter."[83] As we have seen, Semper introduced his argument in a similar way in order to demand cladding for reasons of protection and durability. However, Loos' justification for the precedence of cladding is different: Architecture awakes moods in people and the role of the architect is to "refine this mood": The chamber must appear comfortable, the courthouse threatening and the bank solid.[84] And mood is, above all, a question of cladding. In Loos' dwelling houses the construction is usually highly pragmatic: load-bearing and in-filling

8.50 Curtain Wall House, Tokyo.
Shigeru Ban, 1995.

walls in concrete and brick merge with columns to create the hybrid subgrade while differentiation occurs at the level of the cladding. [Fig. 8.48]

Following this confirmation of the precedence of cladding over construction, Loos states the moral maxim that the possibility of "a confusion of the material clad with its cladding" must be completely ruled out. "That means, for example, that wood may be painted any color except one – the color of wood."[85] A cladding material, writes Loos, can keep its color, if the material to be clad also has this same color. "Thus, I can smear tar on black iron or cover wood with another wood (veneer, marquetry, and so on) without having to color the covering wood; I can coat one metal with another by heating or galvanizing it. But the principle of cladding forbids the cladding material to imitate the coloration of the underlying material. Thus iron can be tarred, painted with oil colors, or galvanized, but it can never be camouflaged with a bronze color or any other metallic color."[86]

Unlike Bötticher, Loos has no interest in the dialectic relationship between cladding and structure. His focus is the appropriateness of the relationship between cladding and space. For Loos, space is, on the one hand, the streets and squares of the modern city; the forum of the modern *"Nervenleben"* (nervous life – a term coined by the philosopher Georg Simmel) which the buildings of Wagner already address with hard crusts and "riveted" armor. Loos' response was to use forms which emerged through reduction and are ostentatious about their desire not to stand out. On the other hand, space for Loos is principally the interior, where "civilized man" luxuriates in his satins and silks and where the cladding must precisely match the moods that the architect deems appropriate. And, despite his sympathy for the classical, Loos sees the coherence of a work not in the "truth" of the relationship between core form and art form but in the ethical relationship between inside and outside, which includes the question of interior and exterior cladding. This is a program for a modern architecture, albeit one which was rejected by the modernist mainstream.

Deep surfaces

"Architecture being the masterly, correct and magnificent play of masses brought together in light, the task of the architect is to vitalize the surfaces which clothe these masses [...]," writes Le Corbusier in his book *Towards a New Architecture* (1922).[87] With the images of his early villas in one's head one can read this statement as a proposal for seeing architecture as a clear volumetric composition and, in doing so, overlook the fact that, in the same sentence, the architect describes the design of the external surface as a primary task. As with Berlage and Behrens before him: Semper's theory of dressing may well be dismissed in the name of *nuda veritas* and yet an alternative theory that would theoretically explain the now undressed form has failed to emerge. As a rule, this gap was provisionally filled by a theory of proportions such as Berlage's system of the Egyptian triangle or Le Corbusier's *Modulor*.

In his book *White Walls, Designer Dresses* (1995), the American architectural theorist Mark Wigley suggests that architects and critics used the color white and fashion as central concepts in order to help modern architecture to victory.[88] In doing so he refers to the debate about *nuda veritas* and *tabula rasa* mentioned above. In contrast with the early modern movement's discussion about unmasking and undressing, the new architecture is a new white dress for the athletic body whose relationship with the institution of fashion is somewhat ambivalent. This appears to contradict the commonly expressed notion that the body of modern architecture is undressed. The architectural critic Jeffrey Kipnis takes up the fashion metaphor when he interprets the buildings of the office of Herzog & de Meuron from the early 1990s as cosmetic: "Cosmetics are erotic camouflage; they relate always and only to skin, to particular regions of skin. Deeply, intricately material, cosmetics nevertheless exceed materiality to become modern alchemicals as they transubstantiate skin into image, desirous or disgusting."[89]

Following a visit to the Alhambra in Granada Jacques Herzog notes in his sketchbook: "Space – the illusion of a plane instead of space or of lattice work in front of the endless space. Surfaces – stone (earthly, heavy) becomes cloth (textile, immaterial). The doors and windows seem like permeable points in a textile fabric; stone, ceramic surfaces – textile effect."[90] The ceramic dressings of the Alhambra "do not trace sculptural components, [...] they cover over the structure [...]."[91] The works of the office display how this interest can result in an architecture which understands the façade as a surface image that can and should be tattooed. In an interview the two architects describe Loos' comments about tattooing as "fairly reactionary and difficult to understand"; they find ornament "interesting [...] if it has a spiritual dimension, if it thus makes sense [...]."[92] One certainly cannot suggest that Loos didn't find ornament interesting – he even used it when he thought it made sense –, but this certainly occurred less frequently with him than with the Basel architects. [Fig. 8.49]

These and similar statements by architects about surface are understood today as an appeal to see materiality as a *surface condition*: as an interface, as an intermediary, meaningful, medial layer between subject and object.[93] "Ce qu'il y a de plus profond en l'homme, c'est la peau" (The deepest thing in man is the skin), as Paul Valéry expressed it in 1960.[94] "The skin of things," the "depth of the surface," texture and facture, *fold* and *fabric* are amongst the many much debated buzzwords in architectural theory at the beginning of the new millennium.[95] In comparison with the complexity of the 19th-century debate about tectonics and dressing, the argumentation of the post-modern aesthetic, Venturi's *decorated shed* or the interest for fashion, dress, masks or cosmetics might appear deceptively simple. In the years after 1968 the rehabilitation of ornament seemed like a rebellious insurrection against the dominant functionalist doctrine and very little more than this was required in order to draw attention to oneself.[96] With Gilles Deleuze and Félix Guattari's rediscovery of the philosophy of Gottfried Wilhelm Leibniz and, thus, the folds of the baroque, surface texture is gaining a depth whose dimensions reach from Issey Miyake's "Pleats Please" collection to Shigeru Ban's Curtain Wall House (1995) and the folded architectural designs of today. [Fig. 8.50]

"In the beginning was cladding."[97] This concise sentence by Loos, published on 4th September 1898 in the newspaper *Neue Freie Presse,* must have appeared to his readers like the opening of a new history of the creation of architecture. Like the Gospel according to St. John in which "the word" is the translation of the Greek *lógos* and, as such, describes not the form but the sense of the word, cladding is also neither a surface nor an outer layer where the building ends but the very meaning of the architecture itself: "In this way" – starting with the protective cladding – "the idea of architecture developed in the minds of mankind and individual men."[98] That is architecture as spatial art, otherwise one begins with sections of walls and "that which is left over around the walls then forms the rooms."[99] Hence, the principle of cladding/dressing means beginning with the space as the content of architecture. Not with abstract, geometrical space, not with grids of columns and wall slabs but with the lived-in space whose quality is inseparable from the materiality of the dressing. In the 1990s a counter movement emerged: The call to order of tectonics directed itself against the spectacularization of the surface which, acting in the name of the sheer greed of global capitalism, reduces buildings themselves to commodities.[100] However, many exponents of tectonics failed to recognize the potential of Semper's suggestion. The principle of dressing sought to focus attention not on ornament but on that layer in the order of things which architecture spreads out between the outside world and the skin: a texture produced by human intelligence and work, which gives pleasure to both the eyes and the hand.

Notes

1   This book principally uses *dressing* as the translation for the German term *Bekleidung,* not least because this is the English word favored by the standard translations of Semper's writings by Harry Francis Mallgrave et al. (see note 18). Not all scholars agree on this matter. Adolf Loos' *Prinzip der Bekleidung* is, for example, generally translated as *The Principle of Cladding* (see p. 255). Á. M.

2   As expressed by Josef Bayer in his essay "Von der Farbe in der Baukunst", in: Bayer, *Baustudien und Baubilder. Schriften zur Kunst,* ed. Robert Stiassny. Jena: Eugen Diederichs, 1919, pp. 245–254, here p. 245.

3   Gottfried Semper, "Preliminary Remarks on Polychrome Architecture and Sculpture in Antiquity (1834)", in: Semper, *The Four Elements of Architecture and Other Writings,* transl. by Harry Francis Mallgrave and Wolfgang Herrmann, Cambridge: Cambridge University Press, 1989, pp. 45–73, On the "admirable" work of Stuart: Ibid., p. 57.

4   James Stuart, Nicholas Revett, *The Antiquities of Athens.* Vol. 1 London: John Haberkorn, 1762, Vol. 2 London: John Nichols, 1787, Vol. 3 London: John Nichols, 1794. Reprint New York: Princeton Architectural Press, 2008.

5   [Antoine-Chrisostôme] Quatremère de Quincy, *Le Jupiter Olympien, ou l'art de la sculpture antique considérée sous un nouveau point de vue.* Paris: De Bure frères, 1815.

6   J[acques Ignace] Hittorff, L[udwig] Zanth, *Architecture antique de la Sicile, ou, Recueil des plus intéressans monumens d'architecture des villes et des lieux les plus remarquables de la Sicile ancienne.* Paris: P. Renouard, without year. [1827?].

7   Owen Jones, *Grammar of Ornament. Illustrated by Examples from Various Styles of Ornament. One Hundred Folio Plates.* London: Day & Son, 1856.

8   Semper, "Preliminary Remarks" (see note 3), p. 65.

9   Ibid., p. 48.

10   Ibid.

11   Ibid., p. 58.

12   Ibid., p. 59.

13   Karl Bötticher, *Die Tektonik der Hellenen,* Volume 1. Potsdam: Ferdinand Riegel, 1852, p. 3. Translation in: Werner Oechslin, *Otto Wagner, Adolf Loos, and the Road to Modern Architecture,* transl. by Lynnette Widder. Cambridge: Cambridge University Press, 2002, p. 190.

14   Ibid., p 188.

15   Ibid., p. 188f.

16   Bötticher, *Die Tektonik der Hellenen* (see note 13), p. XV. Translation by R. H.

17   Karl Otfried Müller, *Ancient Art and its Remains; or a Manual of the Archaeology of Art,* transl. by John Leitch. London: Henry G. Bohn, 1852.

18   Gottfried Semper, *Style in the Technical and Tectonic Arts; or, Practical Aesthetics,* transl. by Harry Francis Mallgrave and Michael Robinson. Los Angeles: Getty Research Institute, 2004.

19   Ibid., p. 113.

20   Ibid., p. 247.

21   Ibid., p. 219.

22   Ibid., p.164.

23   Ibid.

24   Konrad Wachsmann, *Wendepunkt im Bauen.* Wiesbaden: Krausskopf-Verlag, 1959. The author thanks Christian Sumi for drawing his attention to the analogy between the knots of Semper and Wachsmann.

25   Semper, *Style* (see note 18), p. 248.

26   Ibid.

27   Gottfried Semper, "Vergleichende Baulehre. 10. Kapitel" (Manuscript), in: Wolfgang Herrmann, *Gottfried Semper, Theoretischer Nachlass an der ETH Zürich. Katalog und Kommentare.* Basel, Boston, Stuttgart: Birkhäuser, 1981, pp. 191–204, here p. 197. Translation by R. H.

28   Ibid., p. 197.

29   Richard Streiter, *Karl Böttichers Tektonik der Hellenen als ästhetische und kunstgeschichtliche Theorie*. Hamburg und Leipzig: Leopold Voss, 1896, p. 2.

30   Semper, *Style* (see note 18), p. 123.

31   Hermann Weiss, *Kostümkunde. Handbuch der Geschichte der Tracht, des Baues und des Geräthes der Völker des Alterthums*. Stuttgart: Ebner & Seubert, 1860. Semper, *Style* (see note 18), p. 239.

32   Georges Perrot, Charles Chipiez, *Histoire de l'art dans l'antiquité*. Égypte, Assyrie, Phénicie, Judée, Asie mineure, Perse, Grèce, Étrurie, Rom. 8 Volumes. Paris: Librairie Hachette et Cie, 1882–1903. Chipiez published two further volumes after Perrot's death.

33   "On y trouve la confirmation des vues de Semper sur l'origine du décor. Cet écrivain a montré le premier que le vannier, le tisserand et le potier, en travaillant les matières premières sur lesquelles s'exerçait leur industrie, ont produit, par le seul jeu des procédés techniques, des combinaisons de lignes et de couleurs, des dessins dont l'ornemaniste s'est emparé dès qu'il a eu à décorer les murs, les corniches et les plafonds des édifices. Comme ces arts élémentaires sont certainement plus anciens que l'architecture, ces ornements n'ont certainement point passé des murailles sur les nattes, les étoffes et les pots; s'est contraire qui est arrivé! Dans la régularité avec laquelle se répètent les lignes et les couleurs de ces ornements primitifs, on reconnaît aisément la disposition des brins de jonc ou des fils de lin, comme ailleurs on retrouve ces chevrons ou ces cercles concentriques que le doigt du potier ou le tour tracent rapidement sur l'argile humide." Quoted in: Georges Perrot, Charles Chipiez, *Histoire de l'art dans l'antiquité. Tome premier: L'Égypte*. Paris: Librairie Hachette et Cie, 1882, p. 807.

34   Semper, *Style* (see note 18), p. 439.

35   Rudolf Redtenbacher, *Tektonik. Principien der künstlerischen Gestaltung der Gebilde und Gefüge von Menschenhand welche den Gebieten der Architektur, der Ingenieurfächer und der Kunst-Industrie angehören*. Vienna: Verlag von R. v. Waldheim, 1881, p. 233f.

36   Comp. Oechslin, *Otto Wagner*, (see note 13). pp. 64–82.

37   Josef Bayer, "Gottfried Semper geb. 29. November 1803, gest. 15. Mai 1878" (1879), in: Bayer, *Baustudien und Baubilder* (see note 2), pp. 86–128.

38   Semper, "Preliminary Remarks" (see note 2), p. 47.

39   Josef Bayer, "Moderne Bautypen" (1886), in: Bayer, *Baustudien und Baubilder* (see note 2), pp. 280–288.

40   Josef Bayer, "Stilkrisen unserer Zeit" (1886), in: Bayer, *Baustudien und Baubilder* (see note 2), pp. 289–295, here p. 293. Translation by R. H.

41   Roland Barthes, "The Death of the Author", transl. by Stephen Heath in: Barthes: *Image, Music, Text*. New York: Hill & Wang, 1977, pp. 142–148. Here p. 146.

42   Viktor Shklovsky, *Theorie der Prosa*, transl. by Benjamin Sher. Frankfurt am Main: Dalkey Archive Press, 1990.

43   Maurice Merleau-Ponty, *The Visible and the Invisible, followed by Working Notes*, transl. by Alphonso Lingis. Evanston: Northwestern University Press, 1968.

44   Bayer, "Gottfried Semper" (see note 37), p. 118.

45   For more about the iconographic program of the façade see Martin Tschanz, *Die Bauschule am Eidgenössischen Polytechnikum in Zürich. Architekturlehre zur Zeit von Gottfried Semper (1855–1871)*, Zurich: gta Verlag, 2015.

46   Ibid.

47   Edmund W. Smith, *Portfolio of Indian Architectural Drawings*. Part 1. London: W. H. Allen & Co., Kegan Paul, Trench, Trubner & Co., 1897.

48   Otto Antonia Graf, *Otto Wagner*. Volume 1: *Das Werk des Architekten 1860–1902*. Vienna, Cologne, Graz: Hermann Böhlaus Nachf., 1985, p. 41.

49   Josef Strzygowski, *Die Bildende Kunst der Gegenwart. Ein Buch für jedermann*. Leipzig: Quelle & Meyer, 1907, p. 89f.

50   Otto Wagner, *Modern Architecture*, transl. by Harry Francis Mallgrave. Santa Monica, CA: The Getty Center for the History of Art and the Humanities, 1988, p. 109.

51   Ibid., p. 114.

52   John Ruskin, *The Stones of Venice*. Volume 1. London: J. M. Dent, 1907, p. 87.

53   Comp. Ákos Moravánszky, *Competing Visions. Aesthetic Invention and Social Imagination in Central European Architecture, 1867–1918*. Cambridge, Mass.: The MIT Press, 1998.

54   Victor Vasarely, *Vasarely IV*. Neuchâtel: Éditions du Griffon, 1979.

55   Ákos Moravánszky, "Keramik in der ungarischen Architektur der Jahrhundertwende", in: Éva Csenkey (ed.), *Zsolnay. Ungarische Jugendstilkeramik*. Exhibition Catalogue. Vienna: Austrian Museum of Applied Arts, 1986, pp. 27–36.

56 Ákos Moravánszky, "Woven Granite. The Façade of Jože Plečnik's Zacherl House in Vienna", in: Nikolaus Zacherl, Peter Zacherl, Ulrich Zacherl (eds.), *Jože Plečnik – Zacherlhaus/The Zacherl House by Jože Plečnik.* Basel: Birkhäuser, 2015, pp. 54–85.

57 Gottfried Semper, "Der Wintergarten zu Paris" (1849), reprinted in Semper, *Gesammelte Schriften*, ed. von Henrik Karge, Vol. 1.1, Hildesheim, Zurich, New York: Olms-Weidmann, 2014, pp. 243–248, here p. 246.

58 Semper, *Style* (see note 18), p. 659.

59 Wolfgang Herrmann, "Stellung Sempers zum Baustoff Eisen", in Herrmann, *Gottfried Semper* (see note 27), pp. 61–68, here p. 65f.

60 Adolf Max Vogt, "Gottfried Semper und Joseph Paxton", in: Eva Börsch-Supan et al., *Gottfried Semper und die Mitte des 19. Jahrhunderts. Symposion vom 2. bis 6. Dezember 1974, veranstaltet durch das Institut für Geschichte und Theorie der Architektur an der Eidgenössischen Technischen Hochschule Zürich.* Basel, Stuttgart: Birkhäuser, 1976, pp. 175–197, here p. 181.

61 Jean-Baptiste Minnaert, *Henri Sauvage ou l'exercice du renouvellement.* Paris: Éditions Norma, 2002, pp. 166–173.

62 John W. Root, "Development of Architectural Style", published in Vol. XIV, No. 7 (December 1889) to Vol. XV, No. 2 (March 1890) in: *The Inland Architect and News Record.* Comp. Giovanni Fanelli, Roberto Gargiani, *Il principio del rivestimento. Prolegomena a una storia dell'architettura contemporanea.* Rome, Bari: Laterza, 1994, pp. 9–12.

63 Louis Sullivan, "Artistic Brick" (around 1910), in: Sullivan, *The Public Papers,* ed. Robert Twombly. Chicago, London: The University of Chicago Press, 1988, pp. 200–205, here p. 202.

64 Claude Bragdon, "Color and Ceramics", in: Bragdon, *Architecture and Democracy.* New York: Alfred A. Knopf, 1918, pp. 132–147.

65 Ibid., p. 135.

66 Frank Lloyd Wright, "La Miniatura, First-Born of California", in: Wright, *An Autobiography.* New York: Duell, Sloan and Pearce, 1943, pp. 239–255, here p. 246. Comp. Ákos Moravánszky, "The Pathos of Masonry", in: Andrea Deplazes (ed.), *Constructing Architecture. Materials, Processes, Structures. A Handbook.* Basel, Boston, Berlin: Birkhäuser, 2005, pp. 23–31.

67 Ákos Moravánszky, ed., *Architekturtheorie im 20. Jahrhundert. Eine kritische Anthologie.* Vienna, New York: Springer, 2003, p. 132f.

68 Peter Singelenberg, *H. P. Berlage. Idea and Style. The Quest for Modern Architecture.* Utrecht: Haentjens Dekker & Gumbert, 1972, p. 5ff.

69 H[endrik] P[etrus] Berlage, "The Foundations and Development of Architecture" in Berlage, *Thoughts on Style 1886–1909,* transl. by Iain Boyd White and Wim de Wit. Santa Monica: The Getty Center for the History of Art and the Humanities, 1996, pp. 185–258, here p. 234.

70 Ibid., p. 235.

71 H[endrik] P[etrus] Berlage, "Thoughts on Style in Architecture", in Berlage, *Thoughts on Style 1886–1909,* (see note 69), pp. 122–156, here p. 136.

72 Ibid., p. 149.

73 Ibid., p. 136f.

74 H[endrik] P[etrus] Berlage, "Architecture and Impressionism", in Berlage, *Thoughts on Style 1886–1909,* (see note 69), pp. 105–121, here p. 116f.

75 Alfred Gotthold Meyer, *Eisenbauten. Ihre Geschichte und Aesthetik.* Completed by Wilhelm Freiherr von Tettau following the death of the author. Esslingen am Neckar: Paul Neff, 1907.

76 Joseph August Lux, *Ingenieur-Aesthetik.* Munich: Verlag von Gustav Lammers, 1910.

77 Ibid., p. 3f.

78 Peter Behrens, "Kunst und Technik" (1909), in: Behrens, *Zeitloses und Zeitbewegtes. Aufsätze, Vorträge, Gespräche 1900–1938,* ed. Hartmut Frank, Karin Lelonek. Hamburg: Dölling und Galitz, 2015, pp. 300–305, here p. 301.

79 Ibid., p. 302.

80 Adolf Loos, "The Principle of Cladding" (1898), in: Loos, *Spoken into the Void: Collected Essays 1897-1900.* Transl. by Jane O. Newman and John H. Smith, Cambridge, Mass.: The MIT Press (1983), pp. 66–69, here, p. 66.

81 Ibid.

82 Ibid., p. 67.

83 Ibid., p. 66.

84 Adolf Loos, "Architektur", in: Loos, *Trotzdem 1900–1930* (1931). Newly printed and edited by Adolf Opel. Vienna: Georg Prachner 1982, pp. 90–104, here p. 102f.

85 Adolf Loos, "The Principle of Cladding" (see note 80), p. 67.

86 Ibid., p. 68.
87 Le Corbusier, *Towards a New Architecture,* transl. by Frederick Etchells. London: John Rodker, 1931, p. 37.
88 Mark Wigley, *White Walls, Designer Dresses. The Fashioning of Modern Architecture*. Cambridge, Mass.: The MIT Press, 1995.
89 Jeffrey Kipnis, "The Cunning of Cosmetics (A Personal Reflection on the Architecture of Herzog & de Meuron)" (1997), in: Kipnis, *A Question of Qualities. Essays in Architecture*, ed. Alexander Maymind. Cambridge, Mass.: The MIT Press, 2013, pp. 99–113, here pp. 104–106.
90 Quoted in Gerhard Mack, "Architecture as a Multiplicity of Observation. The Architecture of Herzog & de Meuron 1989–1991", transl. by Ingrid Taylor and Katja Steiner in: Mack, *Herzog & de Meuron 1989–1991. The Complete Works*. Volume 2. Basel: Birkhäuser, 1996, pp. 7–13, here p. 7.
91 Ibid.
92 "Minimalismus und Ornament. Herzog & de Meuron im Gespräch mit Nikolaus Kuhnert und Angelika Schnell", in: *ARCH+* 129–130, December 1995, pp. 18–24, here p. 22.
93 As in, for example, Hans-Georg von Arburg, Philipp Brunner, Christa M. Haeseli et al., *Mehr als Schein. Ästhetik der Oberfläche in Film, Kunst, Literatur und Theater*. Zurich, Berlin: diaphanes, 2008; Hans-Georg von Arburg, *Alles Fassade. „Oberfläche" in der deutschsprachigen Architektur- und Literaturästhetik 1770–1870*. Munich: Wilhelm Fink Verlag, 2008; Giuliana Bruno, *Surface, Matters of Aesthetics, Materiality, and Media*. Chicago, London: University of Chicago Press, 2014.
94 Paul Valéry, "L'Idée fixe ou Deux hommes à la mer", in: Valéry, Œuvres II, ed. Jean Hytier. Paris: Bibliothèque de la Pléiade, 1960, pp. 195–275, here p. 215.
95 Arburg et el., *Mehr als Schein* (see note 93).
96 Mentioned here as an example is Michael Müller: *Die Verdrängung des Ornaments. Zum Verhältnis von Architektur und Lebenspraxis*. Frankfurt am Main: Suhrkamp, 1977.
97 Adolf Loos, "The Principle of Cladding" (see note 80), p. 66.
98 Ibid.
99 Ibid.
100 Kenneth Frampton, *Studies in Tectonic Culture: The Poetics of Construction in Nineteenth and Twentieth Century Architecture*. Cambridge, Mass., London: The MIT Press, 1995.

9.
THE APES OF MATERIALS

Materials without Qualities?

In the first volume of *Style* Gottfried Semper reported with great fascination about a new industrial material: "There is an important natural material that has only recently brought about a radical change in many areas of industry thanks to the remarkable flexibility with which it adapts and lends itself to every purpose. I mean gum elastic, or *caoutchouc*, as the Indians call it. It has the broadest stylistic range imaginable, as its natural sphere – imitation – has almost unlimited application. It is, so to speak, the ape of useful materials."[1] It is surprising that caoutchouc is first discussed in the volume about textile art and, hence, as a "simple natural product" alongside animal skins, tree bark, furs, and leather and before flax, wool, and silk. However, the chapter is entitled "Rubber: The Factotum of Industry" and it sits somewhat uncomfortably alongside the "simple natural products" that "do not fundamentally change" as a result of a technical process.[2]

Semper's description of the characteristics of the new material creates the impression that he is seeking the linguistic means to match the incredible transformability of "this remarkable material." The invention of industrial rubber spawns the emergence of a new industry that promises to meet the desire for all new luxury objects imaginable. Semper's list of the objects made of rubber that were on display at the World Exposition in Paris in 1855 covers an entire page: from parasols and saber sheaths to "shoes with fine vents that were impervious to water but allowed perspiration to evaporate."[3] He then closes the chapter with a cry that is as despairing as it is enthusiastic: "A stylist faced with a material of this kind will be at a loss for words!"[4] This is a striking sentence in a "Practical Aesthetics", in which the discussion of individual raw materials and of the history of their processing should reveal the basic rules for their deployment. The great world exhibitions – London 1851 and then Paris 1855 – anchored the new images of industry and industrialization in the public consciousness and delivered systems of classification. Semper had himself contributed to the drawing up of such systems. With his listing of rubber goods that principally owe their comfort to their elasticity, Semper emphasizes the paradisiacal side of industrialization, which the advertising of the time was keen to associate with the tropical origins of the raw material.

When Semper was writing about rubber the material was still young: "Only in the last fifteen years has this material started to attract the attention of industrialists, having previously been used more for gewgaws and for erasers."[5] It was a by-product of the production of gas for street lighting: tar and ammonia-rich fluids, which had first been used successfully as a solvent for natural rubber by the Scottish chemist Charles Macintosh. Macintosh's partner was Thomas Hancock, "the father of the rubber industry", who acquired numerous patents for the manufacture of rubber products after 1820. Hancock's book *Personal Nar-*

9.1 Travelling articles from rubber. Illustration from Thomas Hancock, *Personal Narrative of the Origin and Progress of the Caoutchouc or India-Rubber Manufacture*, London, 1857.

rative of the Origin and Progress of the Caoutchouc or India Rubber Manufacture in England* was published in London in 1857 and contains many examples for the use of rubber including knee protectors for horses and rubber socks for greyhounds and sheep.[6] [Fig. 9.1]

Semper writes that Hancock had "snapped up" the technique of the vulcanization of rubber from the American Charles Goodyear. This invention of 1838 was an important prerequisite for industrial production that made it possible to eliminate such negative characteristics of rubber products as their stickiness or brittleness at low temperatures. This meant that a wealth of rubber products had suddenly appeared on the market that imitated already existing goods but were much more suitable than the electroformed or cast metal alternatives due to their greater malleability.

It is a sign of Semper's openness to new materials that his *Style* includes – and, indeed, gives such prominence – to a material that designers were still ap-

9.2 Baldachin to the staircase in the third courtyard of Prague Castle. Jože Plečnik, 1929/30.

proaching with caution around 100 years later. For rubber is a subversive player that is difficult to accommodate in a strict typology of materials. Rubber is the ape that upsets the harmonious system of the four elements: It can be kneaded or poured like ceramics or metal, woven like textiles or applied in liquid form like varnish. Its properties can be "varied indeterminately."[7] Hence it fails to fit properly into any category.

In the section of *Style* quoted here Semper argues for the use of rubber as an artificial skin "for covering houses" and refers to natural models in doing so: The natural protection of organisms consists of "a continuous *skin system*, impenetrable to water [...] (like that found in plants, in many aquatic creatures such as dolphins, whales, and eels, and also in many land animals such as humans), of a *scale system* [...]."[8] Rubber, the "Factotum of Industry", should therefore principally inspire organic or organ-like forms in architecture. The fascination with this elastic material that is expressed by Semper's description had an impact on architecture around 1900. One can see tensile forms in the work of Otto Wagner and of his employees Joseph Maria Olbrich, Max Fabiani, and, above all, Jože Plečnik. The subject of the animal "skin system" was already occupying Plečnik in such early works as the Zacherlhaus or the St. Charles Borromeo Fountain in Vienna. Published in 1899, Ernst Haeckel's *Kunstformen der Natur* (*Art Forms in Nature*) provided him with inspiration or even direct source material.[9]

This elasticity in the work of Plečnik had nothing to do with the use of rubber but, rather, with the way in which he worked with natural forms and the historic vocabulary of architecture as if he was seeking to test their malleability and the limits to which they could be deformed. His buildings and designs are attempts to communicate ideas of loading, supporting, and movement through the merging of anthropomorphic, sculptural, and architectural forms. His staircase in the courtyard of Prague Castle demonstrates how "skin systems" can serve as a roof covering. [Fig. 9.2]

"A stylist faced with a material of this kind will be at a loss for words!" writes Semper, referring less to the formlessness of rubber than its ability to take on or alter a form. The issue here is not projection or fictive animation, as if the rubber has its own "desired form". Quite the opposite: It can imitate any material.

Yet the material moves all by itself: "[...] it wields to strong pressure but always springs back to its natural density. On the other hand it is more easily stretched and is more inclined to stay in this condition."[10]

The fear of the plastic

Rubber and plastic, seen as materials without identity, triggered not just interest and enthusiasm but also fear and repulsion. For many 20th-century thinkers the very word "caoutchouc" (which in the language of the indigenous peoples of Amazonia means "weeping wood") sounded repulsive, with its undercurrent of chewing-gum-like stickiness. This stickiness has become a metaphor for a general dissolution of solid values, an increasing plasticization of the world. In his essay "Der Ekel" ("On Disgust", 1929) the psychoanalyst and philosopher Aurel Kolnai differentiates between disgust triggered by touch, sight, and smell. He states that "the tactile impression of flabbiness, sliminess, pastiness, and indeed of everything soft, should count among the disgusting."[11] French thinkers such as Georges Bataille and Jean-Paul Sartre read Kolnai's text – probably on the recommendation of Salvador Dalí. In his book *Being and Nothingness* Sartre subsequently established a broad network of phenomenological interrelationships. One can only recall Semper's description of the volatility of rubber when reading Sartre's commentary: "In the very apprehension of the slimy there is a gluey substance, compromising and without equilibrium, like the haunting memory of a *metamorphosis*. To touch the slimy is to risk being dissolved in sliminess. [...] The horror of the slimy is the horrible fear that time might become slimy, that facticity might progress continually and insensibly [...]."[12]

Sartre's reserve was not shared to the same extent by his compatriot Roland Barthes. The French philosopher dedicated an essay in his book *Mythologies* (1957) to the subject of plastic. Barthes writes of the elastic transformation of the traditional aesthetic hierarchies: "The fashion for plastic highlights an evolution in the myth of "imitation" materials [...] But until now imitation materials have always indicated pretension, they belonged to the world of appearances, not to that of actual use; they aimed at reproducing cheaply the rarest substances [...]. It is the first magical substance which consents to be prosaic. But it is precisely because this prosaic character is a triumphant reason for its existence: for the first time, artifice aims at something common, not rare. [...] Plastic is wholly swallowed up in the act of being used: ultimately, objects will be invented for the sole pleasure of using them. The hierarchy of substances is abolished: a single one replaces them all. The whole world *can* be plasticized, and even life itself [...]."[13]

The elasticity and easy formability that Semper, in the mid-19th century, still regarded as a sign of promise are now interpreted by many authors not as advantages but as character weaknesses. Almost a hundred years later, during Germany's post-war reconstruction, Hans Schwippert expressed his doubts about easily shapeable materials when he spoke at the 1952 *Darmstadt Symposium*, which was dedicated to the subject "Man and Technology": "The world of materials has been expanded infinitely. When our understanding of the truth to materials was based on the characteristics of iron and wood then these materials offered very specific characteristics which we learnt to deal with. [...] Now, however, we are confronted by materials that no longer have this sort of character. These new materials are submissive to us in a way that we have never known before. There are plastic materials that simply no longer say: I am like this and you, designer, manufacturer must see how you can deal with me: [...]. These new materials say: Please give me a little of this or a touch of that and I will do what you want. Our task is to confidently master materials in a way we have never done before and this is a task on a scale for which we feel completely unprepared."[14]

The speaking building material is a popular myth in the theory of truth to materials. Nobody expresses the language of building materials as a form of ventriloquism better than Louis I. Kahn in a text in which he speaks about the essence of the brick or, more accurately, lets us hear from the brick himself, who knows how he wants to be laid: "When you are dealing, or designing in brick, you must ask brick what it wants, or what it can do. And if you ask brick what it wants, it will say, 'Well, I like an arch.' And then you say, 'but, uh, arches are difficult to make. They cost more money. I think you can use concrete across your opening equally well.' But the brick says, 'Oh, I know, I know you are right, but you know, if you ask me what I like, I like an arch.'"[15]

According to Alfons Leitl, editor of the journal *Baukunst und Werkform*, the speaking plastic in Schwippert's address and the implication that, in the light of these 'submissive' artificial materials, the concept of truth to materials has become equivocal struck some listeners like a "blow to the solar plexus."[16] "We have known for some time that the truth to materials means very little if this is not accompanied by some notion of form acceptable to humans. We are capable of manufacturing the most horrendous things without violating the law of materials in the slightest way."[17] The anxiety of the designer about having to take full responsibility because the material no longer expresses its own desires could not be better expressed.

In his 1965 lecture "Functionalism Today" the social philosopher Theodor W. Adorno does not mix his words in criticizing artificial materials in the name of truth to materials: Such materials with industrial origins "no longer permitted the archaic faith in an innate beauty, the foundation of a magic connected with precious elements. Furthermore, the crisis arising from the latest developments of autonomous art demonstrated how little meaningful organization could depend on the material itself. Whenever principles rely too heavily on material the result approaches mere patchwork. The idea of fittingness to materials in purposeful art cannot remain indifferent to such criticisms."[18]

In contrast with the "blow to the solar plexus" in Darmstadt artificial materials excited Italian architects from the very beginning. Gio Ponti was convinced that the evolution of architecture would lead from the use of heavy blocks of stone to transparent plastics. "Previously we have said, 'We want the natural product, not the artificial product.' Tomorrow we shall say, 'We want the artificial product because it has all the necessary qualities and the natural product does not have them.' To have achieved an artificial material is a triumph of intellect."[19]

Today, artificial materials such as laminates, plasterboard or silicon are the "true" materials of the globalized city – of, for example, the "generic city" of Rem Koolhaas. Even when one is apparently dealing with wood this is ground, boiled, combined with synthetic resin, and pressed in a mold. In an essay, Andrea Deplazes refers accurately to wood as "indifferent, synthetic, abstract – plastic," as if the organic fibrous structure of wood had previously been the bearer of its former identity.[20]

Concrete as designer

Semper may well have attested to the intelligence of rubber but this was a lower, restricted intelligence – at least in contrast with the personification of other materials. Although Julius Vischer and Ludwig Hilberseimer describe concrete as a designer in the title of their book *Beton als Gestalter* (*Concrete as Designer*, 1928) it was a long time before there was agreement about what this designer was really up to, about the true identity of this material.[21] [Fig. 9.3] In *Ingenieur-Ästhetik* (*Engineer Aesthetic*, 1910) Joseph August Lux criticized the American skyscrapers, which only resembled stone architecture, as being "raised to the sky like rubber." In contrast, concrete architecture appeared to be "leading to a new era of stone building," because it was bound up with "inherent laws that do not emerge from the simple transfer of historical traditions. Even in reinforced concrete construction, which dominates not only functional buildings, aesthetic perfection is only possible if there is no compromise with the traditions of the older art of stone building, as is yet to be proven."[22] In his deliberations about the "nature of the new material" Lux claimed that a "new artificial stone mass that, being fluid, can be given any shape," is not bound to any specific form but, rather, "equipped with an unlimited ability to take on form, which means that the nature of the new material, which may well look like stone, is much closer in essence to that of cast metal."[23] The "artistic possibilities" of stone architecture are unavailable to concrete because it cannot be carved. "In contrast, it can be poured. In this respect, it acts like a teacher of the modern objectivity that indulges in the recognition of naked beauty and in the perfection of the pure and utterly pragmatic form. The fatal timidity, which seeks to wrap this austere beauty with cheaply cast façade decoration, as still occurs in the majority of today's concrete buildings, is then recognized as an outright aesthetic mistake and labeled by noble objective sensibility as scandalous."[24] The artistic potential of concrete building is most apparent in surface decoration that is true to materials, which "is a product of the wooden void into which the concrete mass is poured."[25] The forms incorporated into the formwork "can lead to a rhythmically structured series of relief-like impressions, such as orthogonal recesses which give rise to a technically justified artistic effect."[26]

Lux's argument is only one of a number of ways of looking at and explaining concrete as a ceramic, tectonic, stereotomic or even textile material. For Semper, concrete would have been a key witness for the theory of *Stoffwechsel*, a "factotum of industry" like rubber. The story of early reinforced concrete architecture demonstrates the kaleidoscopic variety of approaches resulting from both the entrepreneurial interests of the engineers as they marketed their patents around the globe and the experimental passion of both architects and fascinated amateurs.

9.3 Cover of the book by Julius Vischer and Ludwig Hilberseimer, *Beton als Gestalter*, Stuttgart, 1928.

The early American concrete skyscrapers were, essentially, steel skeletons that were wrapped in concrete in order to increase the fire resistance and stability of the structure. The European system, which was largely developed and popularized by the engineer and builder François Hennebique – he even published the journal *Le béton armé* –, used reinforcement based on rods and stirrups which were laid parallel and resembled lines of muscles. Hennebique manufactured the first reinforced concrete panel with round reinforcing rods in 1880 and patented his system in 1892. The possibility of pouring the concrete mixture into timber formwork in situ or – as demonstrated by Edmond Coignet as early as 1891 – prefabricating concrete elements in a workshop led to a boom in new methods that allowed concrete structures to be realized in a broad range of styles which even included quasi oriental-exotic forms.

The Church of Saint-Jean de Montmartre in Paris (1894–1904) by Anatole de Baudot is one of the first reinforced concrete buildings to seek its own formal language. De Baudot's starting point was the Gothic but he was soon attempting to free himself from the influence of his teacher and supporter Eugène E. Viollet-le-Duc and to use the new material to create the large spaces that his mentor had failed to build from iron. In order to do this, de Baudot made use of a new method of concrete building that had been developed by the engineer Paul Cottancin. This was based on ribs built from hollow bricks with filigree reinforcement (a mat of iron rods with a diameter of around 4 mm) which were filled with a concrete mixture containing sand and a high cement content. De Baudot was convinced that modern concrete architecture should not be left to engineers because, without the creative cooperation with the architect, the material would be unable to receive the appropriate form. [Figs. 9.4, 9.5]

The brothers Auguste and Gustave Perret developed the idea of the frame system to a point at which its origins in Viollet-le-Duc's "rational" or "modern" Gothic (see p. 67) were barely discernible. Their apartment house in Rue Franklin in Paris (1902–1904) was an impressive demonstration of the potential of the dressed reinforced concrete frame. The path that would lead them to their Church of Notre Dame du Raincy (1922/23, see p. 19) was already quite clear. This development of the modern iron and reinforced concrete frame system provided Sigfried Giedion with enough justification for speaking of threads leading back to the Gothic when he wrote about "the French constructional temperament" in his book *Building in France, Building in Iron, Building in Ferroconcrete*. In his opinion, this "national constant" was associated with the sociological structure, climate, materials, and customs of a country's population.[27]

The Gothic was not the only model that enabled concrete architecture to discover new directions. Giedion pointed to national differences: "Each country must in its own way contribute to collective advancement."[28] Frank Lloyd Wright built his Unity Temple in Oak Park, Illinois (1905–1908) by combining an in situ reinforced concrete structure with prefabricated ornamental elements positioned between the windows. The result, which was completed only a few years after Baudot's church, represents an interpretation of the material which is quite distinct from that of the Church of Saint-Jean de Montmartre. [Fig. 9.6]

In his book *The Ferro-Concrete Style*, which he published in 1928, the architect and professor at the University of Michigan in Ann Arbor Francis S. Onderdonk presented a series of American examples alongside the results of 20 years of studying and visiting European buildings.[29] The book exhibits an interesting collection of the inexhaustible formal potential of the reinforced concrete architecture of the day. The many examples, from romantic villas in Hollywood and a hotel in the ascetic style in California to Erich Mendelsohn's Einstein Tower in Potsdam (1919–1922)[30] and Max Berg's Century Hall in Breslau (now Wrocław, Poland, 1911–1913), document the search for a reinforced concrete style. The author argues that the material should lead to the emergence of a new Gothic but that it is not the forms but the spirit of the style that should be reawakened. The pointed arch is replaced by the parabolic arch and the masonry of the wall by a concrete grid. Onderdonk quotes the Hungarian architect István Medgyaszay (1877–1959), who concluded his analysis of anonymous wooden buildings in Hungarian villages with a proposal for a new "artistic formal language of reinforced concrete." After studying in Otto Wagner's school Medgyaszay had also worked in Hennebique's office in Paris in 1907.[31] Medgyaszay's theater in Veszprém, Hungary (1908) is an important example of pre-First World War reinforced concrete architecture. The almost brutal appearance of the reinforced concrete ceiling in the foyer, the thin, barrel-shaped concrete shells used to cover the auditorium, the perforated concrete grid, and the decorative concrete structure to the windows with their glued glazing were radically new and, in addition to thus, extremely economic

9.4 Façade of the Church of Saint-Jean de Montmartre, Paris. Anatole de Baudot, 1894–1904.
9.5 Vault of the Church of Saint-Jean de Montmartre.

9.6 Unity Temple in Oak Park, Chicago. Frank Lloyd Wright, 1905–1908.

solutions. In his St. Anna's Church in Rárósmulyad (now Muľa in Slovakia, 1909/10) Medgyaszay employed the forms of vernacular wooden architecture. The dome over the central nave consists of thin, prefabricated reinforced concrete segments, which are held together by an externally visible belt weighed down by angelic figures. [Fig. 9.7] In his Vienna lecture, Medgyaszay referred to his travels in Transylvania in 1907 where he prepared drawings for a book on the vernacular art of the Kalotaszeg region.[32] He explained that, rather than being purely decorative additions, the ornamental forms of vernacular art are the results of an instinctive artisanal awareness of the characteristics of the materials and are intended to render such characteristics visible. For example, the decorative motifs of the wooden gateways in the villages represented the separation of the wooden layers of a bent piece of timber before it breaks. On the basis of these observations, Medgyaszay developed his theory of empathy as a means of explaining the logic of both the vernacular and the latest constructional solutions of his time.[33]

Medgyaszay explained metamorphism, the transmission of the forms of village gateways and pergolas into reinforced concrete design, by pointing to the relationship between the material characteristics of wood and reinforced concrete and to the ability of both to withstand both tensile and compressive forces. The buildings of Asia and the equally Asian traits exhibited by the farmhouses and village churches of Transylvania can be seen here as both an inspiration and a model: "the specific oriental character, the extraordinarily logical and honest construction, the artistic relationship of the wooden construction with that of reinforced concrete make these buildings very valuable for our modern efforts."[34] Concrete structures are metamorphoses of tectonic wooden frameworks: Early publications about the new material were already proclaiming reinforced concrete as *Eisengerippe mit Cementumhüllung* (iron skeleton with a

9.7 Reinforced concrete church in Rárósmulyad (now Muľa, Slovakia). István Medgyaszay, 1909/10.

cement envelope).[35] One spectacular example of this concrete technology is the FIAT Lingotto factory in Turin (1915–1926) by Giacomo Mattè-Trucco, which has a test track on the roof. The building succeeded in transforming the rigid framework of slabs and columns into a continuum of movement with the help of the lively dynamic of the ramp as it twists its way up onto the roof. [Fig. 9.8]

In his book, Onderdonk fails to mention the buildings of Irving Gill (1870–1936), who was active in Southern California, despite the striking similarities between his work and that of Medgyaszay. Gill was working in Louis Sullivan's office in Chicago in 1891 when the chief draftsman was a young Frank Lloyd Wright. Two years later Gill set up his own office in San Diego where he soon began to realize buildings with clear, simple volumes and smooth, tinted off-white concrete façades as an architecture for a healthy, hygienic way of life. Amongst the methods that he used was the so-called tilt-slab method: The façade wall was poured in situ in a horizontal formwork before being raised into a vertical position. In contrast with later attitudes to reinforced concrete, concrete was understood here as a natural material whose poured character demonstrates its affinity with mud and adobe. In some of his residential buildings Gill placed leaves into the formwork so that their impressions would appear as natural ornamentation on the concrete skin. His Lewis Courts in

9.8 Ramp in the FIAT factory in Turin-Lingotto. Giacomo Mattè-Trucco,
1915–1926.

Sierra Madre (1910), Horatio West Court in Santa Monica (1919), and Walter
L. Dodge House in Hollywood (1914–1916, destroyed 1970) exhibit a formal
similarity with designs by Tony Garnier – whose vision for a *Cité industrielle*
(1901–1904, first published 1917) proposed concrete houses built with the help
of the Hennebique method – or with houses by Adolf Loos.[36] [Fig. 9.9] Rudolph
Schindler and Richard Neutra, both pupils of Loos in Vienna (Schindler was
also a pupil of Wagner), went to work with Wright in the USA on the recommendation of Loos. In California, they discovered the relationship between
their own ideas and the efforts of Gill. [Fig. 9.10] Echoing the admiration of Josef
Hoffmann and Adolf Loos for the anonymous buildings of the Mediterranean
coast, Gill and Schindler regarded the buildings of America's first inhabitants
and of the Spanish missions as models for a modern architecture. Neutra even
writes of "the cellular domestic structures of the Indians" as the expression of
an "original 'Cubism'" in North America.[37]

In the USA, concrete was also regarded as a freely shapeable material which
lent itself to playful, "naïve" experimentation. In 1907, the tile producer and
art collector Henry Chapman Mercer began to design a large museum for his

9.9 Apartment unit of the Horatio West Court, Santa Monica, California. Irving Gill, 1919.
9.10 Sprayed-on concrete (Gunite) façade of the Lovell House in Los Angeles. Richard Neutra, 1927–1929.

collection of old machinery and tools in Doylestown, Pennsylvania. Fascinated by the new building material he wrote articles in the magazine *Cement Age*. He took an 18th-century farmhouse that stood on his large estate, covered it with concrete and connected it to the large central building. He used timber from demolished buildings and an old bridge as formwork and iron pipes from the local junkyard as reinforcement.[38] [Figs. 9.11, 9.12] Thanks to the rudimentary technique of pouring into a mold, concrete was an almost magical material while, for Gaudí, the direct transfer of natural forms onto his buildings had an almost religious significance.

When the first, timber-built Goetheanum building in Dornach, (1913–1922), designed by Rudolf Steiner as a center for his Anthroposophical Society, went up in flames on the night of 1st January 1923, Steiner immediately declared his desire to reconstruct the building from a solid material. However, many members of the society were unwilling to accept concrete as the material for the second building. Unlike the organic material wood, concrete appeared to them as incompatible with the spirit of anthroposophy. They were finally won over by the argument that the material was a product of the four elements of water, earth, air, and fire. The form of the new concrete building reveals its origin as plastic modeling clay. However, in order to execute the homogenous building volume "in one piece" it was necessary to build a wooden formwork that was not only extraordinarily complicated but also used large amounts of material. [Fig. 9.13] This is the reason why Erich Mendelsohn's Einstein Tower was not built, as planned, from concrete but as brickwork – Mendelsohn's erstwhile employee Julius Posener recalls that highly skilled bricklayers were simply easier to find than boat builders capable of executing the extremely complicated formwork.[39]

Photographs of complex, perfectly executed falsework for concrete bridges, which disappears when the structure has attained the necessary load-bearing capacity, allow us to reflect upon the relationship between formwork and concrete volumes. There is no apparent similarity between the negative and positive forms. According to Semper's system of the four elements, the formwork would be a tectonic construction and the concrete volume a ceramic one which, as Rudolf Schwarz has shown (see p. 80), exhibits similarities with the sedimentation of the earth. However, in the heart of most concrete volumes, in the conglomerate of hardened cement, sand, and gravel, lurks a hidden lattice of reinforcing bars. De Baudot's church is a rare example of the thin iron strands of the filigree form of the building being permitted to appear and dictate the construction. In reinforced concrete beams, the reinforcement absorbs the tensile forces that develop in the constructional element whereas the "concrete dressing" resists the compression. The cracks in a concrete beam are an expression of the contrasting "behaviors" of the two materials. Álvaro Siza and the engineer Cecil Balmond realized a huge hanging canopy for the Portuguese Pavilion at Expo '98 in Lisbon (1995–1998) which recalls the ceremonial gateway to the exhibition *Ein Dokument Deutscher Kunst* (*A Document of German Art*, 1901) at Joseph Maria Olbrich's artists' colony in Darmstadt. Steel cables spanning 70 m were hung between the two freestanding pylons and stabilized by the 20-cm-thin pre-stressed concrete roof elements. The cables are exposed before the concrete canopy meets the pylons. The light falling between the shell and the abutments dramatically increases the contrast between heaviness and dematerialization. [Fig. 9.14]

Siza's monumental canopy would be unimaginable without the light of Portugal: The contrast between the massive pylons and the light concrete sheet is only perceptible due to the brilliant white, homogenous surface of the concrete, the dark shadows, and the blue of the sky and of the Atlantic. Carlo Scarpa's approach to materials was different, although he also worked with the interaction of light and concrete. The light at his Brion Cemetery in San Vito di Altivole (1968–1978) near Treviso is not provided by steady intense sunlight. It varies constantly in line with the movement of visitors and the changing surfaces. Time leaves its traces on the raw concrete; brilliant colored mosaics disrupt the various shades of gray. [Fig. 9.15]

9.11, 9.12 The Mercer Museum in Doylestown, Pennsylvania. Henry Chapman Mercer, 1907–1916.

9.13 Façade detail of the second
Goetheanum building, Dornach.
Rudolf Steiner, 1913–1922.
9.14 The Portuguese Pavilion at
Expo '98 in Lisbon, Álvaro Siza,
1995–1998.

9.15 The Brion Tomb in San Vito di Altivole. Carlo Scarpa, 1968–1978.

The Hungarian architect Béla Sámsondi Kiss (1899–1972) sought new ways of using formwork that, in contrast with the high material consumption and weight of concrete buildings, would permit a constructional method that was as precise as steel building while also dramatically reducing the weight of the structure. He achieved his objective by using formwork lined with porous plasterboard on one side and panes of glass on the other. The plaster draws the water from the extremely thin concrete layer very quickly so that there is no lateral pressure on the glass and the surface of the wall from which the formwork is struck (the plasterboard remains on one side as lost formwork) is as smooth as a mirror. Sámsondi Kiss chose an analogy with textiles in naming the concrete membrane stabilized by the layer of plaster *szövetbeton* (tissue-concrete). He used the method to design residential buildings in Budapest during the war (1942). At his own house in Dayka Gábor Street, the thin concrete membranes were reinforced vertically and horizontally by steel strings, which were pre-stressed with the help of a wooden frame. For Sámsondi Kiss the apartment was part of an integrated urban system, a cell structure, which required the coordination of the dimensions of all elements (including furniture and vehicles). The vertical structure consists of "shelf-pillars" made of tissue-concrete (which can be used as shelves in the interior) and the slabs are thin-wall cellular systems into which the lighting and building services are integrated.[40] [Fig. 9.16a, b]

The use of elastic formwork that may be muter and more destined to disappear but is, at the same time, even more important as a counterpart to the mass plays a defining role in the work of the Spanish architect Miguel Fisac. Fisac described architecture as *un trozo de aire humanizado* (a piece of humanized

9.16 a Study for concrete fabric construction. Béla Sámsondi Kiss.
9.16 b Living room in the architect's house. Béla Sámsondi Kiss, Budapest, 1942.

air).[41] The expressive plasticity of his façades demonstrates how containers can be fashioned for this "humanized air". Dissatisfied with the obligatory impression of the wooden formwork he wanted to lend the concrete a plastic finish that would do justice to its liquid origins. To achieve this, Fisac allowed the concrete mixture to be poured into soft formwork, most commonly using a wooden framework lined with plastic sheets. As a result, the concrete has the appearance of a heavy, coagulated fluid that is causing its container to dilate. Recalling the work of Antoni Gaudí, this is a process that refers to the idea of pouring and is capable of lending a material the appearance of a completely different identity. Liberated from the earthly weight of the poured cement-sand mixture, the elastic concrete cushions are stacked to create façades, appearing to bulge under a pressure that comes from within. [Figs. 9.17, 9.18]

Current images of concrete can be divided between the extreme positions of primitiveness and perfection, between the natural and the technical ideals. Even in Swiss architecture, in which the perfection of the smooth, marble-like concrete surface has become something of a trademark, the rudimentary and the imperfect play an important role. Two family houses by Peter Märkli in Trübbach/Azmoos (1982) demonstrate the expressive potential of the material, this archaic power that is weakened the moment concrete becomes a polished artificial stone with edges as sharp as a blade. The main garden façade of Haus Kühnis has a memorable Palladian physiognomy that contrasts sharply with the lateral façades. The five concrete columns of the central bay at first floor level, which rise from the terrace to the fascia, are equipped with plinths and abacuses. The Minoan-Mycenaean column, whose shaft narrows towards the stone base, has a wooden core that, in Knossos, was covered with clay or stucco and painted. Interpreters of Minoan culture understood this anthropomorphic form to be a representation of the Goddess who can also appear as a tree, column or amphora.[42] The buildings of Jože Plečnik also feature Minoan columns alongside ceramic forms such as amphorae and vases, which are used as architectural elements (Fig. 9.21). At Haus Kühnis Märkli positioned a relief by Hans

9.17, 9.18 Façade of the Mupag Rehabilitation Center in Madrid. Miguel Fisac, 1969–1973.

Josephsohn like an acroterium on the main cornice while also placing a bust of the artist between the Minoan columns of the smaller neighboring house. This strengthens the role of the columns as an intermediary between human figure and building element while even the concrete reveals its origins. [Figs. 9.19, 9.20]

The English word *concrete* emphasizes the specific, tangible, directly experienceable character of this material. Since the 17th century, when the term was

9.19, 9.20 Family house in Trübbach/Azmoos. Peter Märkli, 1982.

first used to refer to artificial stone, concrete has steadily lost concreteness and has perhaps even become the opposite of *concrete* – imaginary, liquid, and almost intangible. In contrast with this, the French word *béton* comes – like bitumen – from the old French *betum* which, in turn, can be traced back to the Latin *pix tumens*, "oozing pitch", "earthly pitch" – whose black and sticky formlessness recalls the disgusting in the writings of Kolnai and Sartre.

In his book *Stones of Rimini* (1934), the English architecture critic Adrian Stokes used Adolf von Hildebrand's psychology of spatial perception as the foundation of an aesthetic in which the subtractive work of the stonemason becomes the paradigm of artistic design. But Stokes complains that stone is no longer the building material of today, "*modern building materials are essentially plastic.* [...] With an armature of steel, Le Corbusier can make you a room of any shape you like."[43] However, the pouring technology of concrete destroys the relationship between spatial imagination and handcraft as a result of which it will kill architecture: "The creations of Le Corbusier and others show that building will no longer serve as the mother art of stone, no longer as the source at which carving or spatial conception renews its strength. Architecture

9.21 Balustrades with ceramic shapes in the Bastion Garden of Prague Castle. Jože Plečnik, 1932/33.

in that sense of the word, indeed in the most fundamental sense of the word, will cease to exist."[44] If growing plasticity gains the upper hand in industry and art then the fine arts, as we know them, will have no future.[45]

The technique of pouring concrete, which does not appear in Semper's *Style*, does indeed represent a major challenge to the system of the four elements and yet it also offers an opportunity to provide the varieties of metamorphism with new examples. Today, concrete has become a hybrid material which circulates in the capillaries of the technical infrastructure which is all around us, and hardens into structures – but only a fraction of it is shaped by architects.

Notes

1   Gottfried Semper, *Style in the Technical and Tectonic Arts; or, Practical Aesthetics*, transl. by Harry Francis Mallgrave and Michael Robinson. Los Angeles: Getty Research Institute, 2004, p. 180f.

2   Ibid., p.169.

3   Ibid., p.182.

4   Ibid., p.183.

5   Ibid., p.181.

6   Thomas Hancock, *Personal Narrative of the Origin and Progress of the Caoutchouc or India-Rubber Manufacture in England*. London: Longman, Brown, Green, Longmans, & Roberts, 1857, newly printed in: *A Centennial Volume of the Writings of Charles Goodyear and Thomas Hancock*. Boston: The American Chemical Society, 1939.

7   Semper, *Style* (see note 1), p. 181.

8   Ibid., p. 185.

9   Ernst Haeckel, *Kunstformen der Natur*. Leipzig, Vienna: Verlag des Bibliographischen Instituts, 1898–1904. Comp. Olaf Breidbach, *Ernst Haeckel. Bildwelten der Natur*. Munich, Berlin, London: Prestel, 2006.

10   Semper, *Style* (see note 1), p. 181.

11   Aurel Kolnai, *On Disgust*, transl. by Elizabeth Kolnai et al. Chicago and La Salle, Illinois: Open Court, 2004, p. 50.

12   Jean-Paul Sartre, *Being and Nothingness. A Phenomenological Essay on Onthology*, transl. by Hazel E. Barnes. New York: Washington Square Press, 1992, p. 777f.

13   Roland Barthes, "Plastic", in: Barthes, *Mythologies*, transl. by Annette Lavers. New York: The Noonday Press, 1991, pp. 97–99, here p. 98f.

14   Hans Schwippert (ed.), *Darmstädter Gespräch. Mensch und Technik. Erzeugnis – Form – Gebrauch*. Darmstadt: Neue Darmstädter Verlags-Anstalt, 1952, pp. 83–86, p. 84f. Translation by R. H.

15   Louis I. Kahn, "I Love Beginnings" (1972), in: Alessandra Latour, ed., *Louis I. Kahn: Writings, Lectures, Interviews*. New York: Rizzoli, 1991, p. 288.

16   Ll. [Alfons Leitl], "Anmerkungen zur Zeit: Ende der Werkgerechtigkeit?" in: *Baukunst und Werkform*, 10/1952, p. 6. Translation by R. H.

17   Ibid.

18   Theodor W. Adorno, "Functionalism Today", transl. by Jane Newman and John Smith in: Peter Eisenman et al (eds.) *Oppositions 17*. Cambridge, Mass.: Institute for Architecture and Urban Studies and MIT Press, (Summer 1979), pp. 31–44.

19   Gio Ponti, *In Praise of Architecture,* transl. by Giuseppina and Maria Salvadori. New York: F.W. Dodge Corporation, 1960, p. 132.

20   Andrea Deplazes, "Wood: indifferent, synthetic, abstract – plastic. Prefabrication technology in timber construction", in: Deplazes, ed., *Constructing Architecture. Materials Processes Structures. A Handbook*. Basel, Boston, Berlin: Birkhäuser, 2005, pp. 77–81.

21   Julius Vischer, Ludwig Hilberseimer, *Beton als Gestalter. Bauten in Eisenbeton und ihre architektonische Gestaltung. Ausgeführte Eisenbetonbauten*. Stuttgart: Julius Hoffmann, 1928.

22   Jos[eph] Aug[ust] Lux, *Ingenieur-Ästhetik*. Munich: Gustav Lammers, 1910, p. 31. Translation by R. H.

23   Ibid., p. 46.

24   Ibid., p. 48.

25   Ibid., p. 49.

26   Ibid.

27   Sigfried Giedion, *Building in France, Building in Iron, Building in Ferroconcrete*, transl. by J. Duncan Berry. Los Angeles: Getty Center for the History of Art and the Humanities, 1995, p. 152.

28   Ibid., p. 53.

29   Francis S. Onderdonk, *The Ferro-Concrete Style. Reinforced Concrete in Modern Architecture*. New York: Architectural Publishing Company, 1928. Reprint Santa Monica: Hennessey + Ingalls, 1998.

30   The Einstein Tower was designed as a reinforced concrete structure but realized as a brick building covered in sprayed plaster due to the difficulty of executing the formwork.

31 István Medgyaszay, "Über die künstlerische Lösung des Eisenbetonbaues", in: *Bericht über den VIII. Internationalen Architekten-Kongress Wien 1908*. Vienna: Verlag von Anton Schroll & Co., pp. 538–554.

32 Dezső Malonyay (ed.), *A magyar nép művészete*. Volume I: *A kalotaszegi magyar nép művészete*. Budapest: Franklin-Társulat, 1907. Reprint Budapest: Helikon Kiadó, 1984.

33 Medgyaszay, "Über die künstlerische Lösung" (see note 31), p. 548.

34 For more on Medgyaszay's approach to architecture see Ákos Moravánszky, "'Die künstlerische Lösung des Eisenbetonbaues'. István Medgyaszays Architektur zwischen Wagnerschule und Nationalromantik", in: Antje Senarclens de Grancy, Heidemarie Uhl (eds.), *Moderne als Konstruktion. Debatten, Diskurse, Positionen um 1900*. Studien zur Moderne 14. Vienna: Passagen Verlag, 2001, pp. 135–152. Translation by R. H.

35 As, for example, in the title of the book by the important German engineer Gustav Adolf Wayss, *Das System Monier. Eisengerippe mit Cementumhüllung*. Vienna: In-house publ., 1887.

36 It has not yet been possible to ascertain whether Loos was aware of Gill's buildings or vice versa. Comp. Thomas S. Hines, *Irving Gill and the Architecture of Reform. A Study in Modernist Architectural Culture*. New York: The Monacelli Press, 2000, p. 132.

37 Richard Neutra, *Amerika: Die Stilbildung des Neuen Bauens in den Vereinigten Staaten*. Vienna: Anton Schroll, 1930, p. 8. Translation by R. H.

38 Thomas G. Poos, *Fonthill: The Home of Henry Chapman Mercer, An American Architectural Treasure*. 2nd Edition. Warminster, Pennsylvania: Manor House, 2008.

39 Julius Posener, *Vorlesungen zur Geschichte der Architektur*, Vol. 2: III, IV, V. Aachen: ARCH+ Verlag, 2013, p. 246.

40 Béla Sámsondi Kiss, *Szövetszerkezetes épületek*. Budapest: Műszaki Könyvkiadó, 1965.

41 Francisco Arques Soler, *Miguel Fisac*. Madrid: Ediciones Pronaos, 1996, p. 248.

42 Walter Pötscher, *Aspekte und Probleme der minoischen Religion. Ein Versuch*. Hildesheim, Zurich, New York: Georg Olms, 1990.

43 Adrian Stokes, *Stones of Rimini*. London: Faber & Faber, 1934. Reprint New York: Schocken, 1969, p. 164.

44 Ibid., p. 165.

45 Ibid., p. 166.

10.
IMMATERIALITY
AND FORMLESSNESS

Does the long process of the metamorphosis of form end with the literal "destruction of reality, of the material" (see p. 196) and its transformation into information? Long before the move from analog to digital modern science began to shift its attention from elementary material particles to the search for other immaterial fundamental entities such as symmetries, force fields or energy flows. This search was focused on primary organizational principles such as symmetry and proportion which occur naturally and also have aesthetic qualities. Modern art and architecture were also significantly emboldened by books such as *Symmetry* by the mathematician, physicist, and philosopher Hermann Weyl (1952).[1] We have already considered Gottfried Semper's Caribbean hut as a concrete early example of the materialization of the principles of dynamic transformation in human production: but as a diagram and not just as an object of sensory perception. This unmistakably represents a continuation of the Greek and, above all, the Platonic search for patterns of organization which requires a unifying examination of the phenomena.

The semiotic approach of postmodernism, its understanding of architecture as a carrier of meaning, has disregarded the specific materiality of objects. But even symbols have their materiality. The façade of the Road Transport Hall of the Swiss Museum of Transport in Lucerne by Annette Gigon and Mike Guyer (2005–2009) consists of a plethora of symbols: The skin of the façade is formed by hundreds of reflective signs mounted on a supporting frame – a "decorated shed", as defined by Robert Venturi; architecture as a carrier of meaning in the narrowest sense of the word.[2] The formal homogeneity of the surface conflicts crassly with the cacophony of meanings of the blue-and-white laminated aluminum signs. But the materiality of these signs seems even stronger; the graphic signs and symbols have become ornaments. So have they lost their meaning? This is a claim that we cannot make. The fact that certain signs (such as that for Route 66), are deliberately "false" for the sake of the onlooking children indicates that the primary semantic meaning of the signs for the observer has indeed been retained. [Fig. 10.1]

In Semper's account of material metamorphosis leather tubes become clay vessels, carpets become brick walls, and wooden triumphal arches become marble buildings or even frescoes. In his studies of polychromy he describes this latter metamorphosis as the elimination of matter: the transformation of real, technically-determined materiality into a representation thereof. He regards the layer of paint as the subtlest and most disembodied form of dressing which the ancients even applied to surfaces that we perceive as blank. "The color crust on marble temples has the appearance of a hard vitreous enamel a half-millimeter thick. [...] The places where the monument was supposed to appear white were by no means left bare, but were covered with a white paint."[3]

10.1 Swiss Museum of Transport, Lucerne. Gigon & Guyer, 2005–2009.

Semper's theories of *Stoffwechsel* and dressing opened the door for a large-scale reduction of the corporeal materiality of the façade and for its interpretation as a carrier of images and, later, as a medial interface. The idea that polychromy as a bearer of meaning was not only the most ephemeral layer of Greek marble façades but had also long since disappeared caused some of Semper's contemporaries to reflect. But Semper never made the claim attributed to him by Leo von Klenze, the court architect of King Ludwig I of Bavaria, that, according to his theory of *Stoffwechsel*, "from wood to metal, from metal to stone, from stone to stain and finally to immaterial color, Greek architecture must ultimately be known as the *Color Style*. This would achieve the spiritualizing reconciliation of structure and dressing, because the *immaterial crust of color* would be the *only solid thing* in the building."[4] Semper's theory sought to explain the relationship between pictorial quality and physicality rather than to speak of the complete dissolution of the material.

The dematerialization of architecture through the use of slender iron structures, which Semper regarded as a threat to architecture (see pp. 242–244), had

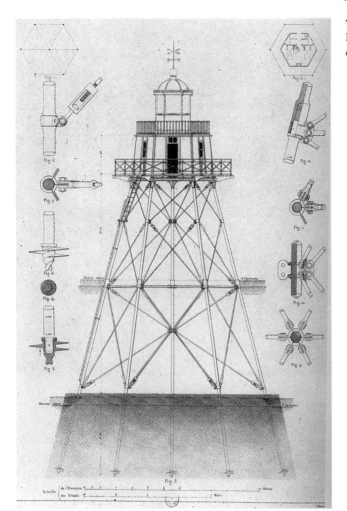

10.2 Walde Lighthouse, Léonce Reynaud, 1859, in Reynaud, *Traité d'architecture. Atlas*, Paris, 1875.

become a promising trend for many architects by the beginning of the 20th century. Hermann Muthesius is one of those who energetically countered the criticism of the immateriality of iron architecture: Semper's "habitual ideal was shaped by the fact that previous generations had built with materials which appeared solid, namely stone and wood; If slender metal bars had been available to them then slenderness would probably be regarded today as the norm and the ideal and solidity would be condemned as unaesthetic."[5] Muthesius points to the beauty of the bicycle: "[…] it is precisely the slenderness of the spokes that gives us this impression of delicacy and elegance."[6] In the mid-19th century the French architect Léonce Reynaud had already presented an extraordinarily filigree structure for lighthouses based on a combination of tensioning ropes and an iron frame in his book *Traité d'architecture*.[7] [Fig. 10.2] The change of attitude in favor of "slenderness" diagnosed by Muthesius is also illustrated by comparing the initial protests of French artists against the construction of the Eiffel Tower in Paris with the later transformation of the "ugly" iron framework into the city's most popular landmark. The support of Hendrik Petrus Berlage,

10.3 Nave of the Church of Notre-Dame du Travail, Paris-Montparnasse. Jules Astruc, 1899–1902.

Peter Behrens or Joseph August Lux for the monumental wrapping of iron construction cited above in the chapter on the theory of dressing (see p. 254) increasingly gave way to the approval of the aesthetic effect of lightness and delicacy. Like Berlage's Stock Exchange, the Church of Notre-Dame du Travail in Paris by Jules Astruc (1899–1902) exhibits the sought-after contrast between power and dematerialization: The Neo-Romanesque façade of brick and rubble gives no hint of the arcade of semi-circular arches made of slender iron profiles which lends the interior the appearance of a line-drawing of a vault. [Fig. 10.3]

Ephemeralization

While Muthesius regarded the filigree construction of the bicycle as expressing the new potential of modern industry, others soon saw the airplane as not only the fulfillment of a dream of flight stretching back across the centuries but also the "symbol of the new age" (Le Corbusier).[8] Flight had been given a boost by a new material: aluminum. Although this metal is an important component of clay it was the mid-19th century before it could be manufactured in a pure form for the first time.[9] Decorative objects made from aluminum alloys were displayed at the World Exposition in Paris in 1878, but industrial scale production was only made possible by the discovery of electrolysis in the 1880s. In the final years of the 19th century aluminum appeared in interiors, most particularly in the form of grilles to lifts and staircases (e.g. in the Monadnock

10.4 Portal of the *Die Zeit* news agency in Vienna, 1902. *Der Architekt*, 1902.
10.5 Glass wall to the staircase in Aarhus City Hall. Arne Jacobsen and Erik Møller, 1938–1941.

10.6 Stair with aluminum balustrade in the vestibule of the Postal Savings Bank in Vienna. Otto Wagner, 1903–1906.

Building by Burnham und Root, 1889–1892). Otto Wagner was the first to use aluminum for the design of structural elements such as columns and brackets, not only due to its lightness but mostly due to its silky-matt metallic surface which, unlike iron, requires no protection against corrosion. Wagner built the portal to the office of the *Die Zeit* news agency in Vienna (1902) entirely out of aluminum. [Fig. 10.4] The caps to the fixing bolts of the façade cladding of the Postal Savings Bank, the thin columns of the canopy, the cladding to the pillars in the banking hall, and, not least, the free-standing columns with the outlets for the air heating system were all made of aluminum. In the entrance hall to the Postal Savings Bank the fine, filigree elements of the aluminum balustrade provide a powerful contrast to the heavy, stereotomic stone construction of the walls to the staircase. [Fig. 10.6] For Wagner, the matt, silvery glow of the metal which, when illuminated, is capable of evoking spatial effects, is even more important than its lightness. He used aluminum fittings combined with dark stained beechwood, satin, and silk in items of furniture such as the armchairs for the boardroom of the Savings Bank (designed 1902, executed 1904). Ludwig

10.7 Aluminum portal to the Retti candle shop, Vienna. Hans Hollein, 1964/65.

Hevesi, the chronicler of the Secession, writes of aluminum as being the "dominant visible metal" in the building and that its use is "almost a good deed" because it "doesn't rust and hence doesn't need to be cleaned."[10] Hevesi highlighted the overall atmospheric effect: "The pillars which support the space, the rows of round radiators in the glass-ceilinged banking hall, the heating grilles, and the light fittings all shimmer in this same metallic silver-gray. This combines with the white tones of the building to create a harmonious whiteness throughout the spaces [...]."[11] Hans Hollein also had such atmospheric effects in mind when he used anodized aluminum in the Retti candle shop in Vienna (1964/65), albeit only in the form of a thin sheet which was perforated by small openings as a way of increasing the effectiveness of the lighting in the interior. [Fig. 10.7]

In the architecture of Wagner the practical advantages of aluminum, its lightness, hardness, and resistance against corrosion, were already inseparable from its aesthetic appeal. The smooth, shimmering surface of the metal is increasingly associated with technology and speed. From the airplane and the

10.8 Assembly of the Zeppelin
LZ 129, from Fritz August
Breuhaus de Groot, *Bauten und
Räume*. Berlin-Charlottenburg,
1935.
10.9 B-Deck of the Zeppelin LZ
129 with aluminum alloy furniture
and inclined Cellon windows,
from Fritz August Breuhaus de
Groot, *Bauten und Räume*. Berlin-
Charlottenburg, 1935.

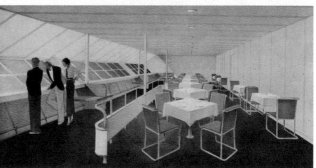

streamlined caravan to the suitcase, aluminum embodies the dream of travel.
The design of the interiors of *LZ 129 Hindenburg* (1933–1936), an airship with a
filigree duralumin skeleton and a length of 245 m, was the work of the architect
Fritz August Breuhaus de Groot. After years of experimentation he launched
the production of furniture built from a number of aluminum alloys "in
order to achieve the optimum in terms of lightness, stability, and comfort."[12]
[Figs. 10.8, 10.9]

While aluminum structures evolved in line with industrial, military, and
transportation needs, a parallel architectural debate developed around this

10.10 Glass cylinders in the *Lichte Erde – Gebrannte Erde* section of the exhibition *Deutsches Volk – Deutsche Arbeit* in Berlin, 1934, by Lilly Reich.
10.11 Tensegrity structure by Richard Buckminster Fuller from the exhibition *Your Private Sky* in Zurich, 2001.

issue of lightness. This was strongly influenced by the utopian crystal cult of the expressionists, the longing to escape the clutches of gravity, and the biological metaphor of the cellular membrane as the building envelope best able to serve the metabolism. In 1926 the former Bauhaus student Siegfried Ebeling published a slim volume entitled *Der Raum als Membran* (*Space as Membrane*) in which he relates his experiences in the research group of the aircraft manufacturer Hugo Junkers, which also developed lightweight methods for the construction of residential buildings. He describes the wall as a means of "climatological differentiation" between inside and outside.[13] The time is right, believed Ebeling, "for a methodical attempt to adapt three-dimensional space, as crudely defined by physics, into a three-dimensional membrane – biologically defined – between our body (as a plasmatic weak substance) and the latent minute forces of the spheres (which are as yet unharnessed by any bio-structure)."[14]

Ludwig Mies van der Rohe was a reader of Ebeling, whose comments about buildings as breathing organisms offered confirmation of his own reading of the works of other vitalist thinkers and, most particularly, of the biologist and natural and cultural philosopher Raoul Francé.[15] Impressed by these theories and, not least, by the new visual methods for representing space described by László Moholy-Nagy in his book *Von material zu architektur* (1929, first American edition: *The new vision: from material to architecture,* 1930), Mies van der Rohe exchanged classical tectonics for his own new vision. As early as 1924 he compared the "ponderous weight of Roman aqueducts" with the "spider-thin power system of a contemporary crane" or "dashing weightlessness of new ferroconcrete structures."[16] This development enabled the wall to increasingly dissolve into a transparent glass surface – up to the point of its very disappearance. His design for a reinforced concrete country house (1923) was an exercise in transforming the traditional structure of the house into a loose collection of vertical and horizontal planes. Mies van der Rohe's collaborator Lilly Reich was extremely interested in light, transparent materials and they jointly designed an exhibition installation for the glass and silk industries in 1927. Given the virtuosity with which this combined various levels of transparency, translucency, chrome shine and reflection, it can be viewed as a preliminary study for the German Pavilion in Barcelona (1929). Reich went on to place huge reflective glass cylinders at the heart of the glass, ceramics, and porcelain section of the exhibition *Deutsches Volk – Deutsche Arbeit* in Berlin in 1934. [Fig. 10.10]

The American inventor, entrepreneur, and visionary Richard Buckminster Fuller started work on his Dymaxion House in 1927. Like Le Corbusier, Fuller was inspired by developments in aircraft design. He used the term "ephemeralization" to describe the tendency towards increasingly slender structural members and an ever better "slenderness ratio."[17] A highpoint in reduction and weightlessness is represented by Fuller's tensegrity structures whose apparently floating struts do not come into contact with each other because they are held in place by fine cables. [Fig. 10.11] Despite their logic these structures seem magical, almost intangible, the struts appearing to float weightlessly in space. In his poetic text "Intuition" (which was also the name that he gave to his sloop). Fuller wrote about the metaphysical reasons for his search for the ephemeral: "the more-with-lessing / Constitutes ever-increasing mastery / Of the physical behaviors of Universe / By the metaphysically operative verb / Mind […]."[18]

For the conservative art historian Hans Sedlmayr the lightness of the modern, its "Denial of the Earth Base", was like an "Attack on Architecture."[19] In his book *Verlust der Mitte* (1948, translated as *Art in Crisis: The Lost Centre*) he writes that the first, still unconscious "Revolution against Architecture", that he identified in the "anti-architectural" designs of spherical buildings by Ledoux and Boullée, was followed by the second: the floating spherical buildings of the utopias of the Russian architects of the revolutionary era. He sees this tendency everywhere in modern architecture. Le Corbusier's Villa Savoye "resting on its supports upon the lawn suggests a space-ship that has just landed. His floating

10.12 Guggenheim Museum in Bilbao. Frank Gehry, 1993–1997.

houses seem to become ever lighter towards their base" for which only "the most insubstantial reasons are given."[20]

The phenomenon that Sedlmayr criticized as the result of revolutions against architecture was described by the art historian Kurt W. Forster in 2004 as "the incessant erosion of the idealized solidity of architecture." As the curator of the 9th Architecture Biennale in Venice – which he entitled *Metamorph* – Forster alluded to the proliferation of computer-generated forms at the end of the Millennium as testimony to a light and transformable architecture. He regards

Frank O. Gehry's Guggenheim Museum in Bilbao (1993–1997), which is often cited as an example of the use of the CATIA software of an aircraft manufacturer, as the best evidence of this development, despite the fact that the form of the building was developed quite traditionally with the help of freehand sketches.[21] The volume of the museum is covered with a thin titanium skin – a moving, animated form reminiscent of the dresses of the women in Botticelli's *Primavera*. [Fig. 10.12]

Immateriality

Much discussed in recent decades in the fields of art and architecture, the subject of immateriality draws together a number of tendencies. It relates to "paper architecture" and the designs of the 1970s which were never intended for realization, the communicative and medial dimension of architecture or immersive, atmospheric spectacularizations. In a broader sense, the above-discussed subjects of lightness and transparency – as represented, for example, by high-tech architecture, the Guggenheim Museum in Bilbao or the structures of engineers seeking to minimize material cross-sections – are also perceived as embodying this tendency to immateriality. In speaking of a "virtualization of matter" the Argentinian designer, painter, and theorist Tomás Maldonado is primarily referring to the growing separation between surface appearance and deep structure.[22] Hence, the term "immateriality" is misleading because – as demonstrated by the examples mentioned above – although material may be reduced in quantity, there is no sense in which it disappears. Rather, it intensifies in significance as its structural performance becomes more significant.

The exhibition *Les Immatériaux*, curated by the French philosopher and theorist Jean-François Lyotard, was held at the Centre Georges Pompidou in Paris in 1985. In describing the exhibition concept Lyotard referred to the extent to which new materials had altered man's relationship with matter: "New materials, in a wide meaning of the term, are not merely materials which are new. They question the idea of man as a being who works, who plans and who remembers: the idea of an author."[23] The notion of matter no longer refers to natural materials which man uses and processes for specific ends. According to Lyotard, electronic methods of payment, serial music, and minimalism in art provide confirmation that the "model of matter" is being increasingly replaced by the "model of language": "The principle on which the operational structure is based is not that of a stable 'substance', but that of an unstable ensemble of interactions."[24]

Today, immateriality is being investigated on two fronts: The first issue is protected space, the construction of which was long considered to be the most important task of architecture. However, a feeling of security can no longer be achieved by walls, ceilings, and door locks alone. Computer viruses or electromagnetic waves require immaterial protective mechanisms. Does this mean that we have to rethink the concept of the "defensible space"? The second issue is the historic development of the architectural profession which, isolated from the materiality of the building site, is increasingly occupied with the design of atmospheres and surfaces. But when the British architect and architectural his-

häufung (haufwerk)

der vierte oft schwer bestimmbare materialzustand ist die regelmäßige, rytmisch
gegliederte oder unregelmäßige häufung. sie ist meist leicht veränderbar.
organische zusammenhänge sind bei häufungen schwer festzustellen; als ganzes
sind sie nicht syntese, sondern addierung. oft sind sie mit „faktur" verwandt,
so daß an sich nichts dagegen spricht, die häufung (das haufwerk) zum zwecke
einer vereinfachung dieser begriffswelt faktur zu nennen. (abb. **32—40**)

es wird nicht behauptet, daß mit der definition der struktur, textur, faktur usw.
eine endgültige formulierung für diese begriffe gelungen ist. es war jedoch
nötig, bei einem pädagogischen vorgehen den versuch dazu zu machen, da sie
bisher gänzlich unfixiert waren.

10.13 Massing (*Häufung*) Old
car tyres. Page from László
Moholy-Nagy, *Von material zu
architektur*, Munich, 1929.

foto: weltspiegel

abb. 32 häufung (faktur)
alte autoreifen

48

torian Jonathan Hill uses this premise as the starting point for drawing up his
"Index of Immaterial Architectures" he lists headings such as acrylic yarn and
aluminum, fireworks, fabric, Nordic Light, and even weather and cloud, all of
which are unthinkable without matter.[25]

Informe: Matter without form

In *The new vision: from material to architecture* Moholy-Nagy presents a heap
of old car tires as an example of 'massing', a material condition which is difficult
to define and comparable with mud bubbling from a volcano in New Zealand
or a sea of open umbrellas.[26] [Fig. 10.13] Formlessness, despite being open to
Kolnai or Sartre's allegation of disgusting sliminess, became a program – which
was first labeled "*informe*" by the French philosopher Georges Bataille in 1929
and then emerged in the 1990s as a central category of postmodern artistic
theory.[27] Forged as a weapon against idealism, but equally deployable against
the idealization of material, Bataille saw formless matter as a sort of waste that,
as an amorphous, mud-like mass of matter, could not be shaped into an image.
As with all concepts critical of art, formlessness was of course immediately

10.14 Remote Material Deposition. Installation, Sitterwerk, St. Gallen.
Gramazio & Kohler, 2014.

absorbed by art. In their publication *Formless*, which appeared in 1997, Yve-Alain Bois and Rosalind E. Krauss write that the operative, performative power of the formless is necessary if one is to understand the artistic practice of Lucio Fontana or Robert Morris.[28]

The term "formless", which strips material of any constructive role, is a difficult one for design and architecture. The exhibition *Formless Furniture* in Vienna's Museum of Applied Arts (2008) offered unmistakable proof of the fact that armchairs by Frank Gehry, Karim Rashid or Gaetano Pesce, produced by exclusive furniture makers, have virtually nothing to do with the artistic concept of formlessness.[29]

In architecture, even the very latest mechanical production processes seem unable to produce more than the apparently archaic, amorphous masses of matter exemplified by the products of the Remote Material Deposition process developed by Gramazio Kohler Architects: A computer-controlled launching device hurls clay projectiles towards predetermined spatial positions where the projectiles should amalgamate to create a wall. The structure is continually measured as it rises and the control mechanism adapted accordingly. [Fig. 10.14]

In this way, digital technologies are paradoxically fulfilling Bataille's wish for

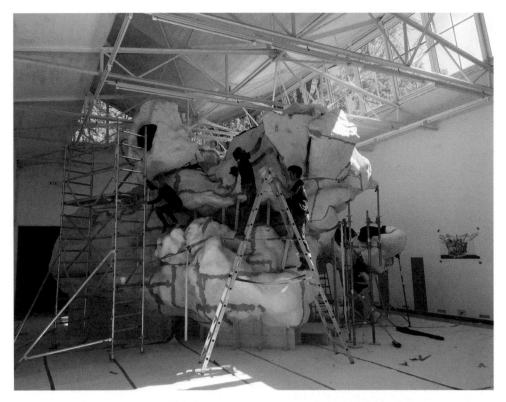

10.15 Installation of the concrete elements of *Incidental Space* in the Swiss Pavilion of the Architecture Biennale in Venice in May 2016. Architect: Christian Kerez, engineer: Joseph Schwartz.

a primary, iconoclastic, "ontological" materiality. Launching devices transfer material to a pile which appears excessively "thrown together", despite the precision of the producing technology. *Incidental Space* by Christian Kerez, the Swiss contribution to the Architecture Biennale in Venice in 2016, is a further radical attempt to address this contradiction. In the atelier, which was "more like a kitchen or a chemistry laboratory than an architectural workshop", the architect and his students sought spatial forms – *objet trouvés*, waste – which were then cast in plaster. The spatial figure which was eventually selected was then scanned and, after being scaled, the elements of formwork were pressed and machined.[30] The result was an empty, amorphous concrete object which awakened associations with, primarily, natural forms (cocoon, cave) – as well as with the work of artists such as Fontana or architects such as Frederick Kiesler. [Fig. 10.15] In the context of a Biennale whose title, *Reporting from the Front*, had been selected by the curator Alejandro Aravena with a view to addressing issues such as ecology, migration or the housing crisis, this contribution met with a widespread lack of understanding. And yet Kerez succeeded in steering attention towards the real expertise of the architect: towards the knowledge of how to manufacture things technically, towards the mastery of practical aesthetics in the Semperian sense. This does not mean that current political issues should be ignored. Like input from engineering and the fine arts, these feature amongst Semper's "external influences" that shape the position of the artist. But the considerable intellectual and material resources invested in the realization of *Incidental Space* are reason enough for not dismissing the result as "formless".

Material ecstasies: Atmospheres

The popular success of immersive artistic environments which work with all the senses such as Peter Zumthor's thermal baths in Vals, Diller + Scofidio's Blur Building (known as "the cloud") at Expo 02 in Yverdon-les-Bains, Ólafur Eliasson's *Weather Project* in London's Tate Modern (2003) or Philippe Rahm's *Digestible Gulf Stream* at the Architecture Biennale in Venice (2008) demonstrates the growing interest in natural phenomena as installations, in atmospheres established by diffuse arrangements which surround the body. In the psychological aesthetic of the 19th century the term "empathy" signified the projection of the feelings of the viewer onto the work of art. It was as if the object was imbued with a real spirit, a form of sympathy between the viewer and the viewed. [Fig. 10.16]

Atmospheres are not subjective moods: As substances which surround and touch us and which we even inhale, they are part of reality.[31] This is why the German philosopher Gernot Böhme, who has dedicated a number of essays to the phenomenon of atmospheres, also speaks of "quasi-objective feelings". In his text "On Synesthesia" he defines atmosphere as the "primary and, to a certain degree, basic object of perception," as the totality "in which all particulars are embedded in which one is able to focus, depending upon the degree of attentiveness and analysis."[32] We can describe that collective act of projection in which society reacts to artifacts by establishing a form of atmospheric space as "social empathy". This is rooted in the political and cultural spheres of a particular age. One reason for the popularity of atmospheres is certainly the potential for dependency set free by always perfect virtual spaces, 3-D projections, and data glasses. The German philosopher Peter Sloterdijk suspects that there is an even deeper connection between the new awareness of atmosphere and the condition of "being-in-the-world" in the technological age.[33] Sloterdijk claims that philosophers have been preoccupied to date with objects and subjects and have hardly noticed that we find ourselves within atmospheric bubbles, globes and foam. Having only been made aware of this condition by the environmental and banking crises we are participants in a collective experiment of global dimensions whose initial hypotheses, arrangements, and relationships are not clear to us.[34] Subterranean spaces are particularly suitable for atmospheric installations because descending into the underworld is already understood as a departure from the everyday. This explains the enormous success of spectacular immersive productions in new metro stations with dynamic lighting effects generated by computer-controlled LED lights. [Fig. 10.17]

Atmosphere and climate are natural categories but also possess other – social and cultural – meanings. This is why many find that the aesthetic of atmo-

10.16 The Blur Building media pavilion of Expo 02 in Yverdon-les-Bains.
Diller Scofidio + Renfro, 2002.

spheres is a suitable way of preparing the ground for a more responsible use
of resources. Böhme writes of an "ecological aesthetics of nature", while Rahm
wants to see architecture as a "new atmosphere and second meteorology", as
the creator of objective, open places "where new social and political relationships can be invented."[35] But is the diffuse "blur", a fusion of esoteric categories
of the immaterial and the atmospheric, truly the medium that will facilitate
the encounter between the subject and the world? As a design task, immersive

materiality must always be confronted with the question of whether this inhalable architecture will allow a perceptive subject to keep a critical distance. Semper's haze of carnival candles as the "true atmosphere of art" and the related concept of the total work of art may signify an interaction between reality and illusion and life and art but not a complete virtualization of reality.

The history of technology as the history of culture

For Semper – the architect, builder of barricades, and political refugee from Germany – the Crystal Palace was the prototype for all future shopping malls. For most visitors, the space below the glazed arch represented the fulfillment of their erotic fantasies, their dreams of colonial domination and technical utopias. In short, it was the image of a globalized world. Scarcely any other heterotopia of this period could have demostrated Semper's ideas more convincingly than the Crystal Palace, whose space ennobled the industrially produced goods with an anthropologically devised family tree.

In 2002, 150 years after the opening of the "Great Exhibition" in London, Jeffrey Kipnis, the curator of the exhibition *Mood River* in Columbus, Ohio, regarded the flow of goods as signifying, above all, abundance. As early as the 1970s, voices amongst Italian architects and designers were already announcing the end of the aesthetic that saw "good form" as the fulfillment of the expectations that had been formulated by the representatives of the Werkbund and functionalism. Emilio Ambasz, curator of the exhibition *Italy: The New Domestic Revolution* (1972) in the Museum of Modern Art in New York, assumed that visitors accustomed to the clear, fixed form of the object might be disturbed by the new "environmental ensembles" whose novel materiality permitted constant metamorphoses and an openness to a range of uses.[36] The organizers of *Mood River* believed that everything was connected by a "vibratory mesh [...] the continuum of resonance" that, despite its apparent discontinuities, creates a "living order larger than meets the eye."[37] The transformation of such objects as toothbrushes, razors, training shoes, lights, surfboards, airplanes or even architectures are unrelated to the circumstances of their manufacture. Their forms are controlled by – and should awaken – feelings. To this extent, the idea corresponds with psychological concepts such as formal desire or empathy which can be traced back to Alois Riegl.[38]

"Omnia mutantur, nihil interit", everything changes, nothing perishes. There is no discipline in which this phrase, which Ovid puts in the mouth of Pythagoras in the final book of the Metamorphoses, is more valid than in architecture. From the pyramids to the door handle we perceive the work of architects as immobile and static, but these are the products of a constant process of transformation, driven by networks of organic and inorganic matter, energy or culture, which pervade and shape cities. Whether waste disposal systems or electric cars, flows of migrants or political demonstrations, global warming or advertising campaigns – these are all factors in the large-scale process of metamorphism of cities and regions. This process also includes destruction, but this is creative destruction in line with Justus von Liebig's characterization of natural metabolism. It is different from nature due to the fact

10.17 Robert Wilson, *By the Sea ... You and me*. Digital print on a lenticular panel with LED lighting, 2012. Toledo metro station in Naples, architect Oscar Tusquets Blanca.

that these transformations are consciously and actively controlled. Semper's emphasis of this difference is proof of his modernity. His theory should provide the foundation for shaping the "free creations of man", which also requires "understanding, observation of nature, genius, will, knowledge, and power."[39] (see p. 176)

For Semper, history was not just about the past but also about the material that the makers of basic objects of use – regardless of whether these were chairs or houses – had had to understand in order to ensure that they produced more than mere meaningless things. In this context, however, 'understand' referred not to the ability to be able to position something chronologically in the history of evolution but to a detailed knowledge of the concrete manufacturing process. The misunderstandings regarding Semper's "materialism" relate to the lack of recognition and appreciation of the materiality of the objects and yet they also demonstrate the almost subconscious suppression of such knowledge by the representatives of the modern scientific approach. This scientific approach is afraid of matter because it lacks the terms and the concepts with which to discuss it. In turn, Semper's idea of culture, his "practical aesthetic", disregards the fine arts which are celebrated elsewhere as our greatest cultural achievement and speaks instead of the aesthetic of technically produced objects. Learning from Semper does not mean proposing his theory of *Stoffwechsel* as the basis for new analog or digital design strategies. The important thing is the task that he set himself: the shaping of a way of observing the continuum of history which, rather than excluding technology, examines this in synthesis with culture. Contrary to C.P. Snow's assertion that the "two cultures" of the sciences and the humanities are a diametric opposition, it is precisely at the interfaces that we should expect to find the new ideas which will enrich our culture.[40]

Notes

1   Hermann Weyl, *Symmetry*. Princeton, New Jersey: Princeton University Press, 1952.

2   Robert Venturi, Denise Scott Brown, Steven Izenour, *Learning from Las Vegas. The Forgotten Symbolism of Architectural Form*. Revised edition. Cambridge, Mass.: The MIT Press, 1979.

3   Gottfried Semper, "Preliminary Remarks on Polychrome Architecture and Sculpture in Antiquity" (1834), in: Semper, *The Four Elements of Architecture and Other Writings*, transl. by Harry Francis Mallgrave and Wolfgang Herrmann. Cambridge: Cambridge University Press, 1989, pp. 45–73, here p. 59.

4   *Bayerische Staatsbibliothek München, Klenzeana I/12*, p. 123. Quoted from Adrian von Buttlar, "Die Unterhose als formgebendes Prinzip? Klenzes Kritik an Sempers 'Stil'", in: Heidrun Laudel, Cornelia Wenzel (eds.), *Stilstreit und Einheitskunstwerk. Internationales Historismus-Symposium Bad Muskau 20. bis 22. Juni 1997*. Dresden: Verlag der Kunst, 1998, pp. 185–194, here p. 193. Translation by R. H.

5   Hermann Muthesius, "Das Formproblem im Ingenieurbau", in: *Jahrbuch des Deutschen Werkbundes 1913: Die Kunst in Industrie und Handel*. Jena: Eugen Diederichs, 1913, pp. 23–32, here p. 26. Translation by R. H.

6   Ibid.

7   Léonce Reynaud, *Traité d'architecture. Première partie: Art de batir. Études sur les matériaux de construction et les éléments des édifices*. 4th Edition. Paris: Dunod, 1875, Plate 79.

8   Le Corbusier, *Aircraft*. London, New York: The Studio Publications, 1935. Reprint Milan: Editrice Abitare Segesta, 1996.

9   Robert Friedel, "A New Metal! Aluminum in its 19th-Century Context", in: Sarah Nichols (ed.), *Aluminum by Design*. Exhibition Catalog. Pittsburgh, Pennsylvania: Carnegie Museum of Art. New York: Harry N. Abrams, 2000, pp. 58–83.

10   Ludwig Hevesi, "Der Neubau der Postsparkasse", in Hevesi, *Altkunst–Neukunst. Wien 1894–1908*. Ed. Otto Breicha. Vienna: Carl Konegen, 1909. Reprint Klagenfurt: Ritter Verlag, 1986, pp. 245–248, here p. 246.

11   Ibid.

12   Fritz August Breuhaus de Groot, *Bauten und Räume*. Berlin-Charlottenburg: Verlag Ernst Wasmuth, 1935, p. 144. Translation by R. H.

13   Siegfried Ebeling, *Space as Membrane*, ed. Spyros Papapetros, transl. by Pamela Johnston. London: Architectural Association, 2010.

14   Ibid., p. 16.

15   R[aoul] H[einrich] Francé, *Die Pflanze als Erfinder*. Stuttgart: Kosmos, 1920.

16   Ludwig Mies von der Rohe, "Building Art and the Will of the Epoch!" in: *Der Querschnitt 4*, 1924, no 1, pp. 31–32. Reprinted in: Fritz Neumeyer, *The Artless Word. Mies van der Rohe on the Building Art*, transl. by Mark Jarzombek. Cambridge, Mass., London: The MIT Press, 1991, pp. 245–247, here p. 245.

17   The Greek word *ephemeros* means "one day long".

18   R[ichard] Buckminster Fuller, *Intuition*. Garden City, New York: Doubleday & Company, 1972, p. 52f.

19   Hans Sedlmayr, *Art in Crisis. The Lost Centre*, transl. by Brian Battershaw. London: Hollis and Carter, 1957, pp. 104–108, here p. 104.

20   Ibid., p. 107.

21   Mark Rappolt, Robert Violette (ed.), *Gehry Draws*. London: Violette Editions, 2004.

22   Tomás Maldonado, *Reale e virtuale*. Milan: Feltrinelli, 1993.

23   Jean-François Lyotard, "Les Immatériaux", transl. by Paul Smith in: Reesa Greenburg, Bruce W Ferguson, Sandy Nairne (eds.), *Thinking about Exhibitions*. London, New York: Routledge 1996, pp. 159–173, here p. 159.

24   Ibid., p. 164.

25   Jonathan Hill, *Immaterial Architecture*. London, New York: Routledge, 2006.

26   László Moholy-Nagy, *The New Vision 1928 fourth revised edition 1947 and Abstract of an Artist*, transl. by Daphne M. Hoffman. New York: George Wittenborn, 1947, p. 27.

27   Georges Bataille, *Visions of Excess. Selected Writings, 1927–1939*, ed. Allan Stoekl. Minneapolis: Minnesota University Press, 1985.

28   Yve-Alain Bois, Rosalind Krauss, *Formless. A User's Guide*. New York: Zone Books, 1997. Comp. Georges Didi-Huberman, *Ähnlichkeit und Berührung. Archäologie, Anachronismus und Modernität des Abdrucks*. Cologne: DuMont, 1999, p. 196.

29   Peter Noever (ed.), *Formless Furniture*, Exhibition Catalogue. Vienna: MAK, Ostfildern: Hatje Cantz, 2009.

30   "Eine gefundene Raumfigur", Interview of Hubertus Adam by Christian Kerez, in: *TEC21*, 142, Volume 23 (3rd June 2016), pp. 22–24.

31   Ákos Moravánszky, "Architectures to be Inhaled. Constructing the Ephemeral", in: Carsten Ruhl, Chris Dähne and Rixt Hoekstra (eds.), *The Death and Life of the Total Work of Art. Henry van de Velde and the Legacy of a Modern Concept*. Berlin: Jovis Verlag, 2015, pp. 226–242.

32   Gernot Böhme, "On Synesthesia", in: Böhme, *The Aesthetics of Atmospheres*. Abingdon, New York: Routledge, 2017.

33   Peter Sloterdijk, *Spheres*. Los Angeles: Semiotext(e), Volume 1: 2011; Volume 2: 2014; Volume 3: 2016; Sloterdijk, *Terror from the Air*. Los Angeles, Semiotext(e), 2009.

34   Peter Sloterdijk, "Atmospheric islands", in Sloterdijk, *Spheres*, Volume 3 (see note 33).

35   Gernot Böhme, *Für eine ökologische Naturästhetik*. Frankfurt am Main: Suhrkamp, 1993; Philippe Rahm, "Thermodynamic Architecture" in *ACADIA 08 › Silicon + Skin › Biological Processes and Computation (Proceedings of the 28th Annual Conference of the Association for Computer Aided Design in Architecture, Minneapolis, Minnesota, 2008)*, pp. 46–51, here p. 47.

36   Emilio Ambasz, *Introduction*, in: Ambasz (ed.), *Italy: The New Domestic Revolution. Achievements and Problems of Italian Design*. Exhibition Catalogue. New York: The Museum of Modern Art, 1972.

37   Sanford Kwinter, "Hydraulic Vision", in: *Mood River*. Exhibition Catalogue. Columbus, Ohio: Wexner Center for the Arts, 2002, p. 33.

38   Chee Pearlman, "Designing Desire", in: *Mood River* (see note 37), pp. 46–48.

39   Gottfried Semper, "On Architectural Styles. A Lecture Delivered at the Rathaus in Zurich" (1869), in Semper, *The Four Elements* (see note 3), pp. 265–284, here p. 268.

40   C[harles] P[ercy] Snow, *The Two Cultures*. London: Cambridge University Press, 1959. p. 3.

BIBLIOGRAPHY

Stan Allen, Marc McQuade (eds.), *Landform Building: Architecture's New Terrain*. Baden: Lars Müller Publishers, 2011.

Günter Bandmann, "Bemerkungen zu einer Ikonologie des Materials", in: *Städel-Jahrbuch, Neue Folge*, Volume 2. Munich: Prestel Verlag, 1969, pp. 75–100.

Günter Bandmann, "Der Wandel der Materialbewertung in der Kunsttheorie des 19. Jahrhunderts", in: Helmut Koopmann, J. Adolf Schmoll gen. Eisenwerth (eds.), *Beiträge zur Theorie der Künste im 19. Jahrhundert*, Volume 1. Frankfurt am Main: Vittorio Klostermann, 1971, pp. 129–157.

Michael Bell, Jeannie Kim (eds.), *Engineered Transparency. The Technical, Visual, and Spatial Effects of Glass*. New York: Princeton Architectural Press, 2009.

Michael Bell, Craig Buckley (eds.), *Solid States. Concrete in Transition*. New York: Princeton Architectural Press, 2010.

Michael Bell, Craig Buckley (eds.), *Post-Ductility. Metals in Architecture and Engineering*. New York: Princeton Architectural Press, 2012.

Michael Bell, Craig Buckley (eds.), *Permanent Change. Plastics in Architecture and Engineering*. New York: Princeton Architectural Press, 2014.

Jane Bennett, *Vibrant Matter. A Political Ecology of Things*. Durham, London: Duke University Press, 2010.

Ernst Bloch, *Die Lehren von der Materie*. Frankfurt am Main: Suhrkamp Verlag, 1972.

Gernot Böhme, *The Aesthetics of Atmospheres*. Abingdon, New York: Routledge, 2017.

Hartmut Böhme (ed.), *Die Elemente der Kunst*. Paragrana. Internationale Zeitschrift für Historische Anthropologie, Volume 5. Berlin: Akademie Verlag, 1996.

Yve-Alain Bois, Rosalind Krauss, *Formless. A User's Guide*. New York: Zone Books, 1997.

Karl Bötticher, *Die Tektonik der Hellenen*, 2 Volumes. Potsdam: Verlag von Ferdinand Riegel, 1852.

Gail Peter Borden, Michael Meredith (eds.), *Matter: Material Processes in Architectural Production*. London, New York: Routledge, 2012.

Martin Bressani, *Architecture and the Historical Imagination. Eugène-Emmanuel Viollet-le-Duc, 1814–1879*. Farnham: Ashgate, 2014.

Giuliana Bruno, *Surface. Matters of Aesthetics, Materiality, and Media*. Chicago, London: University of Chicago Press, 2014.

Victor Buchli, *An Anthropology of Architecture*. London, New York: Bloomsbury Publishing, 2013.

Roger Caillois, *Pierres*. Paris: Gallimard, 1983.

Roger Caillois, *The Writing of Stones*, transl. by Barbara Bray. Charlottesville: University of Virginia Press, 1985.

Adélaïde de Caters, *El despertar de la materia. Aalto, Eisenstein y Proust*. Madrid: Fundación Caja de Arquitectos, 2007.

Charles Chipiez, *Histoire critique des origines et de la formation des ordres grecs*. Paris: Ve A. Morel & Cie, 1876.

Luisa Collina, Cino Zucchi (eds.), *Sempering. Process and Pattern in Architecture and Design*. Milan: Silvana Editoriale, 2016.

Yves Delemontey, *Reconstruire la France. L'aventure du béton assemblé 1940–1955*. Paris: Éditions de la Villette, 2015.

Andrea Deplazes (ed.), *Constructing Architecture. Materials Processes Structures. A Handbook*, 1st Edition. Basel, Boston, Berlin: Birkhäuser, 2005.

Georges Didi-Huberman, "Die Ordnung des Materials", in: *Vorträge aus dem Warburg-Haus*, Volume 3. Berlin: Akademie-Verlag, 1999, pp. 1–29.

Wolfgang Drechsler, Peter Weibel (eds.), *Bildlicht. Malerei zwischen Material und Immaterialität*. Vienna: Europaverlag, 1991.

Caroline van Eck, *Organicism in nineteenth-century architecture. An inquiry into its theoretical and philosophical background*. Amsterdam: Architectura & Natura Press, 1994.

Klaus Eggert, "Gottfried Semper, Carl von Hasenauer", in: Ulrike Planner-Steiner, Klaus Eggert, *Friedrich von Schmidt, Gottfried Semper, Carl von Hasenauer*. Wiesbaden: Franz Steiner Verlag, 1978, pp. 73–225.

Beate Ermacora, Helen Hirsch, Magdalena Holzhey (eds.), *The Forces Behind the Forms: Geology, Matter, Process in Contemporary Art*. Cologne: Snoeck Verlagsgesellschaft, 2015.

Fernando Espuelas, *Madre Materia*. Madrid: Lampreave, 2009.

Giovanni Fanelli, Roberto Gargiani, *Il principio del rivestimento. Prolegomena a una storia dell'architettura contemporanea*. Bari: Laterza & Figli, 1994.

Marco Ferrari, *Architettura e materia. Realtà della forma costruita nell'epoca dell'immateriale*. Macerata: Quodlibet, 2013.

Banister F. Fletcher, *The Influence of Material on Architecture*. London: B. T. Batsford, 1897.

Edward R. Ford, *The Architectural Detail*. New York: Princeton Architectural Press, 2011.

Adrian Forty, *Concrete and Culture. A Material History*. London: Reaktion Books, 2012.

Kenneth Frampton, *Studies in Tectonic Culture: The Poetics of Construction in Nineteenth and Twentieth Century Architecture*. Cambridge, Mass., London: The MIT Press, 1995.

Matthias Frehner, Daniel Spanke (eds.), *Stein aus Licht. Kristallvisionen in der Kunst.* Exhibition Catalog. Kunstmuseum Bern, Bielefeld: Kerber Verlag, 2015.

Christian Fuhrmeister, *Beton Klinker Granit – Material Macht Politik: Eine Materialikonographie.* Berlin: Verlag Bauwesen, 2001.

Maurizio Gargano, *Forma e materia. Ratiocinatio e fabrica nell'architettura dell'età moderna.* Rome: Officina Edizoni, 2006.

Roberto Gargiani (ed.), *La colonne. Nouvelle histoire de la construction.* Lausanne: Presses polytechniques et universitaires romandes, 2008.

Roberto Gargiani, Anna Rosellini, *Le Corbusier. Béton Brut and Ineffable Space, 1940–1965. Surface Materials and Psychophysiology of Vision.* Lausanne: EPFL Press, 2011.

Roberto Gargiani (ed.), *L'architrave, le plancher, la plate-forme. Nouvelle histoire de la construction.* Lausanne: Presses polytechniques et universitaires romandes, 2012.

Sigfried Giedion, *Building in France, Building in Iron, Building in Ferroconcrete,* transl. by J. Duncan Berry. Los Angeles: Getty Center for the History of Art and the Humanities, 1995.

Ulrich Giersch, Ulrich Kubisch, *Gummi – Die elastische Faszination.* Berlin: Nicolai, 1995.

Michael Gnehm, *Stumme Poesie. Architektur und Sprache bei Gottfried Semper.* Zurich: gta Verlag, 2004.

Michael Gnehm, "Bekleidungstheorie" and "Stoffwechseltheorie", in: *ARCH+* 221 (Winter 2015), Special Issue "Tausendundeine Theorie", pp. 33–39, pp. 155–157.

Gramazio & Kohler, *The Robotic Touch. How Robots Change Architecture.* Zurich: Park Books, 2014.

Fabio Gramazio, Matthias Kohler, Silke Langenberg (eds.), *Fabricate: Negotiating Design & Making.* Zurich: gta Verlag, 2014.

Paul M. Graves-Brown (ed.), *Matter, Materiality and Modern Culture.* London, New York: Routledge, 2000.

Alfred C. Haddon, *Evolution in Art as Illustrated by the Life-Histories of Designs.* London: Walter Scott, 1895.

Penny Harvey, Eleanor Conlin Casella, Gillian Evans, Hannah Knox et al., *Objects and Materials: A Routledge Companion.* London, New York: Routledge, 2014.

Joseph Hanimann, *Vom Schweren. Ein geheimes Thema der Moderne.* Munich, Vienna: Carl Hanser Verlag, 1999.

Karin Harather, *Haus-Kleider. Zum Phänomen der Bekleidung in der Architektur.* Vienna, Cologne, Weimar: Böhlau-Verlag, 1995.

Ariane Lourie Harrison (ed.), *Architectural Theories of the Environment: Posthuman Theory.* Abingdon: Routledge, 2013.

Uta Hassler, Christoph Rauhut (eds.), *Bautechnik des Historismus. Von den Theorien über gotische Konstruktion bis zu den Baustellen des 19. Jahrhunderts.* Munich: Hirmer Verlag, 2012.

Uta Hassler (ed.), *Der Lehrbuchdiskurs über das Bauen.* Zurich: Hochschulverlag AG an der ETH Zürich, 2015.

Wolfgang Herrmann, *Gottfried Semper. Theoretischer Nachlass an der ETH Zürich. Katalog und Kommentare.* Basel, Boston, Stuttgart: Birkhäuser Verlag, 1981.

Wolfgang Herrmann, *Gottfried Semper: In Search of Architecture.* Cambridge, Mass.: The MIT Press, 1984.

Jonathan Hill, *Immaterial Architecture.* London, New York: Routledge, 2006.

Francesca Hughes, *The Architecture of Error: Matter, Measure, and the Misadventures of Precision.* Cambridge, Mass.: The MIT Press, 2014.

Yuk Hui, Andreas Broeckmann (eds.), *30 Years After Les Immatériaux. Art, Science, and Theory.* Lüneburg: meson press, without year [2015].

Mari Hvattum, *Gottfried Semper and the Problem of Historicism.* Cambridge: Cambridge University Press, 2004.

Oscar Rueda Jiménez, *Bekleidung. Los trajes de la arquitectura.* Barcelona: Edición Fundación Arquia, 2015.

Sigrid G. Köhler, Hania Siebenpfeiffer, Martina Wagner-Egelhaaf (eds.), *Materie. Grundlagentexte zur Theoriegeschichte.* Frankfurt am Main: Suhrkamp Verlag, 2013.

Susanne Küchler, Daniel Miller (eds.), *Clothing as Material Culture.* Oxford, New York: Berg, 2005.

Petra Lange-Berndt (ed.), *Materiality.* Documents of Contemporary Art. London: Whitechapel Gallery, Cambridge, Mass.: The MIT Press, 2015.

Heidrun Laudel, *Gottfried Semper. Architektur und Stil.* Dresden: Verlag der Kunst, 1991.

David Leatherbarrow, Mohsen Mostafavi, *Surface Architecture.* Cambridge, Mass.: The MIT Press, 2002.

Joseph August Lux, *Ingenieur-Aesthetik.* Munich: Verlag von Gustav Lammers, 1910.

Jean-François Lyotard, *Immaterialität und Postmoderne,* transl. into German by Marianne Karbe. Berlin: Merve Verlag, 1985.

Harry Francis Mallgrave, *Gottfried Semper. Architect of the Nineteenth Century.* New Haven, London: Yale University Press, 1996.

Harry Francis Mallgrave, *Modern Architectural Theory. A Historical Survey, 1673–1968.* Cambridge, New York: Cambridge University Press, 2005.

Josep Lluís Mateo, Florian Sauter (eds.), *Earth Wind Air Fire. The Four Elements and Architecture.* New York: Actar Publishers, 2014.

Hartmut Mayer, *Die Tektonik der Hellenen. Kontext und Wirkung der Architekturtheorie von Karl Bötticher.* Stuttgart, London: Edition Axel Menges, 2004.

Narciso G. Menocal, *Architecture as Nature. The Transcendentalist Idea of Louis Sullivan.* Madison, London: The University of Wisconsin Press, 1981.

Ernan McMullin (ed.), *The Concept of Matter.* Notre Dame, Indiana: The University of Notre Dame Press, 1963.

Daniel Miller (ed.), *Materiality.* Durham, London: Duke University Press, 2005.

Daniel Miller, *Stuff.* Cambridge: Polity Press, 2010.

Matthew Mindrup (ed.), *The Material Imagination. Reveries on Architecture and Matter.* Farnham: Ashgate, 2015.

Ákos Moravánszky, *Die Erneuerung der Baukunst. Wege zur Moderne in Mitteleuropa 1900–1940.* Salzburg, Vienna: Residenz Verlag, 1988.

Ákos Moravánszky, *Competing Visions. Aesthetic Innovation and Social Imagination in Central European Architecture, 1867–1918.* Cambridge, Mass.: The MIT Press, 1998.

Ákos Moravánszky, *Lehrgerüste. Theorie und Stofflichkeit der Architektur.* Zurich: gta Verlag, 2015.

Mohsen Mostafavi, David Leatherbarrow, *On Weathering. The Life of Buildings in Time.* Cambridge, Mass.: The MIT Press, 1993.

Barbara Naumann, Thomas Strässle, Carolina Torra-Mattenklott (eds.), *Stoffe. Zur Geschichte der Materialität in Künsten und Wissenschaften.* Zurich: vdf Hochschulverlag, 2006.

Winfried Nerdinger, Werner Oechslin (eds.), *Gottfried Semper 1803–1879. Architektur und Wissenschaft.* Munich, Berlin, London: Prestel Verlag, Zurich: gta Verlag, 2003.

Werner Oechslin, *Otto Wagner, Adolf Loos, and the Road to Modern Architecture.* transl. by Lynnette Widder. Cambridge: Cambridge University Press, 2002.

Konrad Onasch, *Lichthöhle und Sternenhaus. Licht und Materie im spätantik-christlichen und frühbyzantinischen Sakralbau.* Dresden, Basel: Verlag der Kunst, 1993.

Francis S. Onderdonk, *The Ferro-Concrete Style. Reinforced Concerete in Modern Architecture.* New York: Architectural Publishing Company, 1928. Reprint Santa Monica: Hennessey + Ingalls, 1998.

Georges Perrot, Charles Chipiez, *Histoire de l'art dans l'antiquité.* 8 Volumes. Paris: Hachette, 1882–1889. Translated into English in several volumes by Walter Armstrong. London: Chapman & Hall, 1883–1894.

Antoine Picon, *French Architects and Engineers in the Age of Enlightenment,* transl. by Martin Thom. Cambridge: Cambridge University Press, 1992.

Antoine Picon (ed.), *L'Art de l'ingenieur.* Exhibition Catalogue. Paris: Centre Pompidou, 1997.

Ruggero Pierantoni, *Vortici, atomi e sirene. Immagini e forme del pensiero esatto.* Milan: Mondadori Electa, 2003.

Heinz Quitzsch, *Gottfried Semper – Praktische Ästhetik und politischer Kampf.* Braunschweig, Wiesbaden: Friedr. Vieweg & Sohn, 1981.

Thomas Raff, *Die Sprache der Materialien. Anleitung zu einer Ikonologie der Werkstoffe.* Munich: Deutscher Kunstverlag, 1994.

Rudolph Redtenbacher, *Die Architektonik der modernen Baukunst. Ein Hülfsbuch bei der Bearbeitung architektonischer Aufgaben.* Berlin: Verlag Ernst & Korn, 1883.

Mario Rinke, Joseph Schwartz (eds.), *Before Steel. The Introduction of Structural Iron and its Consequences.* Sulgen, Zurich: Niggli Verlag, 2010.

Mario Rinke, Joseph Schwartz (eds.), *Holz: Stoff oder Form. Transformationen einer Konstruktionslogik.* Sulgen: Niggli Verlag, 2014.

Sascha Roesler, *Weltkonstruktion. Der außereuropäische Hausbau und die moderne Architektur. Ein Wissensinventar.* Berlin: Gebr. Mann Verlag, 2013.

Gillian Rose, Divya P. Tolia-Kelly (eds.), *Visuality/Materiality. Images, Objects and Practices.* Farnham: Ashgate, 2012.

Anna Rosellini, *Louis I. Kahn. Towards the Zero Degree of Concrete 1960–1974.* Lausanne: EPFL Press, 2014.

Dietmar Rübel, Monika Wagner, Vera Wolff (eds.), *Materialästhetik. Quellentexte zu Kunst, Design und Architektur.* Berlin: Dietrich Reimer Verlag, 2005.

Dietmar Rübel, *Plastizität: Eine Kunstgeschichte des Veränderlichen.* Munich: Verlag Silke Schreiber, 2012.

Joseph Rykwert, *The Dancing Column. On Order in Architecture.* Cambridge, Mass.: The MIT Press, 1996.

Andrew Saint, *Architect and Engineer. A Study in Sibling Rivalry.* New Haven, London: Yale University Press, 2007.

Jacques Sbriglio, *Le Corbusier et la question du brutalisme.* Marseille: Parenthèses, 2013.

Walter Scheiffele, *Das leichte Haus. Utopie und Realität der Membranarchitektur.* Leipzig: Spector Books, 2015.

Ulrich Schütte, *Ordnung und Verzierung. Untersuchungen zur deutschsprachigen Architekturtheorie des 19. Jahrhunderts.* Braunschweig, Wiesbaden: Friedr. Vieweg & Sohn, 1986.

Konrad Werner Schulze, *Architektur der Gegenwart.* Volume IV: *Der Ziegelbau.* Stuttgart: Akademischer Verlag Dr. Fritz Wedekind & Co., 1927.

Fritz Schumacher, *Das Wesen des neuzeitlichen Backsteinbaues,* Munich: Verlag Georg Callwey, without year [1920].

Gottfried Semper, *Gesammelte Schriften.* 4 Volumes. ed. by Heinrich Karge. Hildesheim: Olms Verlag, 2008–2014.

Gottfried Semper, *Wissenschaft, Industrie und Kunst und andere Schriften über Architektur, Kunsthandwerk und Kunstunterricht,* ed. by Hans M. Wingler. Mainz: Florian Kupferberg Verlag, 1966.

Gottfried Semper, *The Four Elements of Architecture and Other Writings,* transl. by Harry Francis Mallgrave and Wolfgang Herrmann, Cambridge: Cambridge University Press, 1989.

Gottfried Semper, *The Ideal Museum. Practical Art in Metals and Hard Materials.* Vienna: Schlebrügge Editor, 2007.

Gottfried Semper, *Style in the Technical and Tectonic Arts, or, Practical Aesthetics,* transl. by Harry Francis Mallgrave, Michael Robinson. Los Angeles: Getty Research Institute, 2004.

Mimi Sheller, *Aluminum Dreams. The Making of Light Modernity.* Cambridge, Mass.: The MIT Press, 2014.

Cyrille Simonnet, *Le béton. Histoire d'un matériau. Économie, technique, architecture.* Marseille: Édition Parenthèses, 2005.

Francisco Arques Soler (ed.), *La materia de la arquitectura. The Matter of Architecture.* Ciudad Real: Fundación Miguel Fisac, 2009.

Annette Spiro, Hartmut Göhler, Pinar Gönül (eds.), *Über Putz. Oberflächen entwickeln und realisieren.* Zurich: gta Verlag, 2012.

Philip Steadman, *The Evolution of Designs. Biological Analogy in Architecture and the Applied Arts.* Cambridge: Cambridge University Press, 1979.

Richard Streiter, *Karl Böttichers Tektonik der Hellenen als ästhetische und kunstgeschichtliche Theorie. Eine Kritik.* Hamburg, Leipzig: Verlag von Leopold Voss, 1896.

Richard Streiter, *Ausgewählte Schriften zur Aesthetik und Kunst-Geschichte,* ed. by Franz von Reber, Emil Sulger-Gebing. Munich: Delphin-Verlag, 1913.

Mark Swenarton, Igea Troiani, Helena Webster (eds.), *The Politics of Making.* London, New York: Routledge, 2007.

Chris Tilley, Webb Keane, Susanne Küchler, Mike Rowlands, Patricia Spyer (eds.), *Handbook of Material Culture.* London: SAGE, 2006.

Philip Ursprung (ed.), *Herzog & de Meuron. Natural History.* Exhibition catalogue. Montreal, Canadian Centre for Architecture, Baden: Lars Müller Publishers, 2005.

David Van Zanten, *Designing Paris. The Architecture of Duban, Labrouste, Duc, and Vaudoyer.* Cambridge, Mass.: The MIT Press, 1987.

Anthony Vidler, *The Writing of the Walls. Architectural Theory in the Late Enlightenment.* New York: Princeton Architectural Press, 1987.

Julius Vischer, Ludwig Hilberseimer, *Beton als Gestalter. Bauten in Eisenbeton und ihre architektonische Gestaltung. Ausgeführte Eisenbetonbauten.* Stuttgart: Julius Hoffmann, 1928.

Monika Wagner, *Das Material der Kunst. Eine andere Geschichte der Moderne.* Munich: C. H. Beck, 2001.

Monika Wagner, "Der Holzstil. Expressionistische Beiträge zur ‚neuen deutschen Kunst'", in: Matthias Krüger, Isabella Vogt (eds.), *Im Dienst der Nation: Identitätsstiftungen und Identitätsbrüche in Werke der bildenden Kunst.* Berlin: Akademie Verlag, 2011, pp. 61–76.

Lauren S. Weingarden, *Louis H. Sullivan and a 19th-Century Poetics of Naturalized Architecture.* Farnham: Ashgate, 2009.

Susanne Weiß, *Kunst + Technik = Design? Materialien und Motive der Luftfahrt in der Moderne.* Cologne, Weimar, Vienna: Böhlau Verlag, 2010.

Richard Weston, *Materials, Form and Architecture.* London: Laurence King, 2003.

Jan Peter Wingender (ed.), *Brick. An Exacting Material.* Amsterdam: Architectura & Natura, 2016.

Johann Heinrich Wolff, *Beiträge zur Aesthetik der Baukunst oder die Grundgesetze der plastischen Form, nachgewiesen an den Hauptheilen der Griechischen Architektur.* Leipzig, Darmstadt: Carl Wilhelm Leske, 1834.

David Young Kim (ed.), *Matters of Weight. Force, Gravitation, and Aesthetics in the Early Modern Period.* Emsdetten, Berlin: Edition Imorde, 2013.

Pietro Zennaro, *La qualità rarefatta. Considerazioni sull'influenza del vuoto nella costruzione dell'architettura.* Milan: Franco Angeli, 2000.

Pietro Zennaro, *Architettura senza. Micro esegesi della riduzione negli edifici contemporanei.* Milan: Franco Angeli, 2009.

INDEX

ILLUSTRATION CREDITS

Foreword: Another Brick in the Wall

0.1 Photo: Ákos Moravánszky
0.2 *Encyclopédie. Recueil de planches, sur les sciences, les arts libéraux, et les arts méchaniques, avec leur explication. Architecture, Maçonnerie.* Paris: Briasson, 1769, plt. I. Archive Á. M.
0.3 Photo: Ralph Feiner, courtesy of Gramazio & Kohler Architects
0.4 Photo courtesy of Gramazio & Kohler Architects

1. Introduction

1.1–1.4, 1.6, 1.8, 1.9 Photos: Ákos Moravánszky
1.5 Courtesy of Atelier Peter Zumthor und Partner
1.7 Ernst Gladbach, *Der Schweizer Holzstyl*, 1st Series, Zurich: Caesar Schmidt, 1882, plt. 18. Archive Á. M.

2. Paths to Matter

2.1, 2.3, 2.5–2.13, 2.15, 2.16, 2.18, 2.19 Photos: Ákos Moravánszky
2.2 Photo: Ricardo Joss
2.4 *Encyclopédie: Recueil de planches, sur les sciences, les arts libéraux, et les arts méchaniques, avec leur explication. Marine.* Paris: Briasson, 1769, plt. V. Archive Á. M.
2.14 *Der Architekt* Vol. XIII, 1907, p. 52. Archive Á. M.
2.17 Auguste Choisy, *L'art de bâtir chez les Romains*, Paris: Ducher et Cie, 1873, plt. VIII. Archive Á. M.

3. The Matter of Nature

3.1 M.-A. Laugier, *Essai sur l'architecture*, 2nd edition, 1755. Courtesy of the ETH Baubibliothek Zurich
3.2, 3.4–3.6, 3.10–3.16, 3.18, 3.21–3.32, 3.33b, 3.34–3.37 Photos: Ákos Moravánszky
3.3 William Chambers, *A Treatise on the Decorative Part of Civil Architecture*, London: Joseph Smeeton, 3rd edition, 1791. Archive Á. M.
3.7 [Eugène E.] Viollet-le-Duc, *Entretiens sur l'architecture*, Vol. II, Paris: Vve A. Morel, 1872, p. 84. Archive Á. M.
3.8, 3.9 [Eugène E.] Viollet-le-Duc, *Entretiens sur l'architecture, Atlas*, Paris: A. Morel, 1864, plts. XXI, XXII. Archive Á. M.
3.17 László Moholy-Nagy, *Von material zu architektur*, Munich: Albert Langen, 1929, pp. 36, 41, 43. Archive Á. M.

3.19 Alfred Ehrhardt, *Kristalle*. Hamburg: Heinrich Ellermann, 1939, p. 68. Archive Á. M.
3.20, 3.33a Rudolf Schwarz, *Von der Bebauung der Erde*. Heidelberg: Lambert Schneider, 1949, pp. 23, 29. Archive Á. M.

4. The Four Elements of Architecture

4.1 Victoria & Albert Museum, London E. 339–2007.
4.2, 4.4, 4.11, 4.16, 4.22, Gottfried Semper, *Der Stil*, Vol. 1: Frankfurt a.M.: Verlag für Kunst und Wissenschaft, 1860, Vol. 2: Munich: Friedrich Bruckmann's Verlag, 1863. Archive Á. M.
4.3 Courtesy of MAK – Austrian Museum of Applied Arts Vienna, Vol. 1, 1909, 13
4.5 Photo: Jonas Wirth
4.6–4.8, 4.13–4.15, 4.18, 4.19, 4.25, 4.26, 4.28, 4.29, 4.31–4.33, 4.35 Photos: Ákos Moravánszky
4.9 Dimitris Pikionis, *Architectural Sketches 1940–1955*. Ed. Agni Pikionis, Athens: Bastas-Plessas Publications, 1994, p. 82
4.12 *Vitruvius Teutsch*, transl. by Walther Hermann Ryff, Nuremberg, 1548, pp. 61, 62, 63. Archive Á. M.
4.17 Ernst Gladbach, *Der Schweizer Holzstyl*, Zurich: Caesar Schmidt, 1882, plt. 5. Archive Á. M.
4.20, 4.21 Photo: Filip Dujardin, courtesy of architecten de vylder vinck taillieu
4.23 Photo: Leon Faust
4.24 Giovanni Battista Piranesi, *Le antichità romane*, Vol. IV, Rome, 1784. Archive Á. M.
4.27 Photo: Karl R. Kegler.
4.30 Charles-François-Antoine Leroy, *Traité de stéréotomie*, Vol. II: Atlas, 5th edition. Paris: Gauthier-Villars, 1870, plt. 62. Archive Á. M.
4.34 Harald Szeemann, *Individuelle Mythologien*, Berlin: Merve, 1985, U2

5. The Nature of Matter

5.1 Jean-Nicolas-Louis Durand, *Précis des leçons d'architecture*, Vol. I., Paris: Goeury, 1819. Archive Á. M.
5.2, 5.6–5.11, 5.13–5.18, 5.20, 5.22–5.28 Photos: Ákos Moravánszky
5.3a–d Paul Schmitthenner *Gebaute Form*, ed. Elisabeth Schmitthenner, Leinfelden-Echterdingen: Alexander Koch, 1984, figs. 14, 23, 27, 35. Courtesy of Johannes Schmitthenner
5.4 Augustus Welby Pugin, *Contrasts*, London: Charles Dolman, 1841. Archive Á. M.

5.5 John Ruskin, *The Stones of Venice*, Vol. II, London: J.M. Dent [1907], plt. V. Archive Á. M.
5.12 Photo: Chicago Historical Society
5.19 Paul Graef, ed., *Neubauten in Nordamerika*, Berlin: Julius Becker, 1897, plt. 88. Archive Á. M.
5.21 *Wasmuths Monatshefte für Baukunst*, Vol. XII (1928), p. 147
5.29 Courtesy of Burkhalter Sumi Architekten
5.30, 5.31 Photo: Ralph Feiner, courtesy of Bearth + Deplazes Architekten
5.32 Photo: David Grandorge, courtesy of Sergison Bates architects

6. The Life of Matter

6.1, 6.2 A[loys] Hirt, *Die Baukunst nach den Grundsätzen der Alten*, Berlin: Realschulbuchhandlung, 1809, plts. I, II, XXX. Archive Á. M.
6.3 A[loys] Hirt, *Die Geschichte der Baukunst bei den Alten*, Berlin: G. Reimer, 1821–1827, Atlas, plt. XXX. Archive Á. M.
6.4 Charles Chipiez, *Histoire critique des origines et de formation des ordres grecs*, Paris: A. Morel, 1876, p. 208. Archive Á. M.
6.5 Le Corbusier, *Une maison – un palais*, Paris: G. Crès, 1928, p. 43. Archive Á. M.
6.6 Auguste Choisy, *Histoire de l'architecture*, Vol. I., Paris: Gauthier-Villars, 1899, p. 288. Archive Á. M.
6.7 A[ugustus] Lane-Fox Pitt-Rivers, *The Evolution of Culture and Other Essays*, ed. J. L. Myres, Oxford: Clarendon Press, 1906. Archive Á. M.
6.8a, b Alfred C. Haddon, *Evolution in Art as Illustrated by the Life-Histories of Designs*. London: Walter Scott, 1895, pp. 344, 348
6.9, 6.10, 6.15 Photos: Ákos Moravánszky
6.11 Gottfried Semper, *Ueber die bleiernen Schleudergeschosse der Alten und über zweckmässige Gestaltung der Wurfkörper im Allgemeinen*. Frankfurt am Main: Verlag für Kunst und Wissenschaft, 1859, plts. 2–3
6.12 *Allgemeine Bauzeitung*, Vol. 55 (1890), p. 18. Archive Á. M.
6.13 *Kunstgewerbeblatt*, N.F. 19 (1908), p. 82. Archive Á. M.
6.14 Le Corbusier, *Vers une architecture*, 2nd edition. Paris: G. Crès, 1929, p. 116. Archive Á. M.

7. The Theory and Practice of Metamorphism

7.1 Gottfried Semper, *Der Stil*, Vol. 2, Munich: Friedrich Bruckmann's Verlag, 1863, p. 4. Archive Á. M.

7.2, 7.9–7.13, 7.15, 7.17, 7.18, 7.20, 7.21, 7.24 Photos: Ákos Moravánszky

7.3 S[elim] O[mirovich] Khan-Magomedov, *Ivan Zholtovsky*, Moscow: S. E. Gordeev, 2010, p. 89

7.4 gta Archive, Zurich

7.5 [Eugène E.] Viollet-le-Duc, *Entretiens sur l'architecture*, Atlas, Paris: A. Morel, 1864, plt. 1. Archive Á. M.

7.6, 7.8 Constantin Uhde, *Der Holzbau*, Berlin 1903, figs. 9, 33. Archive Á. M.

7.7 Charles Texier, *Description de l'Asie Mineure*, Vol. 1, Paris, 1839, Archive Á. M.

7.14 Photo: Damjan Prelovšek

7.16 Courtesy of Boris Podrecca

7.19 Archive Á. M.

7.22, 7.23 Photo: Ralph Feiner, courtesy of Bearth + Deplazes Architekten

8. The Principle of Dressing

8.1, 8.9, 8.11 Courtesy of gta Archive, ETH Zurich

8.2, 8.3 Karl Bötticher, *Die Tektonik der Hellenen*, Fünfundvierzig Kupfertafeln. Berlin: Ernst & Korn, 1862, plts. 7, 14. Archive Á. M.

8.4 Gottfried Semper, *Der Stil*, Vol. 1, Frankfurt a. M.: Verlag für Kunst und Wissenschaft, 1860, p. 180. Archive Á. M.

8.5 Akademie der Künste, Berlin, Konrad Wachsmann Archive, No. 164 F.1

8.6, 8.7 Georges Perrot and Charles Chipiez, *Historie de l'art dans l'antiquité*, Vol. I, Vol. V. Paris, 1882, 1890. Archive Á. M.

8.8, 8.10, 8.12, 8.15, 8.16, 8.18–8.24, 8.26, 8.27, 8.30–8.33, 8.35–8.38, 8.40, 8.45, 8.47, 8.48 Photos: Ákos Moravánszky

8.13 Edmund W. Smith, *Portfolio of Indian Architectural Drawings*, London, 1897, plt. XXXIX. Archive Á. M.

8.14 Joseph August Lux, *Otto Wagner. Eine Monographie*. Munich, 1914. Archive Á. M.

8.17 *Allgemeine Bauzeitung* Vol. 65 (1900), plt. 10.

8.25 *Aus der Wagner-Schule MCM*, Vienna: Anton Schroll, 1901, no page. Archive Á. M.

8.28 [Eugène E.] Viollet-le-Duc, *Entretiens sur l'architecture*, Atlas, Paris: A. Morel, 1864, plt. XXIX. Archive Á. M.

8.29 *Moderne Bauformen* Vol. XIII (1914), plt. 2

8.34 Photo: Damjan Prelovšek

8.39 Pierre Chabat, *La brique et la terre cuite*, Paris: 1881. Archive Á. M.

8.41, 8.42 Photos: Adam Shaw

8.43, 8.44 Archive Á. M.

8.46 Jan Gratama, Dr. H. P. Berlage Bouwmeester. Rotterdam: L & J. Brusse's uitgevers-maatschappij, 1925, p. 32

8.49 Photo: Bertalan Moravánszky

8.50 Courtesy of Shigeru Ban

9. The Apes of Materials

9.1 Thomas Hancock, *Personal Narrative of the Origin and Progress of the Caoutchouc or India-Rubber Manufacture*, London, 1857. Archive Á. M.

9.2, 9.4–9.6, 9.8–9.15, 9.17, 9.18, 9.21 Photos: Ákos Moravánszky

9.3 Ludwig Hilberseimer, *Beton als Gestalter*, Stuttgart: Julius Hoffmann, 1928, cover. Archive Á. M.

9.7 Photo: Katalin Moravánszky Gyöngy

9.16a, b Courtesy of György Sámsondi Kiss, Budapest

9.19, 9.20 Courtesy of Studio Märkli

10. Immateriality and Formlessness

10.1 Photo: Heinrich Helfenstein, courtesy of Atelier für Architekturfotografie Heinrich Helfenstein

10.2 Léonce Reynaud, *Traité d'architecture*, Atlas, Paris: Dunod, 1875, plt. 79. Archive Á. M.

10.3, 10.5–10.7, 10.11, 10.12, 10.16, 10.17 Photos: Ákos Moravánszky

10.4 *Der Architekt* 1902, p. 47. Archive Á. M.

10.8, 10.9 Fritz August Breuhaus de Groot, *Bauten und Räume*. Berlin-Charlottenburg: Ernst Wasmuth, 1935, pp. 144*, 145. Archive Á. M.

10.10 Photo: Paul Schulz

10.13 László Moholy-Nagy, *Von material zu architektur*, Munich: Albert Langen, 1929, p. 48. Archive Á. M.

10.14 Courtesy of Gramazio & Kohler Architects

10.15 Photo courtesy of Joseph Schwartz

Prof. em. Dr. Ákos Moravánszky
ETH Zurich, Institut gta

Acquisitions Editor: David Marold, Birkhäuser Verlag, A-Vienna
Project and Production management: Angelika Heller, Birkhäuser Verlag, A-Vienna
Translation: Rupert Hebblethwaite, A-Vienna
Layout and cover design: Ekke Wolf, typic.at, A-Vienna
Printing and binding: Holzhausen Druck GmbH, A-Wolkersdorf

Library of Congress Cataloging-in-Publication data
A CIP catalog record for this book has been applied for at the Library of Congress.

Bibliographic information published by the German National Library
The German National Library lists this publication in the Deutsche Nationalbibliografie; detailed
bibliographic data are available on the Internet at http://dnb.dnb.de.

This publication is also available as an e-book (ISBN PDF 978-3-0356-0806-9) and in a German
language edition (ISBN 978-3-0356-1018-5).

© 2018 Birkhäuser Verlag GmbH, Basel
P.O. Box 44, 4009 Basel, Switzerland
Part of Walter de Gruyter GmbH, Berlin/Boston

© Cover image:
Ákos Moravánszky, Marble quarry near Carrara, 2016.

Printed on acid-free paper produced from chlorine-free pulp. TCF ∞

Printed in Austria

ISBN 978-3-0356-1019-2

9 8 7 6 5 4 3 2 1   www.birkhauser.com